AVERROËS'S THREE SHORT COMMENTARIES ON ARISTOTLE'S "TOPICS," "RHETORIC," AND "POETICS"

STUDIES IN ISLAMIC PHILOSOPHY AND SCIENCE

Published under the auspices of
the Society for the Study of Islamic Philosophy and Science

Averroës's
Three Short Commentaries on Aristotle's "Topics," "Rhetoric," and "Poetics"

Edited and Translated by

Charles E. Butterworth

SUNY PRESS

UNESCO COLLECTION OF REPRESENTATIVE WORKS
ARABIC SERIES
This book
has been accepted
in the Arabic Series
of the Translations Collection
of the United Nations
Educational, Scientific and Cultural Organization
(UNESCO)

First Edition
For information, contact State University of New York Press, Albany, NY

www.sunypress.edu

Printed in the United States of America

Library of Congress Cataloging in Publication Data

Averroës, 1126–1198.
Averroës's three short commentaries on Aristotle's
"Topics," "Rhetoric," and "Poetics."
(Studies in Islamic Philosophy and Science)
Arabic and English.
Includes bibliographical references and index.
1. Aristoteles. Organon. 2. Logic—Early works to 1800.
I. Butterworth, Charles E.
II. Title. III. Series.
B749.A35B87 160 75-4900
ISBN 0-87395-208-1

To My Wife

PREFACE

There was a time when Dante could be certain that even an oblique reference to Averroës would be immediately understood by any of his readers. Indeed, over the course of several centuries, fierce debate raged around the philosophy of Averroës: he was either extolled as the foremost interpreter of Aristotle or vilified as the gravest menace to Christian faith. Schools devoted to the study and propagation of his commentaries on Aristotle flourished, while others zealously committed to combatting the teachings of those commentaries had equal success. Today, mention of his name evokes no passions, prompts no discussions; rather, reference to Averroës is usually met with querulous stares. Even in learned circles, little is known about the man and still less about his teachings.

The contemporary neglect of Averroës can be traced to the very reason for his celebrity during the Middle Ages: his reputation as *the* commentator on Aristotle. Today, few people are interested in either Aristotle or commentary. Philosophic study having been reduced to scientific method or general culture, the passion for serious discussion about perennial problems has waned. Thus knowledge of, much less interest in, the problems raised by Aristotle is slight, and desire for acquaintance with the momentous debates those problems have occasioned nil. Moreover, with the spread of the assumption that all things evolve through time, inventiveness has come to be acclaimed the mark of excellent thought and commentary condemned as imitative or servile. Consequently, Averroës has been judged as neither meriting an important place in the history of philosophy nor deserving particular study.

Even those still attracted to the philosophy of Aristotle are little inclined to study the commentaries by Averroës. They seem to consider the recovery of the Greek manuscripts as having diminished the significance of those commentaries. In their eyes, Averroës performed the historical function of preserving Aristotle's thought until the sources could be recovered, but his importance goes no further. As a result, Averroës has become a figure of mild curiosity, a thinker to be studied by orientalists or backward looking scholastics.

For many reasons, the contemporary neglect of Averroës is unfortunate. Like Aristotle, Averroës addressed himself to theoretical and practical questions of concern to human beings in all ages. As long as it is possible to wonder about the origin of the world or the basis of political justice, serious minds can delight in careful consideration of Aristotle's ideas and in Averroës's interpretative presentation of those ideas. To such minds his use of the commentary can be especially instructive, for the art of commenting was completely transformed in his hands. Far from a servile imitation or literal repetition, Averroës presented a unique interpretation of Aristotle's ideas under the guise of a commentary. Indeed, an attentive reading of Averroës's commentaries with the texts of Aristotle shows that arguments Aristotle had made are often omitted, notions foreign to his thought sometimes added, and on occasion arguments even invented in his name.

Hence the recovery of the Greek manuscripts does not render Averröes's commentaries obsolete. On the contrary, their recovery makes the study of those commentaries immensely more fascinating. As the thought of Aristotle is laid bare and compared with the interpretation presented by Averroës, new questions about the meaning of the interpretation, as well as about the significance of the distortion, arise. At that point the reader can begin to appreciate the special relationship between the scholarly task of uncovering the thought of someone else and the philosophic task of making that thought one's own. Once Averroës's use of the commentary acquires this kind of problematic significance, his reputation as *the* commentator on Aristotle can again occasion serious reflection.

The treatises presented here are especially helpful for reassessing the importance of Averroës. Nowhere has he been so audaciously liberal with the text of Aristotle as in these treatises or in the larger collection from which they are taken. That larger collection has long been presumed to represent Averroës's *Short Commentary on Aristotle's Organon*. It does represent that short commentary, but a short commentary which transforms the *Organon* by adding a non-Aristotelian treatise, as well as Aristotelian treatises not belonging to what is usually understood to be the *Organon*, and by changing the order of the treatises in the *Organon*. More importantly, the treatises presented here—which are short commentaries on individual treatises of the extended *Organon*—offer exciting interpretations and provocative applications of Aristotle's teaching. Consideration of the logical arts appears to be little more than a veil from behind which Averroës evoked the problematic relation between philosophic thought, religious belief, and political conviction. Even the horizons of time and culture peculiar to the discussion serve only as reminders of how unlimited the discussion really is.

It is especially pleasant to be able to express my gratitude to all those who have given so generously of their time and learning and thus facilitated my work on this book, as well as to acknowledge those institutions which have provided material aid.

Without the help of Norman Golb, I would never have been able to undertake this project; he gave unstintingly of his time and learning to teach me how to decipher Judaeo-Arabic manuscripts. Lawrence Marwick and William C. Williams helped me prepare the Hebrew part of the critical apparatus. George N. Atiyeh offered valuable criticism of the Arabic text. If I have a severe but judicious Aristarchus, it must be Miriam Galston; she offered excellent criticism of the finished text and invaluable advice about how to translate technical Arabic into smooth English. Above all, the final presentation of the book owes much to the careful eye and agile mind of Muhsin Mahdi and to his sound advice at each stage of the project. I am especially grateful for the friendly help extended by each of these persons.

I would like to acknowledge the assistance of the Graduate School of the University of Maryland which awarded me a fellowship for the summer of 1970 and a grant for typing expenses. I would also like to acknowledge the assistance provided by a fellowship from the American Research Center in Egypt for the summer of 1972. Finally, I wish to thank the personnel of the Centre Universitaire International in Paris for their helpfulness.

CONTENTS

INTRODUCTION

Born in Córdoba in 1126 C.E. (520 *Anno Hegirae*),[1] Abū al-Walīd Muḥammad ibn Aḥmad Ibn Rushd, known to the West as Averroës, received a traditional education in the principal disciplines of Islamic culture: jurisprudence and theology. He also studied medicine, eloquence, poetry, literature, and philosophy. His reputation as a man of learning brought him to the attention of his sovereign, Abū Ya'qūb Yūsuf, the ruler of the Almohad dynasty, who encouraged him to explain the difficulties in the works of Aristotle and appointed him as a judge, eventually naming him the chief justice of Seville. Except for a brief period of legal exile, Averroës occupied this post, also serving as personal physician and sometime adviser to the Almohad sovereigns, until almost the end of his life in 595/1198. Still, his reputation among learned men of the Middle Ages was due to his skillful interpretations of pagan philosophy and defense of theoretical speculation, rather than to these practical accomplishments. Even today his theoretical accomplishments could interest thoughtful men, but most of his writings are largely inaccessible to them—existing only in medieval manuscripts or barely intelligible Latin translations.

An attempt is made here to fill that void by presenting three treatises of historical and theoretical significance to all interested in philosophic thought. None of these treatises has ever before been edited and published in Arabic or translated into a modern language.[2] Because the Arabic manuscripts were apparently lost at an early date, the closest replicas of the original Arabic version now available to interested scholars are two Judaeo-Arabic manuscripts. They have been used as the basis of this edition. According to the scribe of one of the manuscripts, the copy was completed in 1356 C.E. Unfortunately there is no reliable information about the date of the other manuscript: the date of 1216, written in the kind of Arabic numerals used by Westerners in recent times and in a hand other than that of the scribe, appears on the title page; it has no connection with any of the textual material.

The fourteenth century manuscript contains a Hebrew translation opposite the Judaeo-Arabic text. The Arabic text was first translated into Hebrew in the thirteenth century. Subsequently, it was translated into Hebrew a number of other times, and one translation was eventually published in the mid-sixteenth century.[3] Collating the Hebrew translation with the Judaeo-Arabic manuscripts proved to be of little help for establishing an accurate Arabic text.

Numerous Latin translations of Averroës's works were made in the early thirteenth century, many of which were published in the fifteenth and sixteenth centuries. However, the only known Latin version of the texts presented here is that of Abraham de Balmes who died in 1523 C.E. This translation, made directly from the Hebrew, was published in Venice in the sixteenth century. It has gained wide acceptance and is the principal source cited by those interested in the logical thought of Averroës. It, too, was collated with the Judaeo-Arabic versions, but was of even less help than the Hebrew translation for establishing an accurate Arabic text.

To appreciate why only two manuscripts of such an important work have survived and why those manuscripts have survived in Judaeo-Arabic rather than in Arabic, it is necessary to reflect upon the suspicion in which Averroës was placed as a result of legal exile in the later years of his life. It is also necessary to consider the significance of the purge of unorthodox opinions carried out by the Almohad dynasty shortly after his death. At that time, religious intolerance reached such intensity that books suspected of heresy were frequently burned before the public. It is probable that in this setting works attributed to a figure as controversial as Averroës readily disappeared. However, largely because of Maimonides's influence, Averroës had very early gained such fame in the Jewish community that most of his works were transliterated into Judaeo-Arabic, translated into Hebrew, and widely circulated in North Africa and even France. The collection to which the treatises presented here belong, as well as Averroës's more formal commentaries on works by Aristotle, were of special importance to those members of the Jewish community interested in peripatetic philosophy and were consequently carefully preserved. Even though Latin Aristotelian studies became more prominent than Jewish Aristotelian studies in the later Middle Ages, Jewish interest in Averroës and in Judaeo-Arabic or Hebrew versions of his works did not diminish. As a result, many of the medieval Judaeo-Arabic and Hebrew versions of his works are still available.[4]

However, these considerations do not explain why the treatises presented here have been neglected since their recovery more than a century ago. One reason for that neglect appears to be their subject matter: logic. The writings of Averroës on logic were not studied very carefully by fellow Arabs nor by the Latin Aristotelians who were first attracted to his works. Similarly, even though the academic community knew about the existence of these treatises in Judaeo-Arabic manuscripts and about the existence of the *Middle Commentaries on Aristotle's Organon* in Arabic manuscripts during the latter part of the nineteenth century, scholars preferred to edit Hebrew translations of other works by Averroës while deploring the lack of Arabic manuscripts. It was not until the first third of the twentieth century that one of the logical works was thoroughly edited.[5]

Another reason why these treatises have been neglected is that, as commentaries, they were considered to be less original than other writings by Averroës. Throughout the nineteenth century, the image of an Averroës who was a faithful disciple of Arisotle prevailed. For a long while it was accepted without question and passed on as rigorously confirmed. Only recently has the doctrine begun to be doubted. However, while it reigned supreme, scholars expressed more interest in those works of Averroës which were obviously independent and original. Turning their attention to these works, they left the commentaries, and especially the commentaries on logic, aside.[6]

Whatever the full explanation might be, it is clear that neglect of these treatises has not resulted from an informed judgment about the quality of the arguments they set forth. Far from having thoroughly investigated these arguments, the academic community has never been very knowledgeable about the most superficial aspects of the treatises. When Munk first announced the existence of one of the Judaeo-Arabic manuscripts in 1847, he simply identified it as Averroës's *Short Commentary on the Organon* without any reference to its possible significance. Shortly afterward, Renan reported Munk's discovery, but paid such little attention to the content of the treatise or to its identity that he spoke of the Hebrew version of the *Short Commentary on Logic* (which he called *Abrégé de Logique*) and of the manuscript discovered by Munk (which he called *Abrégé de l'Organon*) without ever associating the two. More importantly, he insisted that the treatises on rhetoric and poetics contained in the Florence manuscript of Averroës's *Middle Commentaries on Aristotle's Organon*, which he had catalogued, were short commentaries. Although he recognized differences between the treatises on rhetoric and poetics in the Florence manuscript and the Latin translations of these works by Hermannus Alemannus and Abraham de Balmes, he never compared them with the manuscript discovered by Munk.[7]

Despite Renan's acknowledgement of the manuscript's existence and Munk's subsequent reminder of its significance as the Arabic source, the German historian of logic, C. Prantl, showed no awareness, as late as 1861, that the treatise existed in any form but the old Latin version. Some years later, Steinschneider attacked Prantl for this apparent lapse of scholarship and used the occasion to announce his discovery of the other manuscript containing the Judaeo-Arabic version of this collection of treatises on the art of logic.[8] Still, nothing prompted anyone to edit the manuscripts. They remained neglected after Father Bouyges mentioned their existence in 1922 and erroneously identified a notebook manuscript he had found in Cairo as a possible Arabic copy of the *Short Commentary on Rhetoric*. Even Wolfson's repeated call for a *Corpus Commentariorum Averrois in Aristotelem* did not lead to an edition of the treatises.[9]

Such neglect must be decried, for, in addition to the historical significance attached to these manuscripts, the treatises are important for other reasons. Above all, they command serious attention because of their daring critique of traditional Islamic thought and of the dialectical theologians who considered themselves its true defenders. Starting with the particular perspective of Islam, Averroës was able to raise the universal question of the relation between philosophy, politics, and religion. These treatises are also of special interest due to their form or literary genre. So little is yet known about the different kinds of commentaries and treatises composed by Averroës or about their functions that careful attention must be paid to examples of each. In that way it may be possible to learn what the art of commentary truly was for Averroës and how he used it to present his own, as well as Aristotle's, thought. Only then will it be possible to form correct opinions about the quality of Averroës's teaching. Finally, these treatises are important because of what they teach about the way Aristotle's logical writings were interpreted at that time.

THE TEXT

BEFORE CONSIDERING the teaching set forth in these treatises, it is appropriate to have an accurate idea of their character. The correct identification of the treatises is linked to the problem of determining their original titles. Moreover, because of the peculiarities present in the formal organization as well as in the substantive arguments of the treatises, serious questions have arisen about their authenticity. Finally, a description of the manuscripts and an explanation of the way they have been edited and translated, though free of controversy, are equally important preliminaries.

In the Munich catalogue, the manuscript is identified as *The Short Commentary on Aristotle's Organon and on Porphyry's Introduction.*[10] Since the manuscript contains no title, this is more a conjectural description of the subject matter and putative identification of the work than a title.The title given the manuscript in the Paris catalogue, on the other hand, only vaguely alludes to the subject matter and to the identification of the commentary: *Summary of Logic.*[11] In his *Index Général*, Professor Vajda listed the manuscript under yet another title: *al-Ḍarūrī fī al-Manṭiq* (*What Is Necessary in Logic*). [12]

Professor Vajda's choice of title is in keeping with a long tradition. In his biographic sketch, Ibn Abū Uṣaybi'ah first referred to one of Averroës's works by something like this title: *Kitāb al-Ḍarūrī fī al-Manṭiq* (*The Book of the Necessary in Logic*). Moreover, among the books of Averroës mentioned in the Escurial manuscript 884 is a work bearing a title identical to the one given by Professor Vajda.The Latin translator Abraham de Balmes also identifed the work by a similar title: *Compendium necessarium Averroys totius logicae.* Steinschneider, who discovered this use of the title by de Balmes, originally questioned the "*necessarium*" and the traditional title because they were reflected in the first few words of the treatise: "*al-gharaḍ fī hādhā al-qawl tajrīd al-aqāwīl al-ḍarūrīyah min ṣinā'at ṣinā'at al-manṭiq* (the purpose of this treatise is to abstract the necessary speeches pertaining to each and every logical art)." However, he settled upon the traditional title in his final description of the two Judeao-Arabic manuscripts.[13]

Steinschneider's earlier doubt about the accuracy of the traditional title was better founded than he realized. The only other Arabic reference to anything resembling the traditional title was Ibn al-Abbār's vague allusion: "his book in Arabic, whose title was *al-Ḍarūrī*." When al-Anṣārī wrote a supplement to Ibn al-Abbār's book, he made no reference to such a title and only spoke generally of Averroës's commentaries on Aristotle's philosophical and logical books. Even the noted historian, master of tradition, and theologian Shams al-Dīn al-Dhahabī, who claimed to cite the works of Averroës according to Ibn Abū Uṣaybi'ah's list, omitted the qualificative "*al-Ḍarūrī*," calling the book simply *Kitāb fī al-Manṭiq* (*Book on Logic*).[14]

An even more important difficulty with the traditional title is that it does not explain what kind of a treatise Averroës wrote. However, Ibn Abū Uṣaybi'ah's list does contain a long descriptive sub-title: *Kitāb al-Ḍarūrī fī al-Manṭiq, mulḥaq bih Talkhīṣ Kutub Arisṭūṭālīs wa qad lakhkhaṣahā Talkhīṣan tamman mustawfan* (*The Book of the Necessary in Logic, Containing His Complete and Exhaustive Middle Commentary on Aristotle's Books*).[15] Although it purports to identify the kind of treatises contained in the collection, it cannot be considered accurate. In the first place, the word "*talkhīṣ*" ("middle commentary"), usually used in contradistinction to "*sharḥ*" or "*tafsīr*" ("large commentary") and "*jawāmi'*" or "*mukhtaṣar*" ("short commentary"), is certainly not descriptive of the treatises contained in this collection. Even if the word "*talkhīṣ*" is understood in the loosest possible sense, these treatises certainly do not provide a "complete and exhaustive" commentary on the art of logic. Averroës admitted as much in the opening words of this collection by saying that the purpose of the work was to provide an abstract or summary ("*tajrīd*") of what was necessary. Moreover, the manuscript copies of the *Middle Commentaries on Aristotle's Organon* have been found; those treatises are much more extensive commentaries on logic than what is found in this collecton. Finally, there is no evidence that Averroës used anything resembling Ibn Abū Uṣaybi'ah's title or subtitle to refer to this work, whereas he did refer to one of his works in terms similar to the title reflected in the Munich catalogue listing and in the way de Balmes used the word "compendium":

at one point Averroës spoke of "our short commentary" (*al-mukhtaṣar al-saghīr alladhī lanā*) on logic.[16]

Consequently, the conjectural title of the Munich catalogue offers the most accurate identification of this collection of treatises. Apart from the negative reasons already considered, there are positive reasons which confirm its appropriateness. In the first place, most of the treatises comment on particular books of Aristotle's *Organon*. In addition, the general logical theory presented in these treatises is basically Aristotelian. Moreover, there are frequent references to Aristotle and explanations of what prompted him to write about each art. Still, there are several superficial and substantive divergences from what might be expected to be the form of a short commentary, and they might call this identification into question.

For example, Averroës introduced the work by a general statement about the reasons for studying logic without ever suggesting that the treatises to follow depended on Aristotle's logical theory. In fact, he never mentioned Aristotle's name in that general statement. Moreover, he began the treatise by commenting on Porphyry's *Isagoge* as though it were a necessary preface to Aristotle's *Categories*.[17] Averroës altered the end of the treatise in a similar manner by including treatises on the arts of rhetoric and poetics. Here, too, the change was effected without elaborate explanation, the only preparation being Averroës's introductory remark that rhetoric and poetics were logical arts as much as demonstration, dialectic, and sophistics.[18]

Nor did Averroës respect the order of Aristotle's *Organon*. For one thing, he transferred the discussion of equivocal terms from the discussion of the *Categories*—where Aristotle had examined the subject —to the treatise concerned with the *Isagoge*, even though Porphyry never discussed that subject.[19] Again, arguing that it was essential to learn how to make syllogisms after having learned how to distinguish their different classes, he placed the discussion of syllogistic topics immediately after the discussion of the syllogism and immediately before the discussion of what he considered to be the most important logical art—demonstration. In terms of the *Organon* Averroës thus placed that which corresponds to Books II–VII of the *Topics* after the *Prior Analytics* and before the *Posterior Analytics*.[20] He also inverted the order of the treatises on the arts of dialectic and sophistry: in this work, the treatise on sophistry follows the discussion of demonstration (i.e., the *Posterior Analytics*) and precedes that on dialectic; in Aristotle's *Organon*, the treatise on dialectic (i.e., the *Topics*) follows the *Posterior Analytics* and precedes *On Sophistical Refutations*.

Finally, there are notable discrepancies in the titles of the various treatises. With the exception of the treatises on the *Categories* (*al-Qawl fī al-Maqūlāt*), the *Posterior Analytics* (*Kitāb al-Burhān*), and *On Sophistical Refutations* (*Kitāb al-Sūfsaṭah*),[21] the traditional titles for the works of Aristotle are not used here. For example, the treatise following that on the *Categories* is entitled *On the Rules Peculiar to Assent* (*al-Qawānīn allatī takhuṣṣ al-Taṣdīq*),[22] rather than *On Interpretation* (*Fī al-ʿIbārah*). Similarly, rather than a title suggestive of *Prior Analytics* (*Kitāb al-Qiyās*), Averroës called the corresponding treatise *On the Knowledge for Bringing about Assent* (*Fī al-Maʿrifah al-fāʿilah li al-Taṣdīq*). When he wrote about the syllogistic topics, he called that treatise *On the Rules by Which Syllogisms Are Made* (*Fī al-Qawānīn allatī taʿmal bihā al-Maqāyīs*)[23] instead of simply *Topics* (*Fī al-Mawāḍiʿ*).

In addition to these superficial divergences from what might be expected to be the form of a commentary, there are substantive divergences. Averroës presented a novel classification of the different kinds of syllogisms and introduced some that were never mentioned by Aristotle. Similarly, his analysis of the matters of syllogisms was foreign to Aristotle's logical thought. In addition, he gave a disproportionate amount of attention to some subjects and completely neglected others. His discussion of the theory of the nondemonstrative syllogism set forth in the *Topics*, for example, was so extensive that the reader might think Aristotle had written a book solely about the dialectical syllogism. Conversely, Averroës's discussion of the art of poetics was completely free of any reference whatsoever to tragedy.

Given all of these divergences, the correctness of calling the collection a Short Commentary might be questioned. In addition to the divergences, there is the massive fact that Averroës never explicitly declared it his intention to set forth the teaching of Aristotle in this collection. It might therefore be argued that the extent to which the treatises differ from Aristotle's logical teaching will cease to be problematic once the collection is no longer thought of as a kind of commentary. Averroës's allusion to his *mukhtaṣar saghīr* could then be understood simply as an allusion to a "short treatise," rather than as an allusion to a "short commentary" on Aristotle. However, such an argument fails to account for the numerous references to Aristotle throughout the text, references which always take Aristotle's correctness for granted—as though Averroës were simply explaining Aristotle's thought. That argument is likewise unable to account for the fact that each treatise ends with remarks about the kind of considerations which first prompted Aristotle to write about the particular art. Above all, that argument is unable to explain why the content of each treatise should correspond roughly to a particular Aristotelian text.

By his frequent references to Aristotle, Averroës gave the distinct impression that his exposition was based on Aristotle's treatises about the logical arts. At the same time, by means of the aforementioned superficial and substantive divergences from Aristotle's *Organon,* he suggested that the exposition was in no way limited to Aristotle's text. Differently stated, while generally oriented toward the logical teaching of Aristotle, these treatises of Averroës were addressed to the larger subject rather than to the particular arguments found in Aristotle's books on the logical arts. Because Averroës presented them as setting forth in summary fashion what Aristotle had fully explained and because he tried to keep the image of Aristotle foremost in the reader's mind, they ought to be considered as commentaries. The kind of freedom from Aristotle's text and attention to the general subject which is permitted by the superficial divergences has been observed to be characteristic of Averroës's procedure in the short commentaries, the middle and large being devoted to an explicit consideration of particular Aristotelian arguments.[24] Consequently, the descriptive title of the Munich catalogue appears to be most accurate and most in keeping with Averroës's own allusions to the work.

There are problems of a similar sort with the titles of the treatises presented here. Despite clear parallels with Aristotle's *Topics*, *Rhetoric* and *Poetics*, as well as references to Aristotle's intention with respect to each work, Averroës used titles which did not suggest that these treatises were commentaries on Aristotle's works. For example, the first treatise is called *The Book of Dialectic* (*Kitāb al-Jadal*).[25] Similarly, the second of the treatises presented here is called *The Speech about Rhetorical Arguments* (*al-Qawl fī al-Aqāwīl al-Khaṭābīyah*),[26] while the last of the three treatises is entitled *About Poetical Speeches* (*Fī al-Aqāwīl al-Shiʿrīyah*).

The reasoning which dictated identifying the larger work as the *Short Commentary on Aristotle's Organon* also dictates identifying these treatises as the *Short Commentary on Aristotle's Topics*, the *Short Commen-*

tary on Aristotle's Rhetoric, and the *Short Commentary on Aristotle's Poetics*. Moreover, despite his recourse to novel titles for these and others of the logical works, Averroës cited them by their traditional titles in the course of his argument. For example, he referred the reader to *Kitāb al-Qiyās* (*Prior Analytics*), rather than to *Fī al-Maʿrifah al-fāʿilah li al-Taṣdīq* (*On the Knowledge for Bringing about Assent*).[27] Similarly, at one point he used the traditional Arabic title for the *Topics*, *Kitāb al-Ṭūbīqī*, rather than *Kitāb al-Jadal* (*Book of Dialectic*) or *Fī al-Qawānīn allati taʿmal bihā al-Maqāyīs* (*On the Rules by Which Syllogisms Are Made*).[28] It should also be noted that Averroës seemed to consider the titles *Kitāb al-Jadal* (*Book of Dialectic*) and *Kitāb al-Ṭūbīqī* (*Topics*) interchangeable: in his introduction to the *Talkhīṣ Kitāb al-Ṭūbīqī* (*Middle Commentary on Aristotle's Topics*), he spoke of both as equally valid titles.[29] Moreover, at the end of the *Short Commentary on Aristotle's Rhetoric*, he referred to that work as the *Book of Rhetoric* (*Kitāb al-Khaṭābah*). Finally, it is clear that Averroës did not consider the treatise *Fī al-Qawānīn allatī taʿmal bihā al-Maqāyīs* (*On the Rules by Which Syllogisms Are Made*) to represent his commentary on the *Topics*, because he so carefully explained to the reader that he was using the topics discussed in this treatise solely to prepare the way for his teaching about demonstration and because he reminded the reader quite frequently that his use of topics here differed from the way they were used in dialectic or rhetoric. Consequently, just as there is no question that the treatises on rhetorical and poetical speeches refer to Aristotle's books on those subjects, so there can be little doubt that the treatise on dialectic refers to Aristotle's book on the art of dialectic—the *Topics*.

Recourse to novel titles for most of the treatises in this collection was one more way for Averroës to indicate the different character of these commentaries to the reader. In the larger commentaries, which were explicitly devoted to explaining Aristotle's arguments in an organized manner, Averroës used the traditional titles. In these Short Commentaries, where the goal was to explain the subject matter in a succinct fashion, the use of novel titles alerted the reader to a special freedom from Aristotle in the commentary. Recognition of the different titles could either spur the imaginative reader to search for other instances in which Averroës took liberties with the Aristotelian teaching or lull the indolent reader into thinking that Averroës's freedom from Aristotle was only superficial.

* * *

Of no less importance than the proper identification of these treatises is confirmation of their authenticity. While Prantl has been the only one to argue that they might be spurious, he has advanced weighty objections worthy of serious consideration.

His suspicions were first aroused because of two innovations he found in the technical vocabulary of the treatises: he was astonished that the Latin terms *definitio* and *demonstratio* had been replaced by the terms *formatio* and *verificatio*. (Both pairs of terms were used to translate the Arabic terms *taṣawwur* and *taṣdīq*). Acknowledging the possible temerity of founding his critique on the Latin translations alone, Prantl insisted that the terminological innovation was of such magnitude that it could not possibly be due to the translator. Steinschneider agreed with Prantl's acknowledgement of temerity, blamed him for failing to note that Munk had never expressed doubts about the authenticity of the treatises, as well as for neglecting Averroës's own reference to his Short Commentary on logic, and then dismissed Prantl's objection by citing similar examples of that innovative terminology in the translated works of al-Fārābī and Avicenna.[30] Later, Lasinio, who agreed with Steinschneider's general condemnation of Prantl's scholarship, made the particular refutation more convincing by citing a passage in which another Latin translator used the terms *formatio* and *verificatio* or *certificatio* for *taṣawwur* and *taṣdīq*, while de Balmes—whose translation had first aroused Prantl's suspicions—used yet other terms.[31]

Another reason for Prantl's doubts about the authorship of these treatises was the difference he observed between Averroës's willingness to preface these treatises with a commentary on Porphyry's *Isagoge* and his reluctance to preface the *Middle Commentaries on Aristotle's Organon* with a commentary on that work. Not believing that such inconsistency could be found in the work of one man and the authenticity of the Middle Commentaries being beyond doubt, Prantl concluded that these treatises were to be rejected as spurious.[32] Because he failed to understand the grounds of Averroës's reluctance, Prantl's conclusion was too hasty. Of prime importance to Averroës was the particular context of the commentary: he considered the Middle Commentaries to be, above all, commentaries "on the books of Aristotle."[33] The introductory remarks to his *Middle Commentary on Aristotle's Categories* limit the collection even more by defining its goal as that of commenting on Aristotle's books about logic, explaining and summarizing them.[34] For that goal it was not necessary to comment on Porphyry.

That same emphasis on the particular context of the commentary explains Averroës's willingness to include remarks on Porphyry's *Isagoge* in the Short Commentaries. Averroës introduced a new ordering of the art of logic in these treatises. He first identified concept (*taṣawwur*) and assent (*taṣdīq*) as fundamental terms and then explained that instruction about each had to proceed from that which prepares the way for it (*al-muwāṭṭi' lah*) and from that which brings it about (*al-fā'il lah*). This meant that the art of logic fell into four parts: (i) that which prepares the way for a concept, (ii) that which brings a concept about, (iii) that which prepares the way for assent, and (iv) that which brings assent about. Averroës's discussion of words and of Porphyry's account of the predicables corresponded to the first part, while his commentary on the *Categories* corresponded to the second part. Had Prantl been aware of the new ordering introduced by Averroës, he would have understood what prompted him to discuss Porphyry's *Isagoge* in these treatises even though he was reluctant to do so in the Middle Commentaries.

Prantl had an additional reason for doubting the authenticity of these treatises. He thought that the clearest indication of their spurious character was the way they were ordered. Recalling Averroës's severe criticism of Avicenna for suggesting that the inquiry into dialectical method (that is, the *Topics*) precede the inquiry into demonstrative method (that is, the *Posterior Analytics*), Prantl pointed to the way the commentary on the *Topics* precedes that on the *Posterior Analytics* in this collection.[35] Still persuaded that Averroës was incapable of such inconsistency, he concluded that the treatises were spurious. Unfortunately for his argument, Prantl failed to understand Averroës's reasons for criticizing Avicenna and failed to grasp the content of the treatise which precedes the *Short Commentary on the Posterior Analytics*.

In criticizing Avicenna, Averroës admitted that probable premises were usually more readily at hand than certain premises, but insisted upon the necessity of understanding the conditions of certainty in order to be able to distinguish among the kinds of probable premises that were so easily found. Consequently, it was logical for the *Posterior Analytics* (insofar as it provided the proofs and rules by which certain premises might be obtained) to precede the *Topics* (insofar as it provided the proofs and rules by which probable premises might be obtained).[36] Averroës did not go against this reasoning by placing the treatise entitled *On the Rules by Which Syllogisms Are Made* (*Fī al-Qawānīn allatī taʿmal bihā al-Maqāyīs*) before the *Short Commentary on Aristotle's Posterior Analytics*. The former work was limited to the discussion of the topics occurring in Books II-VII of the *Topics*, but that discussion was designed to prepare the way to demonstration by explaining how to make demonstrative syllogisms. It was in no way concerned with dialectical reasoning.[37] In fact, dialectical reasoning was not considered until Averroës discussed it in the treatise presented here as the *Short Commentary on Aristotle's Topics*. To impress this order upon the attentive reader, Averroës opened the treatise by declaring that only because demonstrative reasoning had already been considered was it now appropriate to consider dialectical reasoning.[38]

Prantl also failed to note the multiple indications that Averroës was trying to explain the art of logic and the order of the traditionally accepted Aristotelian books on the logical arts in an unprecedented manner. In accordance with the previously mentioned fourfold division of the art, Averroës presented his *Short Commentary on Aristotle's De Interpretatione* as corresponding to the third part of the art, that which prepares the way for assent. This was made clear both by the title of that commentary, *On the Rules Peculiar to Assent* (*al-Qawānīn allatī takhuṣṣ al-Taṣdīq*), and by the opening sentences of the treatise.[39] The *Short Commentary on Aristotle's Prior Analytics* was designed to provide the rules for forming syllogisms, i.e., that by which assent is brought about, and was appropriately entitled *On the Knowledge for Bringing about Assent* (*Fī al-Maʿrifah al-fāʿilah li al-Taṣdīq*). However, Averroës did not consider this kind of exposition to correspond to the part of the art which really treated what brought about assent and therefore classed this treatise as a continuation of the third part of the art, explaining that his treatise *On the Rules by Which Syllogisms Are Made* (*Fī al-Qawānīn allatī taʿmal bihā al-Maqāyīs*) constituted the fourth part of the art. This meant that the *Short Commentary on Aristotle's Posterior Analytics* was an explanation of how one kind of assent—the most noble kind, demonstration—worked. Similarly, the treatises on sophistics, dialectic, rhetoric, and poetics were simply so many illustrations of how the other kinds of assent worked.[40] It is clear, then, that Averroës committed no logical inconsistencies by his novel ordering of Books II-VII of the *Topics* and certainly did nothing to call his authorship of these treatises into question. Consequently, this objection of

Prantl's must be rejected along with his other ones and the treatises constituting the *Short Commentaries on Aristotle's Organon* accepted as authentic.

* * *

Now that the treatises have been properly identified and their authenticity assured, it is appropriate to consider their formal characteristics.

The Munich manuscript contains nine treatises and comprises 86 folios. Each folio measures 21.5 cm. in height and 14.5 cm. in width, with the writing occupying 15 cm. of the height and 8 cm. of the width. Although not completely uniform, the folios usually contain 24 lines of script.

All of the treatises but one are complete, and all are in the proper order. The introductory statement explaining the purpose of the collection (fol. 1^{a-b}) is followed by the commentary on the *Isagoge* of Porphyry (fols. 1^{b}–6^{b}). After these are the commentaries on the *Categories* (fols. 6^{b}–10^{b}), *On Interpretation* (fols. 10^{b}–16^{b}), and *Prior Analytics* (fols. 16^{b}–30^{a}). Then the commentary on Books II–VII of the *Topics* (fols. 30^{a}–41^{b}) follows. The commentary on the *Posteroir Analytics* (fols. 41^{b}–63^{a}) and that on *On Sophistical Refutations* (fols. 63^{a}–72^{a}) come next. They are followed by the commentaries presented here: *Topics* (fols. 72^{a}–77^{a}), *Rhetoric* (fols. 77^{b}–86^{a}), and *Poetics* (fols. 86^{a-b}). Unfortunately, most of folio 86^{b} is missing, but its content can be reconstructed from the Paris manuscript, as well as from the Hebrew and Latin translations.

Some damage has occurred to the manuscript, but it is still quite legible. The first line of the first folio has been somewhat obliterated. In addition, the upper corners of many folios, from folio 63 to the end of the manuscript, have fallen off; as a consequence, portions of the first few lines are sometimes missing. These page corners must have fallen off fairly recently, for Lasinio's copy of the *Short Commentary on Aristotle's Poetics* from the Munich manuscript contains readings which can no longer be found due to those missing corners. Many wormholes may also be found from folio 77 to the end of the volume. These holes are sometimes so large that entire words are missing.

The manuscript has been bound, and the flyleaves of the binding indicate the different stages of recognition of its contents. Thus, on what might be considered to be the title page, the work was first identified as having been written by Averroës, but his name has been crossed out and Avicenna's name written in with both Hebrew and Latin characters. On the same page, the manuscript was identified as "*lib. Medicamenta*" or "*Sefer Refuot*," with an explanation in Hebrew and German that the text is in Arabic with Hebrew characters. The date of 1216 also occurs on this page, written in what seems to be the same handwriting as the Latin and German notations. The other flyleaves contain pencil and pen notes from Steinschneider, dated 1864.

The script, a very old Spanish rabbinical script, is large and clear. Although the script is sometimes almost undecipherable, care has been taken to place points, when needed, over the Hebrew letters used to transliterate two Arabic letters. There is no indication of the name of the scribe. Many corrections of an extensive nature are to be found on the margins and above the lines. They are all written in a hand different from that of the scribe.

The Paris manuscript contains the same nine treatises as the Munich manuscript and comprises 103 folios, on 96 of which are contained the treatises presented in the Munich manuscript. Each folio measures 31 cm. in height and 20 cm. in width, with the writing occupying 17.5 cm of the height and 13 cm. of the width. With few exceptions, each folio contains 25 lines of script.

Although all of the treatises are properly ordered and the manuscript complete, the first folio of the Judaeo-Arabic version is missing. The commentary on the *Isagoge* of Porphyry is contained on the first five extant folios. It is followed by the commentaries on the *Categories* (fols. 6–11), *On Interpretation* (fols. 11–17), and *Prior Analytics* (fols. 17–33). After these is the commentary on Books II–VII of the *Topics* (fols. 33–46). Then there are the commentaries on the *Posterior Analytics* (fols. 46–69) and on *On Sophistical Refutation* (fols. 69–79). These are followed by the commentaries presented here: *Topics* (fols. 79–85), *Rhetoric* (fols. 85–95), and *Poetics* (fols. 95–96). Two short treatises by al-Fārābī are separated from the rest of the collection by a blank folio; both treatises are in Judaeo-Arabic alone: "The Speech about the Conditions of Demonstration" (fols. 98ᵃ–100ᵃ) and "Sections Which Are Necessary in the Art of Logic" (fols. 100ᵇ–103ᵇ).[41]

Unlike that of the Munich manuscript, the script of the Paris manuscript is rabbinic *duktus* tending toward cursive. However, it is much smaller and not as clear as the other. Moreover, no care has been taken to place distinguishing points over the Hebrew letters used to transliterate two Arabic letters. The script is so small that the Paris manuscript is only nine folios longer than the Munich manuscript even though it contains both the Judaeo-Arabic and Hebrew versions of the work. The Hebrew translation is placed opposite the Judaeo-Arabic text, and each page of each version begins and ends with approximately the same words.

The Paris manuscript is in remarkably good condition. Except for the missing page of the Judaeo-Arabic text, no damage has occurred to the manuscript. Each of the section titles is set off by flower-like encirclements in red ink. There are some marginal corrections, many in a hand different from that of the scribe. In a colophon, the scribe identified himself as Ezra ben Rabbi Shlomo ben Gratnia of Saragossa.[42]

Microfilm copies and full-size photographic prints of the manuscripts were used for most of the editing, but both manuscripts have also been examined directly at various stages of the project. For purposes of editing, the Judaeo-Arabic manuscripts were considered to be of equal value. Both are deficient due to lacunae; transposition of phrases, words, or letters; and simple grammatical mistakes. Despite evidence of a later attempt to correct the Munich manuscript (e.g., marginal additions and corrections in a different handwriting), many errors still remain.[43] Those lacunae which have not yet been corrected appear to be simple errors of copying: the scribe often dropped several words which occurred between two identical words on different lines. Such errors make it impossible to depend on the Munich manuscript to the exclusion of the Paris manuscript. The Paris manuscript is faulty in these ways and in other ways. It suffers from numerous lacunae not encountered in the Munich manuscript.[44] The missing passages often refer to technical terms or key verbs for which the scribe usually left blank places, as though he had the intention of filling them in later.

In both manuscripts, fine points of Arabic orthography are missed. This appears to be a consequence of the limitations of Judaeo-Arabic. Generally the orthographic difficulties pose no major problem in discerning the sense of the argument.

When all of the evidence is considered, it appears that the Paris and the Munich manuscripts are independent of each other. In addition to the many instances of simple scribal errors which are not significant, there are numerous instances of errors where each manuscript differs from what might be considered to be the correct reading. Moreover, some passages missing from the Paris manuscript were also originally missing from the Munich manuscript; these were often corrected in the margin, and the corrections must have been inspired by readings from a manuscript other than either the Paris or Munich manuscript.[45] Although such an observation suggests that the manuscripts may still be faulty in ways not yet noticed, it only makes careful study of the texts all the more necessary to those interested in Averroës's teaching.

Another problem arises from the fact that many of the lacunae encountered in the Judaeo-Arabic version of the Paris manuscript do not occur in the Hebrew version. Of the two explanations which may be offered, only one is tenable: to assume that the Judaeo-Arabic version is a poor translation of the Hebrew translation is to reason falsely, for it is unlikely that a scribe could translate from the Hebrew in a manner so faithful to the Arabic style of Averroës. It therefore appears that the Hebrew translation was originally made from a better version of the Arabic text than that which the Judaeo-Arabic version represents. Since the Munich manuscript fills most of the lacunae of the Paris Judaeo-Arabic manuscript, it may very likely be based on, or have been corrected on the basis of, a text closer to the one used by the Hebrew translator.

* * *

In the translation, every attempt has been made to combine readable and intelligible English with fidelity to the original Arabic. For two reasons, it has not always been possible to achieve that goal. In the first place, the technical character of these treatises at times made a certain kind of stiffness unavoidable. Averroës was clearly addressing himself to an audience familiar with the general features of logic and thus did not hesitate to use specialized terminology or to speak in the arid style so appropriate to discourse about logic. Secondly, some awkwardness in style has resulted because insofar as has been consonant with intelligent speech, the same word has been translated in the same way whenever it occurs. Here the idea was that a careful reading of any text will at some point oblige the reader to note the occurence and the recurrence of certain words. If words have been translated differently to suit the taste of the translator, that path is closed to the reader. In sum, while every effort was made to arrive at a faithful and readable translation, the path facilitating instruction was chosen when there was no way to avoid choosing between literal ineloquence and eloquent looseness.

Numerous notes accompany the translation. Their purpose is to help the reader understand the text. For that reason, the notes explain technical terms or give more precise information about references Averroës has made to different authors, books, and opinions. Similarly, the dates of authors and of their writings, as well as page references to their writings, have been included in the notes. When appropriate, references to Aristotle have also been included so that a comparison between Aristotle's definitions and Averroës's explanations may be made. There are no marginal references to the books of Aristotle commented upon in these treatises because Averroës did not follow these works in any orderly manner; as has already been explained, he completely restructured them.

Each treatise or commentary has been divided into paragraphs and into sections to permit the reader to follow Averroës's thought more easily. One rule has been paramount in this task of editing: the stages of the argument must be clearly set forth. Although paragraph division as understood today was not used by Arabic writers in Averroës's time, certain conventions did prevail for denoting the change of thought now expressed in the form of paragraphs. In addition, thick pen strokes were used to indicate the change in argument corresponding to the contemporary division of a treatise into sections. Both of these conventions have been respected in the translation as well as in the edition.

THE TEACHING OF THE TEXT

Averroes's *Short Commentaries on Aristotle's Topics, Rhetoric, and Poetics* are part of a larger work, the collection of *Short Commentaries on Aristotle's Organon*. Yet they differ from the other treatises of the collection in important respects. The other treatises explain the concepts leading up to the kind of reasoning which is based on apodeictic premises and results in apodeictic conclusions—the demonstrative syllogism—and explain how it is used. These three treatises, however, are concerned with arts which use mere similitudes of apodeictic premises and demonstrative reasoning. Moreover, while the other treatises are recommended because they teach how to reason correctly, these three treatises are presented as providing ways of imitating or abridging correct reasoning in order to influence other human beings in any number of situations, but especially with regard to political decisions and religious beliefs.

These three treatises even stand apart physically from the other treatises of the collection. Although neither the *Rhetoric* nor the *Poetics* was traditionally viewed as belonging to the *Organon*, Averroës included the *Short Commentary on Aristotle's Rhetoric* and the *Short Commentary on Aristotle's Poetics* as the last two treatises in this collection of short commentaries on the *Organon*. He also reversed the positions of the *Short Commentary on Aristotle's Topics* and the *Short Commentary on Aristotle's On Sophistical Refutations* with respect to their order in the traditional view of the *Organon*. As a result, the *Short Commentary on Aristotle's Topics*, the *Short Commentary on Aristotle's Rhetoric*, and the *Short Commentary on Aristotle's Poetics* are the last three treatises in the collection. So that the significance of this extensive reworking of the *Organon* not escape attention, Averroës offered another indication of the separate status of these treatises. As justification for having reversed the order of the *Short Commentary on Aristotle's Topics* and the *Short Commentary on Aristotle's On Sophistical Refutations*, he limited the art of sophistry to deception about demonstrative arguments. Entirely without parallel in Aristotle's work, that limitation served to explain why the treatise about sophistical arguments followed the treatise about demonstrative arguments in this collection. Averroës then linked the art of dialectic to the art of rhetoric by extolling its usefulness for bringing about persuasion and linked the art of poetics to the art of rhetoric on the grounds that it could persuade people by means of imaginative representations.[46] All of these observations suggest that while the larger collection does constitute a whole and must be studied as such in order to grasp the full teaching, it can also be divided into two major parts and that either one of these parts can be studied separately with profit.

The reason for studying these treatises, rather than those belonging to the other division, is to acquire an understanding of the relation between politics, religion, and philosophy in the thought of Averroës. Intelligent awareness of such topics is important because of the constant influence they exert over thought and action. Learned as well as unlearned human beings are continuously seeking better ways to live with one another as fellow citizens, as members of different nations, or simply as associates. Similarly, decisions about work, play, and family life are tied to opinions about one's place in the universe and about the kind of life proper to man. Whether those opinions are based upon precepts deriving from a particular revelation or are the result of some kind of independent thought, they play an important role in daily life and demand the careful attention of reflective individuals.

Averroës is an important source of instruction about these topics, because the problem of their relationship occupied so much of his practical and intellectual activity. Exceptionally well informed about the sources and interpretations of the revealed religion which dominated his own community, he applied its precepts to particular matters in his capacity as a supreme judge and speculated about broader aspects of the religion in the political realm whenever he acted as adviser to his Almohad sovereigns. He becomes especially important to us because he did not restrict himself to the notions prevalent in that community. To the contrary, he found rare philosophical insight in the thought of Aristotle—a member of a community not affected by revealed religion—and tried to persuade his learned fellow Muslims of Aristotle's merit by writing explanatory commentaries on Aristotle's thought. On a few occasions, he even directed the argument to the larger public in order to defend philosophic activity against attacks by zealous advocates of religious orthodoxy and in order to explain the theoretical limitations of religious speculation, as well as the political significance of religion.[47]

Among all of his writings, the *Short Commentaries on Aristotle's Topics, Rhetoric, and Poetics* are the best sources for acquiring an understanding of the relation Averroës thought existed between politics, religion, and philosophy. In the first place, his thought about this problem was based on specific ideas about the logical character of different kinds of speech, their proximity to certain knowledge, and the investigative or practical purposes to which each might be put. While these ideas are presupposed in his other works, including his larger commentaries on the logical arts, they are explained in these treatises. Secondly, these treatises contain the fullest statement of the grounds for Averroës's abiding disagreement with those who considered themselves the defenders of the faith. In Averroës's view, these dialectical theologians and masters of religious tradition were responsible for confusing the common people by using extraordinarily complex arguments to speak about simple principles of faith and guilty of attacking philosophy under the pretext of saving the faith they had garbled. Awareness of the reasons for his disagreement with them is important, because it is the background against which he expressed his ideas concerning the relation between political life and religious belief, as well as between religious belief and philosophic investigation.

* * *

However, the substantive teaching of these three treatises is not immediately evident. It is so intimately related to the technical exposition of the different logical arts that the treatises first appear to be purely technical. Even though it is at once obvious that the technical exposition was designed to correct prevalent misconceptions about each one of the arts, the deeper significance of that correction must be ferreted out. For example, another consequence of incorporating rhetoric and poetics into logic is that it allowed Averroës to stress the importance of each art for inquiry and instruction, as well as to allude to the way each art shared in the attributes of logic. He thus countered the prevailing tendency to restrict rhetoric and poetics to eloquence and to examine each solely in terms of style. Then, by reminding the reader that rhetorical proofs were quite far removed from certainty and that imaginative representations were frequently based on the merest similitudes of the real thing, Averroës easily prodded him into thinking about the status of our knowledge with regard to the generally accepted political and religious uses of each art.[48] In this way he brought an apparently abstract, timeless discussion to bear on concrete, actual issues. The advantage of his procedure was that it never obliged him to quit the cloak of scientific detachment.

Nonetheless, to appreciate the cleverness of this procedure, its diaphanous quality must be recognized. Averroës tried to facilitate that recognition by the judicious use of subtle allusions. The first occurs at the very beginning of the larger treatise. There he justified his summary account of the logical arts on the grounds that it provided what was needed if one were to learn the essentials of the arts which had already been perfected in his time. This justification was closely related to the goal of the treatise: to enable the interested person to acquire the concepts by which these already perfected arts could be learned. Realization of that goal necessitated understanding how concept and assent were used in each one of the logical arts, these being identified as demonstration, dialectic, sophistry, rhetoric, and poetics.[49] Although it was never given, the obvious reason for such a goal had to be that knowledge of the essentials of those other, already perfected, arts was somehow important.

In the introduction, the only example of already perfected arts cited by Averroës was medicine. However, in the course of the exposition, he referred less explicitly to other arts—e.g., dialectical theology, traditional theology, and traditional jurisprudence. Even though he explicitly cited the art of medicine in the introduction, he made no attempt to correct it in the course of the larger exposition. Conversely, in the course of the larger exposition he did try to correct those other arts which he had not previously cited in an explicit manner. From this perspective, it appears that the ultimate goal of the treatise was to enable the reader to become competent in logic and especially competent in assessing the different ranks of the classes of concept and assent used in the already perfected arts, not so much in order to learn the essentials of those arts as in order to learn how to evaluate them critically. The identification of that ultimate goal cannot, therefore, be separated from the identification of the already perfected arts. Once both identifications are made, the practical, reformative character of the logical exposition becomes evident.

Another particularly significant hint that these abstract summaries of the logical arts contain a broader teaching occurs at the very end of the whole collection. There, Averroës did not hesitate to place the different logical arts in a definite hierarchy. Whereas the particular skill to be acquired from poetics was explicitly judged to be nonessential for man's peculiar perfection, the proper understanding of logic—that is, knowledge of the ranks of the classes of concept and assent—was explicitly judged to be propaedeutic to the attainment of ultimate human perfection. Ultimate human perfection, moreover, was clearly stated to depend on man's acquiring true theory. The reason for that distinction derives from a prior judgment about the superiority of theoretical knowledge to practical action, and the implication of the distinction is that the things the art of poetics allows one to make and do are inferior to the things the larger art of logic allows one to understand.[50] What is striking about the distinction is that Averroës eschewed the easy subordination of poetics to the larger art of logic on the basis of part to whole, treating them instead as though in competition for supreme recognition. That is, in fact, faithful to the claims of the poetical art's protagonists, and Averroës bore witness to those claims before subordinating poetics to logic in such a definitive manner.

That Averroës concluded the treatise by insisting upon the essential hierarchy is significant because of its easily discernible implications. In the first place, it suggests that the art of logic as a whole is not relative, but is guided by reference to a definite standard. Secondly, it shows that the different logical arts do not have equal claims to priority and that their claims are to be judged in terms of their facilitating the attainment of ultimate human perfection. The basic idea is that if man's perfection consists in theoretical understanding, then his actions or practice should be ordered so as to allow the best development of his theoretical nature. Logic is important because the characteristics of theoretical knowledge are explained in it, and theoretical knowledge is differentiated from other kinds of knowledge. Moreover, it is the only art which shows how to acquire theoretical knowledge.

It was necessary for Averroës to state the merits of logic so clearly, because its use was condemned by some people with extensive influence. Usually, those who argued against logic criticized its foreign origin or claimed that other arts could provide theoretical knowledge in a more direct manner. The general tone of the larger treatise does away with the first kind of argument: logic is treated as an art which belongs to the Islamic world as much as to any other world. Those arts alluded to in the beginning statement of the purpose of logic, the arts whose critical evaluation logic will facilitate, are among the ones thought to have greater merit than logic for attaining theoretical knowledge. It is for this reason that their critical evaluation is of such importance.

* * *

Although prepared by the earlier investigation, the critical evaluation is carried out in these three treatises by means of a very selective presentation of each logical art. Thus, in setting forth his account of dialectic, rhetoric, and poetics, Averroës stressed the technical aspects relating to the first two arts. A very extensive explanation of the way arguments are made in each art, of the way they are employed, and of the value of those arguments took the place of an explicit discussion about how these arts might actually be used, that is, to what substantive use they might be put. As a result, essential features of both arts were neglected. For example, in the *Short Commentary on Aristotle's Topics*, there is an account of the quality of dialectical premises, of the extent of belief dialectical argument provides, and of the proximity of dialectic to demonstration, but there is no mention whatever of its possible use for inquiring into the theoretical arts or into the same subjects as metaphysics—uses clearly indicated in other commentaries.[51] Similarly, in the *Short Commentary on Aristotle's Rhetoric*, the standard uses to which rhetoric may be put—deliberation, defense and accusation, praise and blame—are passed over in silence until the very end of the treatise; even then, they are mentioned only incidentally. The *Short Commentary on Aristotle's Poetics* is presented in a different manner, however. Very little is said about the technical parts of the poetical art, and relatively much is said about the uses to which it may be put. To perceive the details of this selectiveness more clearly and to grasp its significance, it is necessary to look at the summary of each art.

When speaking about the art of dialectic, Averroës emphasized that it should not be confused with demonstration despite the appearance of certainty which its arguments provide. The crucial difference between the two arts is that dialectical premises may be false, whereas demonstrative premises are always certain and true. Consequently, not truth—as with demonstration—but renown is the basic consideration in choosing a dialectical premise. The premises used in dialectical syllogisms differ from those used in demonstrative syllogisms for yet another reason: although universal predicates, they do not encompass all of the universal predicates used in demonstration. Nor are the premises of dialectical syllogisms all that prevent it from being identical to demonstration: in addition, the induction used in dialectic has a very limited use in demonstration. Finally, dialectic differs from demonstration because the classes of syllogism to which it has access are far more numerous than those open to the art of demonstration.[52] Obviously, one should not confuse the art of dialectic with that of demonstration. Still, the whole presentation appears very arid, and one cannot help but wonder why Averroës would have been content to insist upon all these technical considerations in order to make such a minor point.

The answer is relatively simple: the tedious technical discussion is a screen for a more important substantive argument. The long discussion of induction, for example, prepared the grounds for Averroës's criticism of the dialectical theologians. This becomes apparent once the particular induction repeatedly cited by Averroës is carefully considered: it is the one used to prove that all bodies are created because most of those to be seen around us are created. The conclusion of that induction was itself the major premise for the familiar syllogism about the world being created because it is a body. Although he never explicitly refuted either argument, Averroës showed that the use of inductions to arrive at premises of syllogisms was highly questionable logical practice. At the most, inductions could be helpful for affirming something that was already generally acknowledged, but never for discovering what was unknown. His teaching therefore restricted induction to a very limited role in dialectical argument. The implication was that those who used induction extensively and placed no restrictions on its use—as the dialectical theologians did, for example—really knew nothing about the art they claimed to practice.

The best way of indicating this appreciation of their worth was to destroy the grounds of their arguments and to establish the correct basis of the art. That is why Averroës tried to identify the kind of assent dialectic provides, show what the true dialectical argument is and how it is constructed, explain the limits of the premises used in those syllogisms, and relate the art of dialectic to other arts according to the quality of its arguments. Above all, that tactic allowed him to avoid mentioning the dialectical theologians by name, a move that was masterfully subtle: rather than attack them openly here, he pretended to ignore them as though this were not the place to speak of them. The effect of his silence, then, was to suggest that they should not really be associated with the art of dialectic. Even though it was possible to say that they practiced an art in their theological disputations, it was clear that the art was not dialectic.

This interpretation admittedly places extensive emphasis on Averroës's silence about the dialectical theologians. Yet no other explanation can account for the strange character of this treatise, especially as compared to the *Short Commentary on Aristotle's Rhetoric.* If a discussion about the dialectical theologians were to occur in any treatise, it is reasonable that it occur in a treatise about dialectic—the art they claimed to practice. However, Averroës relegated that discussion to his treatise on rhetoric. Even so, he did not completely exclude consideration of the dialectical theologians from this treatise for he made obvious allusions to their favorite arguments. It seems necessary, therefore, to ask about the relationship between the teaching of the treatise and the unexpectedly neglected dialectical theologians. As has already been suggested, the whole movement of the treatise toward a strict interpretation of dialectic then becomes especially significant. In addition, by insisting more upon the limitations than upon the varied uses of dialectic and more upon what it was not appropriate for than what it was appropriate for, Averroës was able to indicate his disagreements with the dialectical theologians.

For example, according to this treatise the art of dialectic would be entirely unsuited for investigation. Averroës remained silent about its investigative possibilities here. He also emphasized the technical differences between dialectic and demonstration, as though he wanted to suggest that dialectic does not have the same force or logical necessity as demonstration. Above all, he explicitly denied that training in dialectic could have any relevance for pursuit of the demonstrative arts, a denial which was simply contrary to Aristotle's view.[53] Clearly, Averroës wanted to show that dialectic ought not to be used to investigate the same subjects the art of demonstration is used to investigate. However, because of the numerous references to the investigative possibilities of dialectic in Averroës's other writings, this presentation must be considered partial or restrictive. The fuller teaching is that dialectic may be used to investigate any subject investigated by the art of demonstration, but that the degree of certainty to be expected of dialectical investigation is inferior to what might be expected of demonstrative investigation.

By presenting this partial or restrictive teaching about dialectic, Averroës enabled the reader to call the whole activity of the dialectical theologians into question. If the art of dialectic cannot be used for most kinds of theoretical investigation, then it cannot support the complicated theological disputes characteristic of dialectical theology. Those disputes presuppose a detailed and deep metaphysical inquiry for which dialectic—as presented here—would be inadequate. Consequently, either the dialectical theologians reached their conclusions by means of another art and then presented them in dialectical terms or they attributed too much certainty to their dialectical arguments. Whatever the explanation, their use of dialectic was erroneous.

Averroës could have made the same point without presenting dialectic in this partial or restrictive manner. In the *Incoherence of the Incoherence*, for example, he used dialectical arguments to counter al-Ghazālī's attacks against philosophy. The subject matter was such that he thus used dialectic to investigate weighty philosophical and theological issues. Yet he never lost sight of the limitations of the art and frequently apologized for the general character of his arguments, explaining that they were based on premises which presupposed a fuller examination of each issue.[54] Although it suggested the problematic character of his own replies to al-Ghazālī, this admission of the limitations of dialectical argument raised a graver problem with regard to al-Ghazālī's original criticisms: on what deeper investigation were they based? The advantage of the partial or restrictive teaching about dialectic in the *Short Commentary on Aristotle's Topics*, then, is that this problem was raised quickly and decisively.

Averroës attempted to restrict his presentation of the art of dialectic in another way. At the very end of the treatise, when enumerating the reasons which prompted Aristotle to write about the art, he described dialectic as an art limited to contentious argument between questioner and answerer and even suggested that Aristotle's major purpose in writing about dialectic was to provide each contender with the tools that would help defeat the opponent. The explanation was that once Aristotle had noted that most well-known premises—the basic elements of dialectical argument—are in opposition and may thus be used to prove or disprove the same proposition, he then recognized how useful the art of dialectic was for training in contentious speech. Again, even though Averroës obviously recognized the need to indicate the partial character of his presentation and thus admitted that dialectic had uses other than contentious argument, he immediately reinforced his partial interpretation by dismissing those other uses as irrelevant for the purposes of this treatise and did so without even listing them. As presented here, the contentious art of dialectic is more like the art of fencing: it is good for contending with someone else, but it should be directed by another art.

This partial or restrictive insistence on the contentious character of the art served two purposes. First of all, it drew attention to the question of the audience whom the dialectical theologians usually addressed. If dialectic is really suited for contentious argument between men of equal capacity, it can have little effect when it is employed by the learned to communicate with the usually uneducated mass of people. It appears that the dialectical theologians were trying to use dialectic for the wrong purpose; the art of rhetoric is much better suited for instructing the general public. Secondly, this partial account of the art provides a very accurate idea of the original duty of the dialectical theologians: contending with each other or with the misdirected in defense of the faith.[55] They seem to have neglected their original duty, which was more consonant with the art of dialectic, to attempt activities for which dialectic is very poorly suited.

These thoughts, prompted by an attentive reading of the treatise, show that in order to uncover Averroës's teaching it is as important to ask about what is implied as to ask about what is said. Because the omissions are as significant as the declarations, the only way to explain the whole treatise adequately is to ask about what is missing. A simple account of the technical description of dialectic would not be sufficient, because that description is at such variance with Averroës's other explanations of the art. Moreover, an account of the technical characteristics of dialectic would neglect the allusions to a broader issue. The interpretation set forth here not only explains all the parts of the treatise, it also provides a means of relating this treatise to the other treatises as part of one teaching.

The striking difference between the *Short Commentary on Aristotle's Topics* and the *Short Commentary on Aristotle's Rhetoric* is the emphasis on the dialectical theologians in the latter. Abū al-Ma'ālī and al-Ghazālī are named a number of times, and there are passing references to the dialectical theologians as a group. In addition, several arguments of Abū al-Ma'ālī and al-Ghazālī are cited in order to illustrate different features of rhetorical discourse.[56] However, very few of the references are favorable. In almost every instance, Averroës cited the argument of the dialectical theologians as a negative example and then went on to suggest the correct rhetorical argument.[57]

It was appropriate to criticize the arguments used by the dialectical theologians according to the standards for rhetorical discourse because the dialectical theologians were so ignorant about the technical characteristics of dialectic that they sought to use it when they should have used rhetoric. Rhetoric is the proper art for instructing the general public or addressing it about any matter. That is why Averroës referred to it as "this art of public speaking" in the opening lines of the *Short Commentary on Aristotle's Rhetoric* and arranged the discussion of rhetoric in the treatise according to the persuasiveness of different subjects. For the same reason, when he set down instructions for constructing rhetorical arguments he emphasized what would have greatest persuasive effect on the audience.[58] In fact, the whole treatise is organized so as to show why rhetoric is more suited for public discourse than dialectic. The basic reason is one that was alluded to in the *Short Commentary on Aristotle's Topics*: rhetoric permits the speaker to pass over difficult matters or even to be deceptive regarding them, whereas such practices cannot be admitted in dialectical argument.[59]

One reason the dialectical theologians might have been so confused about the technical characteristics of dialectic that they would try to use it when rhetoric would have been a better tool is that, superficially, the two arts are quite similar. They both have the same general purpose of bringing about assent. They are also similar in that each art is dependent on a kind of common opinion known as supposition. Averroës did not hesitate to point out these similarities nor to direct the reader's attention to them by talking about rhetorical arguments as though they were special examples of dialectical arguments. The enthymeme was said to correspond to the syllogism and the example to the induction. He even analyzed the forms of the enthymeme according to the categories normally used to discuss dialectical syllogisms and, in the discussion of the material aspects of the enthymeme, implied that parallels with the syllogism could be drawn.[60]

Nonetheless, the similarities between dialectic and rhetoric are only superficial. When the two arts are more closely considered, it becomes readily apparent that they are not identical. For example, even though both arts are used to bring about assent, syllogisms and inductions are used to accomplish this task in dialectic while *persuasive things* are used in rhetoric —that is, even though enthymemes and examples are used, persuasive devices having nothing to do with syllogistic argument may just as easily be used. Then again, while both arts are dependent upon supposition, the particular type of supposition used in rhetoric is of a lower order than that used in dialectic. A corollary of that difference is that rhetorical arguments induce people to belief for reasons which usually do not withstand deeper scrutiny and thus occupy a lower rank with regard to certainty than dialectical arguments.[61] Even the emphasis on the dialectical syllogism served to distinguish the two arts. By constantly drawing attention to the dialectical syllogism, Averroës was able to contrast it with the rhetorical argument *par excellence*, the enthymeme, and to show in what ways they differed.[62]

The superficial parallelism that Averroës drew between the two arts served a dual purpose. In the first place, his explanations that the differences between the two arts were greater than their similarities permitted him to show why rhetoric was better suited for the purposes of dialectical theology than the art of dialectic. At one point, using rhetoric to explain rhetoric, Averroës could even call upon the famous al-Ghazālī for testimony that people with different intellectual capacities needed to be addressed in different ways.[63] Unfortunately, neither al-Ghazālī nor the other dialectical theologians had thought about applying such a principle to their own popular writings. As has been previously noted, however, Averroës had thought about it; most of his criticism of the dialectical theologians and their arguments was directed to that issue. It was in order to show why these arguments could not be used to persuade people, not in order to harm religion, that he pointed out the weaknesses of their theological arguments.

The use of the superficial parallelism also permitted Averroës to make an important substantive argument. When discussing the different uses of enthymemes and examples, as well as their similarities to the dialectical syllogisms and inductions, Averroës twice referred to Abū al-Ma'ālī in order to show how an inadequate grasp of rhetoric led to deeper errors about important theoretical subjects.[64] Because he did not understand how to use a disjunctive conditional syllogism, Abū al-Maʿālī mistakenly believed that he had refuted the idea that the world might have come into being through the uniting of various elements. This mistaken belief not only meant that he failed to refute that idea, it was also a reason for him to abandon further inquiry into the problem. His erroneous belief that it was possible to acquire universal certainty by means of the example led to even more alarming consequences: according to Averroës, to attribute such power to the example would reduce scientific investigation to child's play and render any kind of instruction useless. Thus, in addition to confusing the usually uneducated mass of people by addressing them with complicated arguments, the dialectical theologians led themselves into error by failing to comprehend the deeper significance of their own arguments. Another reason for showing the inadequacies in their arguments, then, was to show why those arguments needed to be examined more carefully and why the possibility for deeper philosophical inquiry needed to be kept open. In both instances, the arguments of the dialectical theologians were refuted in order to suggest how they could be improved.

However, the dialectical theologians were not the only ones to have insufficient knowledge about the characteristics of the logical arts. While they used something like rhetorical arguments without being fully aware of what they were doing, practitioners of other arts used different kinds of rhetorical devices without having an adequate understanding of the limitations of such devices. The last third of the treatise on rhetoric is devoted to a discussion of the persuasive things external to the art of rhetoric, things which are explicitly assigned a lower rank of logical value and rhetorical merit than the enthymeme or example.[65] Central to that discussion was a consideration of how the arguments proper to the traditionalist schools of theology and jurisprudence—testimony, recorded traditions, consensus, and challenging—might be used. The traditionalist theologians and jurists had failed to understand the rhetorical origins of these devices and consequently relied upon them too heavily. As a result, conflict and strife arose concerning things allegedly proven by these devices. To remedy that situation Averroës tried to show the precise limitations of these devices and to clarify their very restricted persuasive qualities.[66]

He identified testimony as being a report about something or a series of reports—i.e., a tradition—about something and said that testimony was about things either perceived by the senses or apprehended by the intellect. Although testimony could be concerned with what we ourselves have perceived or intellectually apprehended, it is unusual to report such matters to ourselves. For that reason, Averroës directed his remarks to an explanation of the extent of belief which ought to be accorded what others claim to have perceived or to have intellectually apprehended.[67] His argument was that unless we ourselves have perceived what has been reported or are able to form an imaginative representation of it, reporting can lead to essential certainty only if it can be proven by a syllogism.[68] Although he did not go into extensive detail about these conditions, it is not difficult to think of situations in which they might be applied. What, for example, would be a convincing imaginative representation of divine revelation to a particular individual? Or how could a syllogism about the event be constructed? The problem becomes more difficult when the reports concern sense-perceptible matters which have never been perceived; for instance, a secret and solitary voyage by an easily recognizable and famous figure.

Averroës also tried to explain the kinds of problems which arise with regard to what has been intellectually apprehended. Testimony about this sort of thing can be of value only to those unable to apprehend it, e.g., the usually uneducated mass of people.[69] Still, for testimony to be effective in this instance, something more is needed. The audience must have some notion of the significance of what is being reported, and that can be acquired only by careful explanation. For example, it is not enough to report that a particular individual received a special revelation from a divine agent. In addition, an effort must be made to explain what revelation is, how it can be transmitted, and what that means for the people exposed to the revelation.

His basic argument was that, whether the matter reported about had been intellectually apprehended or perceived by the senses, recourse to reports could not replace intellectual understanding. Reports are nothing more than persuasive devices and are subject to the same kinds of limitations as other rhetorical devices. For this reason he criticized those who sought to derive certainty from reports by enumerating conditions with which to judge the quality of different reports.[70] Averroës's goal was to underline the suppositional character of reports so that those who used them could begin to think about the problems of communicating the meaning of these reports to others.

Throughout the discussion he tried to insist that testimony or reporting was only of persuasive value; the fuller context of the report had to be understood and explained before it could have any wider value.

When discussing the other persuasive devices external to the art of rhetoric, Averroës reached similar conclusions. He did not consider it possible, for example, to cite consensus to prove the validity of anything. As al-Ghazālī had admitted, there was such confusion about the whole notion of consensus that agreement about the exact definition of the term was lacking.[71] Averroës never questioned the principle that when the community of Muslims agreed upon something, their agreement was infallible. He simply argued that it was not possible to ascertain how that agreement might be determined and thus not possible to use it for deciding whether a person or doctrine had violated the consensus.

Even accomplishing miraculous feats in order to challenge others to belief had definite limitations according to Averroës, since the ability to perform miracles is no sign of special wisdom. At the most, Averroës conceded that such an ability ought to induce people to have a good opinion of the person who performs such feats and to be disposed to believe him. But the more important question was how to acquire some kind of knowledge that would permit a sound judgment about the teaching that this miracle-worker would then set forth. Once again Averroës was able to cite al-Ghazālī as an eminent witness who shared this point of view.[72]

The teaching about these persuasive devices which are external to the art of rhetoric is that they cannot be used as evidence of certain knowledge, except under limited conditions. Averroës also explained that these devices may stand in need of the enthymeme to achieve even their limited effect. The significance of a report, for example, might become clear only when explained by an enthymeme. For that reason, the art of rhetoric should be organized in a way that permits the enthymemes to have their rightful precedence. By organizing the art according to such a hierarchy, another benefit is acquired: to the extent that enthymemes are like syllogisms, this organization of the art insures the possibility of acquiring certainty. When the enthymemes take precedence, it is easier to guide rhetoric by a more rigorous syllogistic art. Averroës thought that the ancients had understood the art in this way and he tried to preserve that understanding.[73]

However, in presenting this view of the art, Averroës restricted rhetoric in an important respect. Until the very end of the treatise, rhetoric was discussed in a context that made it seem to have use only for the popular discussion of religion or for instruction. Every effort was made to show the similarities and differences between dialectic and rhetoric. It is only in the penultimate paragraph, just before turning to a consideration of poetics, that the political uses of rhetoric are mentioned. The earlier portions of the treatise concentrated on the technical aspects of the art and stressed its superficial similarities with dialectic. The end of the treatise stresses the uses to which rhetoric can be put, and these uses turn out to be very similar to those of the art of poetics.

For the purposes of this collection of commentaries, then, rhetoric can be said to occupy a middle ground between the art of dialectic and the art of poetics. It is similar to dialectic in that its arguments can be discussed and analyzed in terms of their formal characteristics; it is similar to poetics in that it has great usefulness for political matters. By neglecting the political uses of rhetoric and concentrating on the ways rhetoric could be used in the popular discussion of religion or for instruction, Averroës was able to set forth his criticisms of dialectical theology. Since he could not remain completely silent about the political uses of rhetoric, he did the next best thing and acknowledged those uses briefly at the very end of the treatise when discussing the reasons which prompted Aristotle to study the art of rhetoric. Such a tactic allowed him to avoid explicit endorsement of Aristotle's views while suggesting at least tacit agreement with them. More importantly, that reference to Aristotle's views was sufficient to remind the thoughtful reader of what had been omitted from the preceding discussion and thus to underline the corrective teaching about the dialectical theologians.

Emphasis on the political usefulness of poetics is the dominant theme of Averroës's *Short Commentary on Aristotle's Poetics*. He began the treatise with a statement about the political uses to which the art of poetics might be put and later explained how recognition of these uses had prompted Aristotle to write about poetics. While the acknowledgement of Aristotle's recognition of the political uses of rhetoric was perfunctory in the *Short Commentary on Aristotle's Rhetoric*, the acknowledgement of his recognition of the political uses of poetics is given more attention in this treatise. Here, the acknowledgement is preceded by Averroës's own recognition of those uses, and it is complemented by the art being recommended to our attention because of its suitability for political uses.[74] Essentially this treatise differs from the other two treatises in that the technical aspects of poetics are almost passed over in this treatise in order to stress the political uses of the art. In each of the other two treatises, the practical uses of dialectic or of rhetoric were almost passed over in order that the technical aspects of either of those arts might be stressed. An example of the way technical explanations are almost passed over in this treatise is the absence of a discussion about the amount of assent provided by the speeches used in poetics. In fact, the word "assent" (*taṣdīq*) does not even occur in the treatise. Such indifference to the technical aspects of the art is counterbalanced only by explicit admissions about the potentially deceptive quality of poetics and by attempts to explain those admissions.[75]

Poetics is potentially deceptive because of the character of the speeches used in the art. The poet may strive to make these speeches rhythmical in order to move the souls of the listeners as he desires, but he gives no consideration to ordering these speeches in order to bring them closer to truth or to certainty. To the contrary, poetic speeches are explicitly said to be usually of little value for seizing the essence of anything.[76] The reason is that although they are meant to give an imaginative representation of something, the resulting imaginative representation is not designed to portray the object as it really is. Consequently, a literal interpretation of poetic speeches will quite probably lead to error. However, listeners can just as readily be deceived by poetic speeches if they make a mistake about the way in which the imaginative representation is couched: even though the listeners may know better than to take the speech literally, they could fall into error by taking the speech as a metaphor when it is really a simile or vice versa.[77]

Still, all of these errors can be traced to simple confusion on the part of the listeners about the meaning of the particular poetic speeches. Closer attention to the rules of the art and to the speeches themselves would help to avoid these kinds of errors. In these cases the error can be corrected by using another kind of speech to describe the thing in question. When the sea is spoken of as being "the sweat of the earth brought together in its bladder," for example, it is readily apparent that a simple physical explanation of seawater and of the topography of the earth would dispel any tendency to literal belief in this poetic image.[78] However, there are things which cannot be conceived of at all or which are extremely difficult to form a concept about except by the kinds of allusions given in imaginative representations. Unfortunately, poetic speeches about these kinds of things lead to error even more frequently.[79] Moreover, to the extent that it is impossible or extremely difficult to explain such things by any other kind of speech, there is little chance of removing the error once it occurs. Averroës gave only one example of these kinds of things: a being which is neither in the world nor outside of it, that is, God.[80] Admittedly, it is extremely difficult, if not impossible, to conceive of God by means of anything other than imaginative representations. Nor can it be denied that confusion, if not error, about God is widespread.

These things which are difficult or impossible to conceive of seem to differ in additional ways from the other things which are also represented by poetic speeches but are easily conceived of. Although Averroës nowhere admitted as much, clearly it is only with regard to the former kinds of things that the practical uses of poetics come into play. These uses include moving the souls of the listeners to predilection for something or to flight from it, moving them to believe or disbelieve in something, and moving them to do or not do certain kinds of actions. The art of poetics may also be used simply to move the souls of the listeners to awe or to wonder because of the delightfulness of the imaginative representation.[81] While the souls of the listeners may be moved to predilection for God or to a desire to flee from Him because of the poetic speech presented to them, it is unlikely that a poetic speech about the sea would have such an effect. A poetic speech about natural phenomena would arouse such emotions only to the extent that the listeners were moved to contemplate the cause of such pleasing or terrifying things, but that too would be linked closely to the notion of God. The contrast becomes starker upon considering the usefulness of poetic speeches for inducing belief or disbelief in something. Similarly, imaginative representations about natural phenomena are not designed to move the listeners to action. At the most, poetic speeches about natural phenomena arouse feelings of awe or wonder in the souls of the listeners; such speeches instruct the listeners about the beauty or the awesomeness of the surrounding world.

When these explanations about the potential for deceptiveness in poetic speeches—especially those speeches about things which it is impossible or extremely difficult to conceive of except by poetic speeches—are carefully considered and compared to the emphasis on the practical uses of poetics, a new significance of the treatise comes into focus. In addition to its political uses, poetics would seem to have patent religious uses. The reasoning behind this conclusion is that influencing the opinions or beliefs and the actions of others is as much a concern of religion as it is of politics. This is especially true of the kind of religion which strives to provide for the welfare of a community of believers, that is, of a religion like Islam.[82] Another way of stating this would be to say that politics is seen to be more than secular. By introducing the idea of speaking about God and showing how it is related to the practical uses of poetics, Averroës has suggested that political concerns are necessarily related to religious concerns.

Although it becomes most apparent in this treatise, that relationship is not introduced for the first time here. The argument of the other two treatises presupposed the interplay between religion and politics. In the treatises on dialectic and rhetoric, a major effort was made to correct the evils wreaked by the dialectical theologians and to establish principles which would prevent those evils from recurring. While the evils in question derived primarily from the realm of religious opinion or belief, they clearly had consequences in the political realm. The treatise on poetics differs from those two treatises because the interplay between religion and politics is made more apparent and because there is a very explicit emphasis on how the art can influence actions. There is, then, a movement or a shift in emphasis in these treatises, a movement from concern solely about opinions or beliefs to concern about both belief and actions. That movement is symbolic of the movement from a narrow concern with religion and politics to a more inclusive concern with both. Insofar as the treatise on poetics represents the culmination of that movement, it stands apart from the other two treatises.

A sign of the different status of the treatise on poetics is the absence of any reference to the dialectical theologians or to the problems they caused. The emphasis here is massively on what the art is for, not on ways that it might be corrected. That does not mean, however, that this treatise occupies a higher rank than the other two treatises. Indeed, the art of poetics as presented here is hardly free from major difficulties. The primary difficulty is the apparent inevitability of deception in the poetic speeches that deal with concepts like God. Implicitly, the argument is that such deceptiveness is part of poetic speeches qua poetic speeches, as though the art of poetics had no internal standards. Averroës brought the problem into sharper perspective by suggesting that speeches about such subjects, insofar as they were deceptive, were more characteristic of sophistry than of poetics.[83]

Although he did not explain what he meant by drawing the parallel with reference to these speeches, he made a similar observation about poetics in the subsequent paragraph. He noted that poetics was classed among the syllogistic arts even though the syllogism is used in it only to make poetic speeches deceptively resemble speeches of other arts.[84] The implication is that poetics can be used for willful deception. When the poet pretends to have proofs about what he says without really having them, poetics strongly resembles sophistry. In that instance his use of syllogistic arguments would not be in accord with the logical rules for their use, but would be deceptively structured in order to receive greater credibility than they might otherwise receive.

Such a possibility arises because, with poetics as with rhetoric, there is no internal control to keep it from being used for deceptive purposes.[85] With dialectic and demonstration, however, the rules of syllogistic reasoning must be followed. Any purposely deceptive use of the arguments belonging to those arts is external to the art. Because poetics is not structured in that way and can therefore be used as sophistry would be, the deceptiveness of its speeches—especially those concerning things which cannot be conceived of at all or only conceived of with difficulty by other speeches—seems inevitable. By linking poetics and sophistry on this issue, Averroës suggested that he drew the same conclusion.

Yet that conclusion is not without exception. The inevitability of deception about this kind of poetic speech depends on a very basic limitation in the explanation, a limitation Averroës need not have imposed. Confusion about the subjects treated by this kind of poetic speech could be removed by metaphysical investigation. However, Averroës remained silent about that possibility. Through his silence he presented as restrictive a teaching about poetics as he did about dialectic.

In part, this restrictive teaching about poetics allowed him to criticize the way the art was being used. That he was not more explicit in his criticism can be understood by reflecting about the generally accepted view among Muslims that the Qur'ān is the best example of poetic excellence in Arabic. Without becoming involved in that controversy, he nevertheless managed to make certain suggestions about Qur'ānic exegesis. His belief about the potential deceptiveness of poetic speeches carried the implication that it was necessary to keep imaginative representations simple and as direct as possible. In this respect, the treatise on poetics, like the treatise on dialectic and rhetoric, contributes to a solution of the fundamental practical issue. By emphasizing the dangers of poetic speech and its politico-religious uses, this treatise subtly urges great care upon those who would use such speech to communicate with most people and especially upon those who might seek to interpret such speech to the people. However such advice is never given; to the extent that it is a consequence of the argument, it is only an implicit consequence. The treatise on poetics remains at a certain level of abstraction at all times.

The restrictive teaching about poetics also allowed Averroës to put the general argument of these three treatises into the proper perspective. Because the potential deceptiveness of poetic speeches brought the art into close relationship with sophistry, Averroës insisted at the very end of the treatise that perfect skill in poetics was foreign to ultimate human perfection.[86] He explained this judgment in his summary of the whole collection of short commentaries by noting that ultimate human perfection depended on correct theoretical knowledge.[87] It was clear from the preceding exposition that poetics could not furnish such knowledge. It is equally clear from the presentation of dialectic and rhetoric that they could not furnish such knowledge either. For the attainment of ultimate human perfection or correct theoretical knowledge, another art was needed—an art based on a full mastery of logic.

Such a judgment was not meant to suggest that these arts were without value. In the first place, it is reasonable that a similar conclusion be drawn at the end of a collection of short commentaries on logic. After all, the study of logic is a preliminary for the pursuit of theoretical knowledge. Even the general order of this collection suggests the primary importance attached to theoretical knowledge. The first few treatises prepared the reader for the study of demonstration, and it was presented as the pinnacle of logical thinking. Thus the first few treatises were steps up to demonstration. From that peak, the treatises on the logical arts concerned with opinion represented a kind of descent: they were based on varying degrees of opinion, while demonstration was based on certainty; they were used to discuss particulars while demonstration was used to discuss universals. It is also possible to discern a descending order among these treatises concerned with opinion, a movement from opinion bordering on certainty to representations bordering on error. Of the three arts, dialectic most resembles demonstration and poetics is least similar to it. By placing these treatises after the discussion about demonstration, Averroës also indicated that one can understand how to work with opinions only after adequately learning how to acquire certain knowledge.

However, Averroës never insisted here that practical life had to be guided by theoretical knowledge. To the contrary, the basic and explicit argument of these treatises is that opinion usually suffices for decent human life. The virtues, for example, are presented as moral habits based on what is generally accepted, not on what is certain.[88] In a similar manner, the restrictive presentation of each of these three treatises served to delineate an area of action in which popular opinion is sufficient. Thus, while his silence about the theoretical uses of dialectic indicated that dialectic should not be used for philosophical pursuits, he argued for the art being used with confidence in other domains.

The goal was to show why the arts based on opinion were best suited for certain functions but also why they had to be limited in their application to those functions. In most practical situations, time restrictions and the intellectual shortcomings of other people make it difficult to attain demonstrative certainty. All that is necessary is that theoretical knowledge not be endangered by opinions used in the practical situations. Averroës attacked the dialectical theologians because they had become confused about the pursuit of theoretical knowledge and had set forth opinions which were harmful to further theoretical investigation. At the same time he attempted to indicate how common opinion should be viewed and what its limitations were. It might be said that he rehabilitated common opinion. He did so by making a strong defense of its practical merits, by proving that those who were most scornful of common opinion were actually most dependent upon it for their own reasoning, and by showing how it might be used in public speech. In that way he was able to indicate the need for eliminating the confusing and complicated speech usually used for public discourse. Similarly, his identification of the limits and different ranks of common opinion served to restrain those who would hastily conclude that all inquiry was relative and perhaps cause greater political harm. Moreover, by insisting that the standard against which common opinion was to be judged was its approximation to certain knowledge, Averroës kept alive the possibility of coming very close to the ideal of ultimate human perfection. His rehabilitation of common opinion in no way lowered the goal of practical life.

However, the larger problem behind all of this is that of the relationship between politics, religion, and philosophy. As these treatises have been examined, it became clear that religious belief was shaped and molded by each of the different arts. It also became evident that religious belief was prior to political action and influenced political action. Moreover, to the extent that these arts depend on correct theoretical knowledge, the way religious belief is shaped and molded depends on correct theoretical knowledge. Differently stated, sound belief depends on sound investigation. While there is a large area in which belief is sound on its own principles, that independence should not be mistaken for opposition to theoretical investigation. The mark of good belief is that it not destroy the possibility of further theoretical inquiry; the mark of good theoretical inquiry is that it protect sound belief and further its acceptance by those unable to pursue theoretical knowledge.

Short Commentary on Aristotle's "Topics"

Outline of Argument for the *Short Commentary on Aristotle's "Topics"*:

Invocation and Title

A. Introduction: The purpose of this commentary is to discuss dialectical arguments and the extent of assent they provide (para. 1).

B. The extent of assent provided by dialectical arguments (paras. 2–4):
   1. They provide belief approximate to certainty (para. 2).
   2. However, because of the kinds of premises used in dialectical arguments, that belief only approximates certainty (para. 3).
   3. That is due to the premises of dialectical arguments often being partially false (para. 4).

C. Classes of dialectical arguments which bring about assent, according to their forms (paras. 5–12):
   1. There are three different kinds of syllogisms used in dialectic (para. 5).
   2. The induction (para. 6):
      a. how it differs from the syllogism (paras. 7–8).
      b. how the way dialectic uses induction sets it apart from rhetoric (para. 9).
      c. because of the limits of the induction, it is best used for generally accepted premises (para. 10).
      d. nonetheless, there are instances when it can be used in demonstration (para. 11).
   3. Summary (para. 12).

D. Classes of dialectical arguments leading to assent, according to their material aspects (paras. 13–19):
   1. The different classes of generally accepted premises (para. 13).

2. These premises are universal predicates or predicables (para. 14).
3. But only five of the eight universal predicates are used in dialectic (para. 15):
    a. a general definition of each of the five universal predicates (para. 16).
    b. although not complete, these definitions offer a sufficient idea of the universal predicates for present purposes (para. 17).
    c. because of the way dialectical syllogisms are constructed, their classes may be twice as numerous as those of demonstrative syllogisms (para. 18).
4. Logical arguments are still another class of argument leading to assent (para. 19).

E. Summary Statement (para. 20).

F. What prompted Aristotle to write about dialectic (para. 21).

Dedication

In the name of God, the Merciful, the Compassionate.
[I beseech] your succor, O Lord![1]

THE BOOK OF DIALECTIC

[INTRODUCTION]

(1) Since we have spoken about the things by means of which the certain assent[1] and the complete concept[2] are distinguished and subsequent to that have spoken about the things which lead to error concerning them, let us speak about dialectical and rhetorical assent and the extent each one provides. For our purposes, it is not necessary to speak about what makes these arts complete. Let us begin, then, with dialectical arguments.[3]

[THE EXTENT OF ASSENT PROVIDED BY DIALECTICAL ARGUMENTS]

(2) We say: the extent [of assent] they provide is supposition[1] which approximates certainty. In general, supposition is believing that something exists in a particular kind of way, while it is possible for it to be different than it is believed to be. Therefore, its peculiar characteristic[2] is that it may be eliminated through opposition; demonstration differs in that it has the peculiar characteristic of not being eliminated through opposition. There are two divisions of supposition. With one, namely dialectical supposition, opposition to it is not noticed; if it is noticed, the supposition can only exist with difficulty. With the other, which is rhetorical, opposition to it is noticed.

(3) That this is the extent of assent this art provides is apparent from the definition of the arguments providing it, since the dialectical argument is a syllogism composed from widespread, generally accepted premises.[1] Now assent about the widespread, generally accepted premise results from the testimony of all or most people, not from the matter being like that in itself—contrary to the way it is with demonstration. Indeed, with demonstration, we arrive at assent which is certain through our assenting to premises because to our minds they appear just as they are externally, not because they are someone else's opinion.

(4) Since that is the case, dialectical premises are often partially false. If they are found to be entirely true, that occurs by accident, that is, because it happens that what is generally accepted is the same outside the mind as it is inside the mind.[1] However, as we have said, we do not take it from this aspect in these syllogisms, but only from the aspect of it being generally accepted. Therefore, a syllogism of sound figure[2] composed from premises like these necessarily provides a probable supposition.

[CLASSES OF DIALECTICAL ARGUMENTS BRINGING ABOUT ASSENT, ACCORDING TO THEIR FORMS]

[THE SYLLOGISM]

(5) Since the extent of assent which this art provides has now been made clear,[1] we shall speak about the classes of arguments causing it. Accordingly, we say that the figure of syllogisms bringing about something like this supposition approximate to certainty must necessarily be sound; otherwise, they would be sophistical, contentious arguments. Therefore, the specific kinds of syllogism used here are the three specific kinds mentioned in the *Prior Analytics*, i.e., the categorical,[2] the conditional,[3] and the contradictory syllogism[4]—the simple and the complex ones. Indeed, it might be possible both to establish and to refute complex problems by means of complex, dialectical syllogisms like these, since generally accepted premises leading to the thing sought are right at hand.

[THE INDUCTION]

(6) This art might use another specific kind of assent which is particular to it, namely, induction. With this specific kind of thing which causes assent, an affirmative or negative universal judgment is asserted about a universal matter because that judgment applies to most of the particulars subsumed under that universal matter. An example of that is our asserting that every body is created because we find that most bodies are of this description. That is an argument which has the force of a syllogism in the first figure,[1] since the minor term[2] is that universal matter, the middle[3] the particulars, and the major[4] the judgment. Nonetheless, the procedure is contrary to the way it is in the syllogism.

(7) That is because with the syllogism we always proceed to the verification of the unknown, partial matter from the universal known to us or we proceed from the equally known to the equally unknown. However, we do not take the equally-known, universal [matter] as a major premise[1] here due to its being equally- [known], but due to its being universal—whether that be by nature or by convention. Our proceeding to the verification of the partial matter from the universal [known] to us is like our explaining that every man is sense-perceiving because every animal is sense-perceiving. For man, which is the minor term here, falls under the major premise and is encompassed within it.[2] An example of our proceeding from the equally-[known] to the equally-[unknown] is our explaining that every man is a laughing being insofar as every man is a speaking being.[3] For speaking is equivalent to laughing. But laughing is generally taken as being encompassed within speaking and subordinate to it, even though it might be equivalent to it—since there is no harm in doing this.[4] For that reason we say that something like this is universal by convention.

(8) With induction, we always proceed from the particular to the universal. Therefore, if we have, for example, explained by means of the induction that every body is created because we have found some bodies to be created, it is clear that we proceed to this universal proposition—which is that every body is created—insofar as we have found some bodies to be created, like earth, water, air, fire, and others. Thus, the composition of the argument which has the force of the syllogism in the first figure is brought forth like this: "Fire, air, water, and earth are bodies; they are created; so body is created." Yet when the induction is used all by itself to explain an unknown problem,[1] it is not very persuasive. That is because if by means of the induction it appears that the predicate applies to the subject, then that problem was not unknown, but was a self-evident premise made apparent by the induction.

(9) Insofar as this art uses the sound syllogism for an unknown problem, it does not take what is known in itself as being a problem; rather, something like this is more appropriate to rhetorical methods. Accordingly, in this art induction tends to be used mainly for verifying the major premise.[1] But in something like this as well, induction is useless. That is because if we have already inductively examined most of the particulars falling under the major premise and not one of those

which we have thereby inductively examined is the subject of the problem, then how did it occur to us that it was encompassed within the major premise? And in general, how did certainty that that premise is universal occur to us? If the subject of the problem was among the [particulars] which we have inductively examined, the very problem reappears as a premise made clear by induction; and the first doubt reappears.[2] However, the art of dialectic does not carry the matter out in such a manner; rather, it asserts that a judgment applies to all [of something] because it applies to most of it, for it is generally accepted that the lesser follows the greater.

(10) Even if all of the particulars are exhausted, induction—insofar as it is induction—does not by itself and primarily set forth the essentially necessary predicate. For it is not impossible for that universal to be a predicate of all of those particulars accidentally—like someone who holds the opinion that everything which comes into being comes into being from what already exists. Therefore, premises such as these are generally accepted. Now the induction used in demonstration is only used for guidance toward certainty, not for providing it primarily and essentially. There is a major difference between what is used for guiding [toward certainty] and what is used for providing [certainty] by itself. Therefore, with regard to the premises about which the induction provides certainty, we do not require that all of the particulars be scrutinized; rather, it is sufficient to scrutinize some.

(11) There are only two circumstances in which using induction [in demonstration] is required: (a) for that general sort of premise none of whose individual cases has happened as yet to be perceived, for example, someone who has never perceived that scammony relieves bile. In cases like this, induction is needed to reach the essential predicate. Now these are known as experiential premises, and these premises vary in the number of individual instances which need to be perceived [so that] certainty about them then results. That is different for each specific matter:[1] for some, a single individual instance need be perceived—as with many of the arithmetical premises—and with some more than one need be perceived. The other circumstance which requires using induction in demonstration occurs because (b) many people do not admit the universality of many premises but admit one of their particulars—like someone who admits that knowledge of health and sickness belongs to one science, which is the science of medicine. Now if he were told that the science of opposites is one,

he would not admit this generalization until it had been made inductively clear to him. At that time, he would reach certainty about its universality.

(12) This, then, is the form of dialectical arguments leading to assent.

[CLASSES OF DIALECTICAL ARGUMENTS LEADING TO ASSENT, ACCORDING TO THEIR MATERIAL ASPECTS]

(13) Their matters, as has been previously [explained],[1] are the generally accepted premises. These are of [different] classes:

(a) Some are generally accepted by everybody, and this is the most noble class. It is possible for all of the different nations to meet in agreement on this one despite the variance in their sects and in their natural dispositions. An example is [the premise] that it is good to thank a benefactor or that it is necessary to respect one's parents.

(b) Some of them are generally accepted by most people, without there being any disagreement among the rest about that. An example is [the premise] that God is one.

(c) Some of them are generally accepted

(i) by learned men and wise men, or by most of them without the rest disagreeing with them, for example, [the premise] that knowledge is virtuous in itself; or

(ii) by most of them, for example, [the premise] that the heavens are spherical.

(d) Some of them are generally accepted

(i) by the practitioners of the arts, without the multitude disagreeing with them about that, for example, [the premise] in the art of medicine that scammony relieves bile and that the pulp of the colocynth relieves phlegm; or

(ii) by those renowned for skill in the arts, without the practitioners of the art disagreeing with them, for example, the argument of Hippocrates that weakness arising without any precedent cause is a warning of sickness;[2] or

(iii) by most of them.

(e) The likeness of what is generally accepted is also generally accepted; for example, if it were a generally accepted [premise] that the science of opposites is one in itself, then sense-perception of opposites would be one in itself.

(f) A thing opposed to what is generally accepted is also generally accepted. For example, if it were a generally accepted [premise] that one ought to do good to friends, then one ought to do bad to enemies.

Now the most noble of all of these is that which is attested to by everyone or by most people; anything else will become generally accepted solely because of the testimony of everyone or of most people to it. Thus the opinions of learned men become generally accepted because everyone or most people hold the opinion that their opinions ought to be accepted. The same thing holds for the opinions which are particular to the arts and for the rest.

(14) These generally accepted premises are necessarily universals, since particulars change and are not perceived by everybody in the same way. If they were, they would be taken indefinitely in these syllogisms, and there would be no concern about stating the ellipsis explicitly. That is why these syllogisms do not lie by means of the particular.[1]

(15) As has been previously [explained], there are eight classes of universals, both simple and complex; genus, species, differentia, property, accident, definition, description, and the statement which is neither definition nor description.[1] Since this is so, dialectical predicates are necessarily one of these classes. However, because species[2] is predicated only of an individual and a proposition whose predicate is an individual is not used in this art, it is not enumerated here as a predicate. Description[3] is subsumed under property, since they have the same force. Similarly, the statement which is neither definition nor description[4] is subsumed under accident. It turns out, then, that there are five classes of dialectical predicates: definition, genus, differentia, property and accident.[5]

(16) It is sufficient here to describe definition as a statement pointing to that meaning of a thing by means of which its basic structure and its being are explained.[1] Genus is defined here as being the predicate, from the aspect of essence, of several things which differ according to species.[2] Differentia is also the predicate of several things which differ according to species, [but it is predicated] from the aspect of quality.[3] Property is the predicate which does not point to the essence of the thing, but applies to all of it, it alone, and always.[4]

Accident is described here in two ways: one is that it is that which applies to the thing and is not genus, differentia, property, or definition; the second is that it is that which might apply to one specific thing and might not apply to it. It is described here in two ways because, taken together, they lead to accident being conceived of absolutely. That is because the first of the two descriptions makes specific what is not distinctive about accident, and the second what is distinctive.[5]

(17) It is clear that the descriptions [given] here are not sufficient for each one of these to be conceived of completely, but for them to be conceived of in this way is sufficient here. That is because a perfect concept of the things from which definitions are put together is [given] in the *Posterior Analytics*.[1] Likewise, what is included in the definition of genus here is clearly the ultimate genus of the genera.[2] Likewise, it is not sufficient for the differentia to be a predicate from the aspect of quality without it applying specifically to the thing for which it is a differentia.[3]

(18) If the predicates pertaining to dialectical premises are one of these five classes, the types of dialectical syllogisms must correspond to what is composed from these five the way they are conceived of here. Thus,[1] they might be taken as a predicate according to the natural course and then converted, and the three terms in the syllogisms might then be related to each other either by a single one of these five relations (like definition or some other relation) or by a combination of them (like one of the terms being related as a differentia and the second as an accident or some other relation). Similarly, they might be taken in another way; that is, two of the terms might always be related to the third—either the major term and the middle to the minor, or the minor and the middle to the major—but the two related terms would be related to each other only by the predicate of accident. This, too, might occur in two ways. Either the two terms might be related to the other term in a single way (like the major term and the middle being related to the minor only as definition or any other one of the five relations). That might be also be done in an opposite manner (i.e., the minor and the middle might be related to the major in this way or in any other one of the relations). The other way is for both terms to be related to the other term in two ways (like the major term being related to the minor as definition and the middle being related to the minor as differentia or some other relation). That, too,

might be done in an opposite manner (i.e., the minor might be related to the major as definition and the middle might be related to the major as differentia or some other relation). Then if these syllogisms were enumerated in this manner, there would be twice as many types of dialectical syllogisms as demonstrative syllogisms. That is because with [dialectical syllogisms] no attention is paid to whether a predicate is made naturally or essentially. Because of their strong resemblance and closeness to the types of demonstrative syllogisms, many people suppose that several types of demonstrative syllogisms are missing in Abū Naṣr [al-Fārābī's] book.[2] In truth, they are dialectical syllogisms.

(19) There is another class of arguments here which lead to assent, those known as logical arguments. This class is composed from true premises which are not essential but are more general than the genus in which they are used. So insofar as it is true, it is supposed that this class should be counted among the classes of demonstrations; while insofar as it is non-essential, it is supposed that this class is dialectical. Themistius[1] explicitly stated that this class is not dialectical. However, from the force of Abū Naṣr [al-Farabi's] argument, it appears that it is dialectical.[2] Now I say unless certainty that a predicate is contained in the substance of a subject or a subject in the substance of the predicate causes assent about a given, generally accepted problem, assent is only caused by general acceptance or by induction. And what is of this sort is necessarily dialectical. But syllogisms such as these are of a higher rank than dialectical syllogisms, since they are neither false nor partial.

(20) Now we have said enough for our purposes here.

[CONCLUSION]

(21) When Aristotle distinguished these dialectical arguments from the demonstrative, not only with regard to the matters, but according to the [form of the] argument[1] as well, he was of the opinion that syllogisms like these—even if they were not demonstrative—had uses for training due to their being more generally accepted. That is because, since several of the generally accepted premises are opposites, it is possible on the basis of these premises to establish and refute the very same thing. That is to say, he was of the opinion that if two

disputants use syllogisms like these in which two opposing premises are joined to a minor premise[2] in order to establish or refute something, on the condition that one wants to defend it and the other to refute it, then this will result in great training for them—the way it does with arts directed toward other ones, like the art of fencing and others. On account of this, this art is made [to be exercised by] a questioner and an answerer. The questioner's role is to get the answerer to admit what will refute his position, and the answerer's role is to refrain from admitting anything which will refute his own position. It was for this that Aristotle set forth all of the topics from which syllogisms concerning every problem are derived, whether the problem be one in which the subject is investigated absolutely or in conjunction [with something else], like seeking whether it is genus, definition, or [another] one of the five relations.[3] Then Aristotle set forth, in addition, how the questioner asks questions and the answerer answers. Furthermore, he set forth particular instructions for the questioner and for the answerer. Therefore this art is defined as an aptitude (a) enabling the questioner to make a syllogism from generally accepted premises for refuting either of two extremes of the contradiction to which he gets the answerer [to admit] and (b) enabling the answerer not to admit anything to the questioner from which the contradiction of what he posits would necessarily follow. There are other uses of this art already enumerated in the *Topics*.[4] However, training like this seems unnecessary for the perfection of the demonstrative arts.But if it were, without a doubt, it would be from the standpoint of the most excellent [kind of training].

The *Topics* is finished. Praise be to God and His Succor.

Short Commentary on Aristotle's "Rhetoric"

Outline of Argument for the *Short Commentary on Aristotle's "Rhetoric"*:

INVOCATION AND TITLE

A. Introduction (paras. 1–3):

1. Purpose: Discussion of persuasive things and the amount of assent they provide (para. 1).
2. Persuasive things are divided into speeches and external things (para. 2).
3. Order of presentation: First persuasive speeches, then the other persuasive things (para. 3).

B. Persuasive Speeches (paras. 4–32):

1. The Enthymeme—a syllogism based on unexamined previously existing opinion (paras. 4–25).
   - a. The forms of syllogisms bring about conclusions by their special construction (paras. 5–15).
     - i. categorical syllogisms (paras. 6–7):
       - (a) how this works in the first figure (para. 6).
       - (b) how this works in the second and third figures (para. 7).
     - ii. conditional syllogisms are of two kinds (paras. 8–13):
       - (a) conjunctive—how it becomes an enthymeme (para. 8).
         - (i) an example of an erroneous use of this by Galen (para. 9).
         - (ii) how to assure the success of this kind of syllogism when the conclusion is sound (para. 10).

(b) disjunctive—how it becomes persuasive (para. 11).

(i) an example of an erroneous use of this by Abū al-Ma'ālī (para. 12).

(ii) how to assure the success of this kind of syllogism when dealing with negations (para. 13).

iii the contradictory syllogism (para. 14).

iv. summary (para. 15).

b. Material aspects of the syllogism—a division based on the premises of the syllogism (paras. 16–25).

i. these premises are considered from the aspect of their being generally accepted by unexamined common opinion and fall into two classes (paras. 17–19):

(a) proofs are taken from sense-perceived things and have a further division into proofs proper and signs (para. 18).

(b) generally received propositions—examples of them (para. 19).

ii. examples of different kinds of proofs (paras. 20–22):

(a) examples of proofs proper, i.e., those proofs in the first figure (para. 20).

(b) examples of signs in the second figure (para. 21).

(c) examples of signs in the third figure (para. 22).

iii. major distinction for rhetoric is the status of premises with regard to unexamined opinion, not their status as necessary or more possible (para. 23).

iv. in rhetoric, as in dialectic, the premises used may be adapted to the ends of the speaker (para. 24).

v. summary: justification of the division of premises according to the necessary and the possible (para. 25).

2. The Example (paras. 26–32).

a. Different instances of the kinds of examples (para. 26).

b. Difference between example and induction (para. 27).

c. Examples are based on two kinds of likeness, and these have certain restrictions (paras. 28–31):

i. with an example, it is not possible to make a particular judgment on the basis of a universal (para. 29).

ii. examples always remain close to unexamined opinion (para. 30).

iii. Failure to recognize these restrictions led Abū al-Ma'ālī astray (para. 31).

d. Summary (para. 32).

C. Persuasive Things Not Occurring by Speeches (paras. 33–44).

1. General enumeration of the 11 persuasive things not occurring by speeches (para. 33).

2. Some of these need a further explanation (para. 34).

a. Testimony (paras. 35–40):

i. testimony is a kind of report (para. 35).

ii. the groups of theologians differ according to their opinions about its sufficiency for intellectually perceived matters (para. 36).

iii. testimonies about sense-perceived matters are strengthened when a large number of people report having seen the matters (para. 37).

(a) certainty can be attained about such matters (para. 38).

(b) such reports can even bring about certainty concerning matters that have not been perceived. (para. 39).

iv. there is no stipulated number of reporters necessary for certainty to be brought about (para. 40).

b. Recorded Traditions: Their strength in persuasion comes from people being brought up according to their dictates (para. 41).

c. Consensus: Although it has a religious basis, it is not yet clear how inviolable it is (para. 42).

d. Challenging: It is most useful with those who claim to be able to work miracles (para. 43).

3. Summary: Although all of these have persuasive value, enthymemes are more noble (para. 44).

D. Conclusion (paras. 45–46).

1. Aristotle wrote about these things when he saw their value for public discourse about political matters (para. 45).

2. The purpose of this treatise has now been fulfilled (para. 46).

Dedication

In the name of God, the Merciful, the Compassionate,
[*I beseech*] *your succor our Lord*![1]

THE SPEECH ABOUT RHETORICAL ARGUMENTS[1]

[INTRODUCTION]

(1) Since we have finished speaking about dialectical syllogisms and the extent of assent they provide, let us speak about persuasive things and the extent of assent they too provide. It is apparent that persuasion is a kind of probable supposition[1] which the soul trusts, despite its awareness of an opposing consideration. In what preceded, we already defined supposition.[2]

(2) From scrutiny and inductive investigation,[1] it appears that the things effecting persuasion can first be divided into two classes: one of them consists in arguments, and the second is external things[2] which are not arguments—like oaths, testimonies, and other things we will enumerate. Similarly, from scrutiny it also appears that the arguments used in public speaking[3] fall into two classes: example and proof. (In this art, the latter is called enthymeme.) That is because when someone advises[4] someone else to take a certain kind of medicine he says to him: "Use it because so-and-so used it, and it helped him." He thus persuades him by citing an example. Or he says to him: "You have a disease like this or like that." It is like that with every single thing concerning which people converse with one another.

(3) Since it has become apparent that this sort of speaking uses these two classes of arguments, we will speak about them first. Then, after that, we will go on to speak about the other persuasive things, for the former are more worthy of being considered persuasive than the latter and are prior by nature.

[THE ENTHYMEME]

(4) We say: the enthymeme is a syllogism leading to a conclusion which corresponds to unexamined opinion previously existing among

all or most people. Unexamined previously existing opinion is opinion which strikes a man as a probable supposition and which he trusts as soon as it occurs to him, even before he has examined it. Syllogisms become conclusive according to unexamined previously existing opinion either because of their forms or because of their matters.[1] This happens because of their forms when they are conclusive according to unexamined opinion. It happens because of their matters when their premises are true, once again according to unexamined opinion.

[FORMS OF SYLLOGISMS]

(5) The forms of syllogisms become conclusive according to unexamined opinion by not being strict with regard to them and by omitting from them the thing which causes the conclusion to follow necessarily, the way the multitude is usually content [to do] when speaking to one another. Therefore, we ought to consider this notion in connection with each specific kind of syllogism we have enumerated;[1] for, by such an enumeration, we will arrive at the types of all the persuasive syllogisms with respect to their forms.

(6) Thus we say: from what has preceded it is clear that the universal premise[1] is what causes the conclusion to follow necessarily in the first figure[2] and that the conjunction[3] is caused by the minor premise[4] being affirmative. Since this is the case, if the major premise[5] is omitted or taken indefinitely the first figure will be persuasive. However, to omit it—as those engaged in demonstration do—is more persuasive, because omitting it may lead people to fancy: (a) that it was omitted because there was no point of contention about it and (b) that it is extremely clear. Similarly, in some instances the first figure may become persuasive by omitting the minor premise or by taking it negatively.[6]

(7) Since it is not clear at the outset which premise brings about the conclusion[1] nor which causes the conjunction in the second[2] and the third[3] figures, but it may be the minor premise or the major premise, there would be no harm in explicitly stating both premises in these two [figures]. But, when this is done and neither one has been omitted, both of them ought to be taken indefinitely; otherwise, no point of contention would remain in these two [figures] at all. Moreover, among the kinds of inconclusive combinations are those that are thought to be conclusive according to unexamined opinion without

really being so. Now these kinds of arguments are still persuasive because of their forms. An example of this is the combination of two affirmative [premises] in the second figure. Similarly, the conclusive types [of syllogisms] which are in the third figure are of this kind when their conclusions are taken in a universal manner.[4] However, in spite of this, one ought not to state the ellipsis in them explicitly but ought to take them indefinitely so that the point of contention in them might be more obscure.

(8) CONDITIONAL SYLLOGISMS are disjunctive—as previously stated—and conjunctive. The conjunctive syllogism is made an enthymeme by leaving a point of contention in it also. It has already been explained in the *Prior Analytics*[1] that the conjunctive syllogism becomes conclusive when the consequence is valid and when the selected term[2] becomes evident by means of a categorical syllogism.[3] If the selected term is self-evident, the consequence must necessarily be explained. It was also explained there that the selected term and the conclusion cannot be just any chance conditional or conditioned term.[4] Since this is the case, this kind of syllogism is only made into an enthymeme by placing some of these restrictions upon it. However, it becomes persuasive primarily by the omission of the selected term. It may become persuasive regardless of which term—that is, the conditional or the conditioned term—or which of their contraries is brought forth as a conclusion. In spite of this, however, when there is an invalid conclusion, the selected term leading to it usually should not be stated explicitly for fear the opponent might notice it—like the man who selects the conditioned term itself and brings forth the conditional term as a conclusion or who selects the contrary of the conditional term and brings forth the contrary of the conditioned term as a conclusion.[5] Still, one might explicitly state the selected term in something like this, and the argument will be persuasive; e.g., the argument of one of the ancients: "If being is created, it has a beginning; but it is not created, thus it does not have a beginning."

(9) Galen[1] and many anatomists use this kind of syllogism to deduce the unknown causes of animal actions. For example, he says: "When the reflexive nerve is eliminated, the voice is eliminated; thus, when the reflexive nerve exists, the voice exists."[2] But it does not necessarily follow as stated: for when animals are eliminated, man is eliminated; yet, from the existence of animals, the existence of man does not necessarily follow.[3]

(10) In the instance when the conclusion [brought forth] is valid (for example, when it is the very opposite of the conditioned term or of the conditional term), one must not state the selected term explicitly. Otherwise, unless the conjunction is omitted and is not stated explicitly, no point of contention will remain in the argument.

(11) The disjunctive syllogism becomes persuasive when more than two opposing considerations exist and they are not all carefully examined or when all of the selected terms are not carefully examined. This syllogism does not become persuasive when the selected term is omitted; rather, when that is done, it remains in the very form in which one seeks to clarify one of the two antitheses into which the problem is divided.[1]

(12) The argument of Abū al-Ma'ālī [al-Juwaynī],[1] in his book called *The Spiritual Directive*[2] when he wanted to refute [the notion of] creation from the elements, is an example of that in which all of the opposing considerations are not carefully examined. For he said: "If a created thing were to have been brought into existence from the four elements, then that could not help but be (a) by means of some bodies intermixing with others until the mass came together in one place or (b) by each one of them independently and separately arising in the composition; and both of these classes [i.e., alternatives] are absurd. Thus, that there should be one being created from more than one element is absurd."[3] Now one thing which ought to have been set down in opposition in the syllogism has been eliminated from this argument, namely, that an existent thing may come into existence in the manner of a mixture, as is seen with oxymel[4] and with other artificial things.

(13) The type [of disjunctive syllogism] in which one begins with a negation and arrives at a negation only becomes persuasive when the selected term is omitted and the conclusion is stated explicitly. Indeed, when the selected term and the conclusion are both omitted, the hearer does not know which thing you intend to conclude. Here, it is not possible for the explicitly stated selected term to be any chance thing nor for it to be according to unexamined opinion; rather, it is always the assertion[1] which is selected and the negation which is brought forth as a conclusion. However, when that is done, no subject of persuasion remains in it.

(14) THE CONTRADICTORY SYLLOGISM.[1] If we wish the contradictory syllogism to be persuasive, the doubt-provoking subject and the

consequent absurdity ought to be stated explicitly, while suppressing the premise from which the absurdity necessarily follows. Still, it might be explicitly stated when the consequence is not apparent. This would be like our argument: "If every man is not sentient, then every animal is not sentient; for every man is an animal."[2] This consequence is in the third figure.

(15) These are the classes of enthymemes according to their forms. They correspond absolutely to the classes of syllogisms.

[MATERIAL ASPECTS OF SYLLOGISMS]

(16) With respect to their matters, syllogisms should be divided into classes in the same way premises themselves are divided, especially the major premise, since it is the one which brings about the conclusion. With the minor premise, however, it is possible to pay no attention whatever to whether it is persuasive, generally accepted, or anything else.

(17) Thus we say that the premises used in this class of arguments, especially the major premise, are taken here insofar as they are generally accepted according to unexamined common opinion. In what preceded, we have defined what unexamined opinion is[1] and that dialectical premises are used only insofar as they are truly generally accepted.[2] Now just as generally accepted things may accidentally be true and may not, similarly, premises which are based on unexamined opinion may accidentally happen to be generally accepted or true and may not. However, in general, they are taken here insofar as they are generally accepted according to unexamined opinion, just as dialectical premises are taken solely insofar as they are truly generally accepted. What is generally accepted according to unexamined previously existing opinion is divided into (a) generally received propositions—and these are premises which are taken universally according to unexamined previously existing opinion—and into (b) sense perceptible things which are taken as proofs of other things, also according to unexamined opinion.

(18) Among these proofs are (a) those that are taken as proofs of the existence of a thing without restriction[1]—like our taking the empty vessel as proof of the existence of void—and (b) those that are taken as proofs of the existence of a predicate for a subject. When the latter are more universal than the subject and more particular than, or similar

to, the predicate, they belong in the first figure; these were specifically assigned the name "proof" by the ancients.[2] If they are more universal than the two extreme terms, they belong in the second figure. If they are more particular than both [of the extreme terms], they belong in the third [figure]. These latter two were specifically assigned the name "sign" by the ancients.[3] The proofs which are taken up here may be matters which are subsequent to the thing proved—e.g., its consequences—and they may be prior [to it]—e.g., its causes.

(19) Now each of the two classes of premises—the generally received propositions and the proofs—may occur in matters which are necessary, possible for the most part, and equally possible. An example of the generally received propositions occurring in the necessary matter is: "everything which is done has a doer." An example of those occurring in the matter which is possible for the most part is: "any sick person who obeys his passions and does not heed the saying of the doctors will not be cured." An example of those occurring in the equally possible is: "whatever is more agreeable and easier is preferable." However, in itself, this could be used to allege that the matter is not preferable.

(20) Proofs. The one in the necessary matter in the first figure which is what is specifically assigned the name "proof," is like our argument: "The brightness of the moon increases bit by bit, so it is spherical." What occurs in the matter which is possible for the most part is like our argument: "So-and-so is gathering men, preparing arms, and fortifying his towns. There is no enemy near him. He is, therefore, resolved upon revolting against authority." This was known among the ancients as "specious proof." Those occuring in the matter which is equally possible are like our argument: "So-and-so did not budge from his position, and all of his companions retreated so that he was felled. He is, therefore, courageous." However, in itself this may also be used as proof of the cowardice which prevents a man from fleeing. This proof, too, the ancients identified as "doubtful proof."[1]

(21) Signs. The ones occurring in the necessary matter in the second figure are like our argument: "The nerve grows out of the brain because it is implanted in it." What occurs in the matter which is possible for the most part is like our argument: "So-and-so showed the enemy the vulnerability of the town because he climbed up on the wall

and watched for the enemy, and the one who points out the vulnerability [of the town's walls] does that." Those occurring in the matter which is equally possible have the same force as the proofs which occur in this matter, since the universals in it have the same force as particulars and particulars may be converted and brought back to the first figure. So if they were taken universally, their falsity would be as great as the falsity of particulars. For this reason, the ancients rejected the type of signs which occur in this matter.

(22) PROOFS WHICH ARE IN THE THIRD FIGURE.[1] The ones in the necessary matter are like our argument: "Time is the celestial sphere, because all things are in time and all things are in the celestial sphere." Those occurring in the matter [which is possible for the] most part are like our argument: "Wise men are virtuous, because Socrates was a virtuous wise man." The reason for rejecting those occurring in the matter which is equally possible [in the third figure] is the very same reason for rejecting those in the second figure.

(23) You ought to be apprised that this division—i.e., the division into the necessary and the possible—is not essential to the premises of enthymemes inasmuch as they are premises of enthymemes. That is because the premises of enthymemes are taken insofar as they are generally received according to unexamined opinion—as we have said[1]—or insofar as they are signs and proofs according to unexamined opinion, not insofar as they occur in a necessary or possible matter. For it is with regard to demonstrative syllogisms that premises are taken according to this description; i.e., they are the ones which take premises insofar as they are necessary or possible for the most part. Thosc which are equally possible are thought to be more characteristic of these arguments, since the demonstrative art does not employ them. But this art—i.e., the art of rhetoric—does not employ them from the standpoint of their being equally possible either; for if it were to employ them from this standpoint, one thing would not be more likely to follow from them than would its opposite. Rather, they are used insofar as one of them preponderates, even if slightly, according to unexamined opinion, either at a certain moment or in a certain condition. Some people who were ignorant of this idea, denied that this art could employ a proof occurring in the matter which is equally possible, for they claimed that no persuasion is brought about by that which is equally possible.

(24) As has been said, this art does not have a particular subject, just as the art of dialectic does not have a particular subject. For the premises employed in these two arts are not grasped in the mind in the same way as they exist outside the mind. Rather, a predicate is always asserted to apply to a subject because of what is generally accepted, either according to unexamined opinion or according to the truth, not because it is of the nature of the predicate to apply to the subject or of the nature of the subject that the predicate should apply to it. Nor does this art only take premises insofar as they are widespread according to unexamined opinion, without qualifying them with regard to mode of existence. Rather, it may take the necessary as though it were possible according to unexamined opinion and, similarly, the possible as though it were necessary. As for taking the necessary as though it were possible, that is like someone who fancies that the heavens could possibly exist in another form and that it is possible for everything to be created out of any chanced-upon thing. As for imagining that something is impossible when it is possible, there are many things whose existence is not difficult when the beliefs of the multitude about them are considered. However, the kind of assent to which we have inclined since youth is that all things are possible—to the extent that the argument of anyone who says this thereby loses its necessary character. For instance, in Plato's confutation of Protagoras, when Protagoras said: "there is nothing that is perceived," Plato replied: "there, now, is something that is perceived"—meaning this assertion Protagoras had made.[1]

(25) Now we have finished what we were about. So let us go back to where we were and say that it appears likely that what compelled the ancients to divide the premises of enthymemes in accordance with their matters is that premises which are widespread according to unexamined opinion are invested with weakness and strength in accordance with each particular matter. For that reason, premises according to unexamined opinion are more persuasive when they happen to occur in the matter which is possible for the most part than when they occur in the equally possible. Now it has become clear from this argument how many classes of enthymeme there are from the standpoint of form and matter.

[THE EXAMPLE]

(26) We ought to speak about the example. There are [different] classes of the example. (a) With one, it is decided whether a predicate applies to a subject or does not apply to it because of that predicate applying to the likeness of that subject or because of it not applying, when it is better known whether the predicate applies to the likeness or not; like our argument that the heavens are created because the wall is created. (b) With another, we decide whether a predicate applies to a subject or does not apply to it because the likeness of that predicate applies to that subject or does not apply to it, when it is better known whether that likeness applies to the subject or does not apply; for example, our deciding that the heavens are changeable because of the fact that they move. (c) With yet another, we decide whether a predicate applies to a subject or does not apply to it because the likeness of that predicate applies to the likeness of that subject or does not apply to it, when it is better known that the likeness of the predicate applies to the likeness of that subject or when it is better known that it does not apply; for example, "honey dilutes because sugar dissolves."

(27) The judgment may be universal, while the likeness is particular, e.g., our argument: "Pleasures are bad because wine is bad." Now the difference between this and induction is that in induction we confirm the universal by the particular, whereas here we confirm one thing by another insofar as it is a likeness—not insofar as one of them is particular and the other universal.

(28) LIKENESS. There are two classes: either a likeness in a common matter or a likeness by analogy. An example of the likeness in a common matter is what preceded. An example of the likeness by analogy is our argument: "The king in the city is like the deity in the world, and just as the deity is one, so too ought the king to be."

(29) In general, regardless of the example, judgment about a particular based on a universal does not occur in it, because neither one of the two similar things is more general than the other. Nor do they exist as similars in this respect. It is clear from what preceded in the *Prior Analytics*[1] that the apodeictically conclusive speech is the one in which the particular is explained by the universal. Since that is the case, no other argument follows apodeictically from the example, nor is it essentially conclusive. An example of that is our deciding

that the heavens are created due to their similarity to created bodies with respect to extension, alteration, connectedness, and other things. For the heavens in this argument are the minor term in the syllogism, since they are the subject of the problem;[2] being created is the major term, since it is the predicate of the problem; and the middle term is extension and alteration. Now when we compose the syllogism, we speak in this manner: "The heavens have extension, and what has extension is created, thus the heavens are created."

(30) However, it is not sufficient that our saying "what has extension is created," be taken indefinitely, if we want "the heavens" to be encompassed apodeictically under it; rather, we should even take it universally, i.e., "every extended thing is created." Now if this universal had resulted from our scrutiny of some extended things in the way particular premises result, then to state it explicitly by an example would be superfluous—unless it were taken as a means of instruction and guidance for bringing about certainty concerning the universal. But if our having perceived some of the extended things as created did not lead us to universal certainty and this premise remained indefinite for us, nothing would result necessarily from our perceiving it—except according to unexamined opinion. From this it appears: (a) that with regard to these kinds of premises, certainty about the universal is not attained by sense perception but by another power, since by sense perception only individual instances of a limited number are discerned and (b) that the ranks of supposition[1] are in accordance with their nearness and their distance from this universal decision. In general, supposition is a universal judgment based on sense perception alone.

(31) Because one of the later dialectical theologians[1]—and he is the one called Abū al-Maʿālī [al-Juwaynī]—was not aware of this, he said: "The example provides certainty as a means of guidance, not only as a way toward the syllogism and scrutiny."[2] However, since he did not speak of the syllogism of a valid figure, it would follow for him that all of the sciences are preexistent. Thus, nothing would be known by means of the syllogism, so that it could happen, for example, that a man who has not theoretically investigated anything at all relating to geometry would be able to read the *Book of the al-Magest*[3] and that the origin of the world would be self-evident.

(32) The rank of the example with regard to assent has now been explained. In this art it corresponds to the induction in dialectic, just as the enthymeme here corresponds to the syllogism in dialectic.

[PERSUASIVE THINGS WHICH DO NOT OCCUR BY ARGUMENTS]

(33) After this, we ought to proceed to speak about the persuasive things which do not occur by arguments and about the extent of assent they provide. All together, there are thirteen kinds of persuasive things:[1]

[1]. Among them is [proclaiming] the virtue of the speaker and the defect of his opponent, for it is clear that by this a man acquires a good reputation and acceptance of what he is saying.

[2]. Among them is bringing the listeners around to assent by means of the passions; for example, strengthening the passions in the soul of the listener so that he must assent because of fanaticism, mercy, fear, or anger. Now it is evident that this also inclines a man to assent.

[3]. Among them is what inclines the listeners by means of moral speeches; this is done, just as Galen used to do, by making them imagine that the chaste, the people of preeminent character, and those who are neither sullied by corrupt thought nor false [in their thoughts] accept their speech.

[4]. Among them is extolling and belittling the matter which is spoken about, for when the speech is extolled, the soul is more inclined to it. On the contrary, when it is deprecated, the soul avoids it; and no inclination for it takes place.

[5]. Among them is consensus.

[6]. Among them are testimonies.

[7]. Among them is awakening a desire for, or apprehension about, something.

[8]. Among them is challenging and betting.

[9]. Among them are oaths.

[10]. Among them is for the quality of the speech, the voice, and the inflection to be in such a condition that they cause the existence of the matter whose affirmation is desired to be imagined; for example,

someone whose face has already become pale and whose voice has already risen recounting a fearful matter.

[11]. Among them is distorting speeches and dropping much from them and putting them into a form in which their repulsiveness appears and opposition to them is simplified; now these enter more into sophistry than they do into rhetoric.

These, then, are all of the external persuasive things.

(34) With many of these, it is immediately evident that they only provide persuasion; with others, that may be somewhat obscure. We will speak about the latter.

[Testimony]

(35) Testimony holds the most powerful rank. In general, testimony is a certain kind of report. Those who bring the report can either be one or more than one. When they are more than one, they may either be a group which it is possible to enumerate or they may be a group which it is not possible to enumerate. Things reported are either perceived by the senses or intellectually apprehended. Those who report things perceived by the senses are either those who have perceived these things themselves or those who report them from others like, fewer, or more numerous than themselves. Now things perceived by the senses which are reported either concern past matters that we have not perceived or matters occurring in the present but absent from us.[1]

(36) Reports about those things we have perceived by the senses are of no use or benefit. It seems this is likewise the case concerning intellectually apprehended things for those practitioners of arts whose habit it is to deduce such intellectually apprehended things in their art. For the multitude, however, testimony about them may possibly bring about persuasion. For this reason, you will find that the sect among the people of our religious community known as the dialectical theologians does not limit itself only to the testimony of the Legislator [Muḥammad] concerning knowledge of the origin of the world, the existence of the Creator, and other things; rather, concerning knowledge of that, it also employs syllogisms. Now the sect known as the *Ḥashawīyāh*[1] rejects that.

(37) Assent to testimonies and reports of sense-perceived matters which have not been witnessed is strengthened and weakened in accordance with the number of the reporters and other considerations relating to them. Thus, the most powerful assent resulting from reports is what a group which cannot be enumerated reports it has perceived or what a group reports on the authority of another group which cannot be enumerated but which has perceived it. Now it [powerful assent about the report] is like that, however much the group increases in size, to whatever extent it reaches, if in the beginning, the middle, and the end it remains the same in that determining their number is either impossible or difficult. This class of reports is the one that is called continuous tradition.[1]

(38) Certainty with regard to diverse matters—like the sending of the Prophet, the existence of Mecca and Medina, and other things—may result from this. But we should theoretically investigate the manner in which this results, for there are some things that produce assent essentially and some accidentally. Now it is clear that assent about the existence of sense-perceived matters results, primarily and essentially, through sensation. Thus, whoever loses some kind of sense, loses some kind of sense perception. Nor does [assent to] the existence of sense-perceived things result essentially only through sensation; indeed, it may also result through an imaginative representation of them according to their essence.[1] Then, too, certainty about the essential existence of sense-perceived things may result through the syllogism; an example of that is: "This wall is built; thus, it has a builder." However, the essential form of the particular builder does not result through it.

(39) Certainty may be obtained about the existence of sense-perceived matters which have never been perceived and whose existence we have no way of apprehending by means of a syllogism, but very seldom—just as we very seldom manage to conceive of them according to their essence.[1] However, even if individual instances of such matters cannot be distinguished by sensation, there is no doubt but what their names or what indicates them can be distinguished by it. Now for the greater number of people, assent to something like this comes about by means of the continuous tradition and exhaustive reports.[2] However, it is clear that this is an accidental effect, because that about them which brings about assent rarely follows from what

is presumed[3] to be its cause, namely, the reports—just as effects[4] rarely follow from their accidental causes.[5]

(40) In this science, it is not necessary to dwell upon the cause for this accidental certainty resulting nor upon how it results; for it has already been spoken about in *Sense and Sensible Objects*.[1] When some people became aware of this, they wanted to set down as conditions for reports a specific number from which certainty would result essentially. When this did not succeed for them, they said: "In itself it results, even if it does not happen for us." Now this is a clear falsification, for if there were some essential number which would lead to certainty, continuous accounts with respect to the number of reporters would not vary, and it would be possible to perceive and to grasp this number. But the many and the few are closely related. Thus, when some of them wanted to set down conditions with regard to the continuous tradition which would lead to certainty and they did not succeed at it, they said; "One of its conditions is that it lead to certainty." Since that is the case, there is no condition at all which could be set down and no means by which certainty could result essentially. Now this art employs the reports and the testimonies in the manner in which they are taken for the most part, which is according to supposition. For it is very seldom concerned with something which no art employs at all.

[Recorded Traditions]

(41) The situation with regard to quoting recorded traditions is also clear; however, whatever assent to them results because of being brought up with them or because of habit is very powerful. Thus, you see many who are brought up according to the ignorant ways of life believing fables from which we are not able to turn them away.

[Consensus]

(42) The foundation for the persuasiveness of consensus—which is the mutual understanding of the people of the religious community and their agreement about something pertaining to the religious community—is the Divine Law's testimony to them about their infallibility.[1] When a group of people became aware of this they said: "He who departs from consensus is not an infidel." Abū Ḥāmid [al-Ghazālī]

explicitly[2] stated this idea about consensus in the first part of his book called *The Distinction Between Islam and Atheism.*[3] He said: "What consensus is has not yet been agreed upon."[4]

[CHALLENGING]

(43) A challenge may be made by means of different things. However, the most persuasive of challenges is the one that is made by means of the completely unprecedented miracle, i.e., by the performance of something considered impossible by mankind. But it is obvious, even if the feat is extremely marvelous, that it provides nothing more than good opinion[1] about the one who performs the feat or nothing more than trust in him and in his excellence when the feat is divine. Now Abū Ḥāmid [al-Ghazālī] has explicitly stated this in his book called *The Balance.*[2] He said: "Faith in the Messengers [i.e., the Prophets] by the way of the miracle, as the dialectical theologians have described it, is the popular way; and the way of the select few is other than this."[3]

(44) These external matters which we have enumerated are the ones from which it is supposed that certainty will result. The persuasiveness of the others is self-evident. Now the enthymemes are more noble and take precedence over these, because they may be used to establish those which are neither clearly existent nor clearly persuasive. For example, when the moral excellence of the speaker is neither evident nor generally accepted, they are used to make it evident. Similarly, when someone supposes that he who claims to be a miracle-worker is not a miracle-worker, they are used to make it clear to him that he is a miracle-worker. The same holds with testimonies, traditions, and other things when the opponent contests them. All of these persuasive things —whether they be arguments or external matters—may be used in all of the reflective arts in the way that those ancients who preceded used to use them, because they supposed that they were ways to certainty.

[CONCLUSION]

(45) When Aristotle became aware of the rank of these [arguments and external things] with regard to assent, he saw that these things which bring about assent were valuable because the multitude used

them with one another for particular voluntary things which judges decide are good or bad. Among the voluntary things which judges decide are good or bad, some are to be found in a man himself and in the present time; these are virtues and vices. Some are to be found in the present time in another person; that is injustice and justice. Some will occur to him in the future; these are useful and harmful matters. Now speech addressed to others about the first kind of things is called contradictory [epideictic];[1] when it is about the second kind of things, it is called forensic;[2] and when it is about the third kind of things, it is called deliberative.[3] Moreover, to the extent that man is a social being and a citizen, he necessarily uses rhetorical arguments about these three categories of things. [Once he recognized all of this,] Aristotle began[4] to set forth rules and things which would enable a man to persuade about each and every one of these things in the best possible manner with regard to that thing. Therefore, this art is defined as being the means by which man is able to effect persuasion about each and every one of the particular matters and to do so in the most complete and most artful manner possible with regard to each thing.

(46) Now we have said enough for our purposes.

All of the *Rhetoric* is completed. Praise be to God the Exalted.

Short Commentary on Aristotle's "Poetics"

Outline of Argument for the *Short Commentary on Aristotle's "Poetics"*:

INVOCATION AND TITLE.

A. The character of poetical speeches (para. 1).

B. Problems arising from the way poetical speeches are understood (para. 2).

C. The syllogistic limits on the art of poetry (para. 3).

D. Why Aristotle wrote about poetical speeches (para. 4).

E. The ultimate purpose of the collection of Short Commentaries on the logical arts (para. 5).

In the name of God the Merciful, the Compassionate.[1]

ABOUT POETICAL SPEECHES[1]

(1) Poetical speeches are rhythmically balanced speeches. With them, one strives for an imaginary representation or exemplification of something in speech so as to move the soul to flee from the thing, or to long for it, or simply to wonder because of the delightfulness which issues from the imaginary representation. They are set down in a rhythmically balanced way, because they thereby become more complete in imaginary representativeness. Now just as the sense-perceptible matters which many of the arts—like the art of decoration and others—cause to be imagined are not really sense-perceptible matters, likewise, speeches which cause something to be imagined are not speeches which make its essence understood.

(2) There are two classes of representations: either (a) the class in which one thing is likened to another by one of the particles of simile[1] or (b) a representation taken as though it was the very thing being represented, and that is by means of substitution[2] and metaphor, like our saying: "He is the sea in whatever way you approach him."[3] Some of these representations are closely similar and others are far-fetched. Now it is evident that this art does not take the representations of something as though they were the thing itself. But many people might err about that and thus take the representation of something as though it were the thing itself; for example, the speech of Empedocles about the water of the sea being the sweat of the earth brought together in its bladder.[4] Now one errs with regard to these representations when they are set down as a substitution and no particle of simile is offered. For the most part these representations cause error concerning the things which can be conceived of only by their representations or which can be conceived of only with difficulty; thus, there is much error about the latter, as with someone who is not able to conceive of a being which is neither inside the world nor outside it. But the most suitable place for this kind of error is the book *On Sophistry*.

(3) Even though this art is syllogistic, the syllogism is not actually used in it, nor is there any kind of syllogism peculiar to it; rather, when a syllogistic argument is actually used in it, it is in the manner of deceit and in order to make it similar to another art.

(4) Aristotle came to the opinion that this art was highly useful, because by means of it the souls of the multitude could be moved to believe in or not believe in a certain thing and towards doing or abandoning a certain thing. For that reason, he enumerated the matters which enable a man to devise an imaginative representation for any particular thing he wishes and to do so in the most complete manner possible for that thing. Thus, the art of poetics is that which enables a man to devise an imaginative representation of each particular thing in the most complete manner possible for it. However, these are perfections external to the primary human perfection.

(5) In sum, anyone who has understood what we have written in these treatises[1] and had no knowledge about all this by nature is now able to discern the rank of every argument he hears with respect to assent or concept. This rank [of understanding] is part of what is noble because man is prepared for ultimate perfection through it. For if man's perfection comes about by his attaining true theory and if he becomes prepared to accept it by this amount [of logical study], then by this amount [of logical study] he attains the rank which prepares him for ultimate perfection.

God is the One who gives success to what is correct.[1]

NOTES

1. Henceforth, the dates of the *Anno Hegirae* will be given first and separated from the corresponding date of the Common Era by a slash (/) mark; for example, the above date would read 520/1126.

2. In the nineteenth century, the Italian orientalist Fausto Lasinio transliterated the Judaeo-Arabic manuscripts of Averroës's *Short Commentary on Aristotle's Poetics* into Arabic and published the transliteration. Lasinio used a copy of the Munich manuscript (cf. infra, n. 10) sent to him by the well-known German orientalist, Moritz Steinschneider, to the point where the Munich manuscript broke off; then he used a copy of the Paris manuscript (cf. infra, n. 11) sent to him by Moise Schwab of the Paris Bibliothèque Nationale. Because he did not have a full copy of the Paris manuscript, Lasinio had no way to control the Munich manuscript readings. This transliteration appeared as an appendix to his edition of Averroës's *Middle Commentary on Aristotle's Poetics*; cf. Fausto Lasinio, "Il Commento Medio di Averroe alla *Poetica* di Aristotele" in *Annali delle Università Toscane* XIII (1873), Parte Prima, pp. xvii-xviii, Appendix A.

More attention has been paid to the *Middle Commentary on Aristotle's Poetics*. Lasinio's edition was based on a single Arabic manuscript (Florence Laurenziano Manuscript CLXXX, 54). Once he became aware of the existence of a second manuscript (University of Leiden 2073), Lasinio printed the variants and suggested better textual readings; cf. *ibid.*, pp. 1–45 (Arabic) and "Studi sopra Averroe, VI" in *Giornale della Società Asiatica Italiana* XI (1897–1898), pp.141–152 and XII (1899), pp. 197–206. 'Abd al-Raḥmān Badawī reprinted Lasinio's 1873 edition of the Middle Commentary; cf, *Talkhīṣ Kitāb Arisṭūṭālīs fī al-Shi'r* in *Arisṭūṭālīs*: *Fann al-Shi'r* (Cairo: Maktabat al-Nahḍah al-Miṣrīyah, 1953), pp. 199–250. Apparently, Badawī knew nothing about Lasinio's later publication of the variants. More recently Salīm Sālim has published a new edition of the same commentary using all the available manuscripts; cf. *Talkhīṣ Kitāb Arisṭūṭālīs fī al-Shi'r* (Cairo: Dār al-Taḥrīr, 1971). It is not believed that Averroës wrote a Large Commentary on the *Poetics*.

There are no Arabic editions of the *Middle Commentary on Aristotle's Topics* by Averroës, even though it is known to be extant in the Florence and Leiden manuscripts. It is not believed that Averroës ever wrote a Large Commentary on the *Topics*.

Lasinio also published an early edition of part of Averroës's *Middle Commentary on Aristotle's Rhetoric*. His edition, based on both the Florence and Leiden manuscripts, stopped shortly before the end of the first *maqālah* of Averroës's commentary; cf. Fausto Lasinio, "Il Commento Medio di Averroe alla *Retorica* di Aristotele" in *Pubblicazioni del R. Instituto di Studi Superiori Pratici e di Perfezionamento in Firenze, Sezione di Filosofia e Filologia, Accademia Orientale*, I (1878), pp. 1–96 (Arabic). 'Abd al-Raḥmān Badawī was the first to edit the whole book; cf. *Talkhīṣ al-Khaṭābah* (Cairo: Maktabat al-Nahḍah al-Miṣrīyah, 1960). Salīm Sālim has also edited the work; cf. *Talkhīṣ al-Khaṭābah* (Cairo: Dār al-Taḥrīr, 1967). It is not believed that Averroës wrote a Large Commentary on the *Rhetoric*.

3. The French orientalist and historian Ernest Renan identified Jacob ben Abba-Maria ben Anatoli as the first to translate this collection of treatises on the art of logic into Hebrew. Although Renan did not state the precise date that Anatoli completed the translation, the context suggests it was completed between 1230–1232. Renan also cited a translation of the collection made by Rabbi Jacob ben Makhir ben Tibbon of Montpelier—known among the Christians of his time as Profatius Judaeus—and claimed it was completed in 1298. Cf. Renan, *Averroès et l'Averroisme* ((Paris: Michel Lévy Frères 1866), 3rd. edition, pp. 188–189.

Some years later, Steinschneider challenged Renan's identification of Anatoli as a translator of this collection, asserting that Anatoli had translated nothing more than the *Middle Commentaries on Aristotle's Organon* in 1232. He also contended that the first translation of this collection was Rabbi Jacob's and that it was completed in 1289, not 1298. (This date corresponds to the one given in the Paris catalogue: *Kislew* 5050; cf. *Manuscrits Orientaux*: *Catalogue des Manuscrits Hébreux et Samaritains de la Bibliothèque Impériale* [Paris: Imprimerie Impériale, 1866], p. 160). Steinschneider also noted that Samuel ben Yehuda of Marseilles expressed displeasure with Rabbi Jacob's translation (which is, incidentally, the translation published at Riva di Trento in 1559 as *Kizzur mi-kol Meleket Higayyon*, that is, *Summary of the Whole Art of Logic*) and did a translation of his own in 1329 or 1330. Cf. M. Steinschneider, *Alfarabi* in *Mémoires de l'Académie Impériale des Sciences de St. Petersbourg*, VIIe série, XIII (1869), no. 4, p. 147 and *Die hebräische Übersetzungen des Mittelalters* (Berlin: Jtzkowski, 1893), p. 54, n. 55.

(The dates 1189 and 5 Kislew 50 in the latter work are obvious misprints and should read 1289 and 5 Kislew 5050 respectively).

4. Cf. Renan, *op. cit.*, pp. 29–42, 79–84, and 173–199. Consider as well the remarks of the noted French orientalist, S. Munk, in the article "Ibn Roschd" in *Dictionnaire des Sciences Philosophiques* (Paris: L. Hachette et Cie., 1847), Vol. III, pp. 163–164 and in *Mélanqes de Philosophie Juive et Arabe* (Paris: A. Franck, 1857), pp. 422–429 and 439–440. Léon Gauthier also discussed this problem in his study of Averroës; cf, Léon Gauthier, *Ibn Rochd* (*Averroès*) (Paris: Presses Universitaires de France, 1948), pp. 9–11.

5. Father Maurice Bouyges edited the *Middle Commentary on Aristotle's Categories* in 1932; cf. *Averroès Talkhiç Kitab al-Maqoulat* (Beirut: Imprimerie Catholique, 1932). In the introduction to this edition, he noted that the work had been neglected in the West and among the Arabs; only Jewish Aristotelians seemed to have had any concern or knowledge about it (pp. v–vi). Cf. also R. de Vaux, "La Première Entrée d'Averroès chez les Latins" in *Revue des Sciences Philosophiques et Théologiques* XXII (1933), p. 193.

Renan first described the Florence Laurenziano Manuscript CLXXX, 54 to the learned community in a letter from Rome dated 27 February, 1850; cf. "Lettre à Reinaud" in *Journal Asiatique* XV (1850), Série IV, pp. 390–391. By 1874, Lasinio was aware of the existence of the University of Leiden Manuscript 2073; cf. "Studi sopra Averroe, V" in *Annuari della Società Italiana per gli Studi Orientali* II (1874), pp. 234–267. For the Judaeo-Arabic manuscripts, cf. infra, p. 4, n. 7.

6. Although still under the influence of the older opinion to some extent, Gauthier noticed a tendency toward independence in Averroës's thought; cf. *op. cit.*, pp. 15 with 257–258 and 278–281. Like Gauthier, Alonso could not deny that Averroës explicitly differed with Aristotle on certain issues; however, he could not completely relinquish the notion that the commentaries were less original than the other works; cf. P. Manuel Alonso, *Teología de Averroes* (Madrid: Maestre, 1947), pp. 26, 36–41 with pp. 33, 89, and 99.

In recent years, there have been more careful arguments about the way in which Averroës is to be considered a disciple of Aristotle. Cf. Michel Allard, "Le Rationalisme d'Averroès d'après une Étude sur la Création" in *Bulletin d'Études Orientales* XIV (1952), pp. 21, 23, 25, and 53–55; G.F. Hourani, *Averroes on the Harmony of Religion and Philosophy* (London: Luzac and Co., 1961), p. 25; H. Blumberg, *Averrois Cordubensis Compendia Librorum Aristotelis qui Parva Naturalia vocantur* (Cambridge: The Mediaeval Academy of America, 1954), p. xi, and *Averroes Epitome of Parva Naturalia* (Cambridge: The Mediaeval Academy of

America, 1961), pp. xiii–xiv; Herbert A. Davidson, *Averroes Middle Commentary on Porphyry's Isagoge and on Aristotle's Categoriae* (Cambridge: The Mediaeval Academy of America, 1969), pp. xiii–xiv, xv, and xix. While the argument that Averroës differed from Aristotle only because he did not understand the text still attracts some attention (cf. Francis Lehner, "An Evaluation of Averroes' Paraphrase on Aristotle's *Poetics*" in *The Thomist* XXX [1966], pp. 38–65 and "The Lambda-Ennea Case" in *The Thomist* XXXII [1968], pp. 387–423), there is a new willingness to consider Averroës capable of intentionally differing from Aristotle (cf. Helmut Gätje, "Averroës als Aristoteleskommentator" in *Zeitschrift der deutschen morgenländischen Gesellschaft* CXIV [1964], pp. 59–65).

7. Cf. Munk, article "Ibn Roschd," *op. cit.*, pp. 161–162, 164. As part of his general presentation of Averroës, Renan sought to explain the difference between the Great Commentary (*Grand Commentaire*), Middle Commentary (*Commentaire Moyen*), and Short Commentary (*Analyse*, *Paraphrase*, or *Abrégé*). However, he mistakenly identified the *Commentary on the Rhetoric* and the *Commentary on the Poetics* contained in the Florence Laurenziano Manuscript CLXXX, 54 as "les paraphrases sur la *Rhétorique* et la *Poétique*." That is, according to his own terminology, as "Short Commentaries." This is one of the two manuscripts used by Badawī and Sālim in their editions, and it fits Renan's own definition of a middle commentary perfectly. Cf. Renan, *op. cit.*, p. 68 with p. 53, and pp. 58–61 with pp. 82–83.

8. Cf. Renan, *op. cit.*, p. 83 (the first edition of this work was published in 1852); Munk, *Mélanges*, *op. cit.*, p. 140, n. 1; and C. Prantl, *Geschichte der Logik im Abendlande* (Leipzig: S. Hirzel, 1861), Vol. II, p. 374 ff. Prantl's error is all the more surprising as he cited both Munk and Renan. Cf. also Steinschneider, *Alfarabi*, *op. cit.*, pp. 148–149.

In an earlier publication, Steinschneider had hinted at his discovery. Among fragments of Munich Codex Hebraicus 356, he had found a loose folio which he recognized as belonging to a commentary on the *Poetics*; it was a misplaced folio, number 86, of the Munich Judaeo-Arabic manuscript. Cf. "Über die Mondstationen (Naxatra), und das Buch Arcandum" in *Zeitschrift der deutschen morgenländischen Gesellschaft* XVIII (1864), p. 169, n. 65. Only after additional searching was he able to bring all the material together; cf. *Hebräische Bibliographie*, "Briefkasten," VIII (1865), p. 32 and "Hebräische Handschriften in München über arabische Philosophie" in *Serapeum* IX (1867), p. 138.

9. Cf. Bouyges, "Notes sur les Philosophes Arabes Connus des Latins du Moyen Age" in *Mélanges de l'Université Saint-Joseph* (*Beyrouth*) VIII

(1922), p. 10. The Cairo publication which Father Bouyges cited bears no resemblance to the *Short Commentary on Aristotle's Rhetoric* presented below, but is simply a haphazard copy of different paragraphs occurring in the first *maqālah* of Averroës's *Middle Commentary on Aristotle's Rhetoric*. Apparently, these paragraphs were taken from Lasinio's early partial edition of that middle commentary; cf. Lasinio, "Il Commento Medio di Averroe alla *Retorica* di Aristotele," *op. cit.* In short, the Cairo publication cited by Father Bouyges is of no value for the serious study of Averroës's rhetorical thought.

Cf. also Harry A. Wolfson, "Plan for the Publication of a *Corpus Commentariorum Averrois in Aristotelem*" in *Speculum* VI (1931), pp. 412–427 and "Revised Plan for the Publication of a *Corpus Commentariorum Averrois in Aristotelem*" in *Speculum* XXXVIII (1963), pp. 88-104. The extent to which the existence of the Judaeo-Arabic manuscripts has been neglected in the academic community is amply illustrated by the fact that, as late as 1943, Wolfson appeared to have no knowledge of either manuscript and restricted himself to the Riva di Trento Hebrew translation and the Venice 1574 Latin translation for speculations about the Arabic equivalents of certain Hebrew words appearing in the text; cf. Harry A. Wolfson, "The Terms *taṣawwur* and *taṣdīq* in Arabic Philosophy and their Greek, Latin, and Hebrew Equivalents" in *The Moslem World* XXXIII (1943), p. 114, n. 9 and p. 115, notes 20, 23, and 25. Similarly, as late as 1969, a scholar publishing a logical work as part of the *Corpus Commentariorum Averrois in Aristotelem* project was unaware of the Munich Judaeo-Arabic manuscript; cf. *Averroes Middle Commentary on Porphyry's Isagoge and on Aristotle's Categoriae*, *op. cit.*, p. xii, n. 8.

10. Cf. *Verzeichnis der orientalischen Handschriften der K. Hof- und Staatsbibliothek in München* (Munich, 1875), Vol. I, *pars quarta*, p. 162: *Die Epitome des Organon von Aristoteles mit der Einleitung des Porphyrius*, Arabisch von Averroes. The manuscript is identified in the catalogue by the number 964, but it carries the number 650a in the Munich Codex Arabicus and is also identified by the number 309 in the Munich Codex Hebraicus.

11. Cf. *Manuscrits Orientaux*: *Catalogue des Manuscrits Hébreux et Samaritains de la Bibliothèque Impériale*, *op. cit.* p. 182: "*Résumé de la Logique*, par Averroès en arabe et en caractères hébreux." It is not clear whether "*la Logique*" refers simply to the art or alludes to "*la Logique d'Aristote*." The manuscript is classified as number 1008 in the Hebrew collection and carries the additional classification of "SI 835 [7A] [FALSAFA]." This is the same manuscript that formerly carried the index number 303.

12. Cf. Georges Vajda, *Index Général des Manuscrits Arabes Musulmans de la Bibliothèque Nationale de Paris* (Paris: Centre Nationale de Recherches Scientifiques, 1953), pp. v and 320.

13. Renan published the biography by Ibn Abū Uṣaybi'ah in the second and third editions of his study; cf. *op. cit.*, pp. 448–456, and especially p. 454. Born in 600/1203 in Damascus, Ibn Abū Uṣaybi'ah was a renowned physician who composed a book of biographies about famous physicians and professors of medicine: *'Uyūn al-Anbā' fī Ṭabaqāt al-Aṭibbā'*. The selection published by Renan is taken from that book. Ibn Abū Uṣaybi'ah died in Sarkhād, near Damascus, in 668/1270.

Renan also published a copy of the Escurial manuscript 884, folio 82; cf. *ibid.*, p. 462.

Cf., as well, Steinschneider, "Une Dédicace d'Abraham de Balmes au Cardinal Dom. Grimani" in *Revue des Études Juives* V (1882), pp. 115-117. This use of the title occurs in Vatican manuscript 3897, which contains a translation by de Balmes of Ibn Bajjah's *Risālat al-Wadā'*. Cf. also Steinschneider, *Die hebräische Übersetzungen*, *op. cit.*, p. 54, n. 54.

14. Ibn al-Abbār, an historian and master of tradition, was born in Valencia in 595/1199 and died in Tunis in 658/1260. He wrote *Kitāb al-Takmilah li Kitāb al-Ṣilah*, a supplement to the biographical dictionary, *Kitāb al-Ṣilah fī Ta'rīkh A'immah al-Andalus* (*Biographical Dictionary about the Leading Men of Andalusia*), of the master of tradition from Córdoba, Ibn Bashkuwāl (494/1101—578/1183). Renan reprinted the portion of Ibn al-Abbār's book relating to Averroës; cf. *op. cit.*, pp. 435–437, esp. p. 436. Although al-Anṣārī's dates are not known, he obviously lived after Ibn al-Abbār, for Renan presented the selection from his book as a supplement to the books of Ibn Bashkuwāl and Ibn al-Abbār; cf. *op. cit.*, pp. 437–447, esp. p. 444.

Shams al-Dīn Muḥammad ibn Aḥmad ibn 'Uthmān al-Dhahabī was born in Damascus in 673/1274 and died there in 748/1348 after travel and residence in many other cultural centers of the Muslim world. Although the list of works given by al-Dhahabī is not as exhaustive as Ibn Abū Uṣaybi'ah's, it does follow that list quite faithfully, except in this instance. Cf. Renan, *op. cit.*, pp. 456–460, esp. p. 457.

15. There are some technical problems with Ibn Abū Uṣaybi'ah's subtitle. First, the text reads "*Kitāb Arisṭūṭālīs* (*Aristotle's Book*)," not "*Kutub Arisṭūṭālīs* (*Aristotle's Books*)" as given here; the plural object "*hā*" of the verb "*lakhkhaṣ*" dictates the correction. Secondly, the text continues after "*mustawfan*" with the words "*Talkhīṣ al-Ilāhīyāt li*

Nīqūlāwus (*Middle Commentary on Nicolas' Metaphysics*"). These words are presented as belonging to the *Kitāb al-Ḍarūrī fī al-Manṭiq* subtitle, but that makes no sense. Consequently, it was decided to read them as a title of another work by Averroës of which nothing is known. H. Jahier and A. Noureddine also understood these words as a separate title in their edition and translation of the text: *Ibn Abī Uçaibi'a*: *'Uyūn al-Anbā' fī T'abaqat al-At'ibbā'*, *Sources d'Informations sur les Classes des Médecins, XIIIe Chapitre*: *Médecins de l'Occident Musulman* (Alger: Librairie Ferraris, 1958), pp. 136–137.

16. The *Middle Commentaries on Aristotle's Organon* are contained in the previously mentioned Florence Laurenziano Manuscript CLXXX, 54 and the University of Leiden Manuscript 2073. There is no other reference to a *talkhīṣ* on logic in Ibn Abū Uṣaybi'ah's list, which suggests possible confusion on his part about the logical treatise he was listing. However, the Escurial manuscript refers to this collection and also to a *Talkhīṣ Kitāb Arisṭū fī al-Manṭiq* (*Middle Commentary on Aristotle's Book about Logic* or *Middle Commentary on Aristotle's Organon*); that title corresponds perfectly to the work contained in the Florence and Leiden manuscripts.

Cf. also Averroës *Rasā'il Ibn Rushd* (Hyderabad: Maṭba'ah Dā'irat al-Ma'ārif al-'Uthmānīyah, 1947), pp. 2–3. In this context, Averroës was contrasting his *mukhtaṣar ṣaghīr* on logic to books on logic written by al-Fārābī. Cf., as well, *Averroes*: *Compendio de Metafísica*, ed. and trans. by Carlos Quirós Rodriguez (Madrid: Maestre, 1919), p. xxxiii, as cited by Alonso in *Teología de Averroes*, *op. cit.*, pp. 55–56.

17. Porphyry was born in Tyre in 232 C.E. and died in Rome in 305 C.E. A zealous student of Plotinus, he had the reputation of being a Neo-Platonist. Porphyry's treatise was translated into Arabic very early and quickly gained wide acceptance. It was considered a good introduction to logic by al-Fārābī and by the time of Averroës was the customary preface to discussions on logic. Cf. *Averroes Middle Commentary on Porphyry's Isagoge and on Aristotle's Categoriae*, *op. cit.*, p. 6: "The intention of the present work is to explain the contents of Porphyry's introduction to the science of logic. [I am undertaking this commentary] because it has become customary for the logical corpus to open with the *Isagoge*."

Cf. also Prantl, *op. cit.*, Vol. I, pp. 626–631; J. Langhade and M. Grignaschi, *Al-Fārābī*: *Deux Ouvrages Inédits sur la Rhétorique* (Beirut: Dar el-Machreq, 1971), pp. 130–131, n. 4; and Ibrahim Madkour, *L'Organon d'Aristote dans le Monde Arabe* (Paris: Vrin, 1969), 2nd. ed., pp. 9–11, and 70–75.

18. Apparently, the inclusion of rhetoric and poetics among the

logical arts can be traced back to two representatives of the Alexandrian school, Olympiodorus and Elias; cf. Richard Walzer, "Zur Traditionsgeschichte der Aristotelischen Poetik" in Richard Walzer, *Greek into Arabic, Essays on Islamic Philosophy* (Oxford: Bruno Cassirer, 1962), pp. 129–136, esp. pp. 133–135; originally published in *Studi Italiani di Filologia Classica*, N.S., Vol. XI (1934), pp. 5–14. Although al-Fārābī and Averroës followed the idea of including rhetoric and poetics among the logical arts, neither accepted it without preliminary consideration; cf. al-Fārābī *Iḥṣā' al-'Ulūm*, ed. 'Uthmān Amīn (Cairo: Dār al-Fikr al-'Arabī, 1949), pp. 63–74 and Averroës *Talkhīṣ al-Khaṭābah*, ed. 'Abd al-Raḥmān Badawī, *op. cit.*, 4, 9–10, 11–13, 18, and 248–249.

19. Cf. the Munich Judaeo-Arabic manuscript (hereafter referred to as M.), folios 1b line 24–3b line 2 and also the Paris Judaeo-Arabic manuscript (hereafter referred to as P.), folios 2a line 2–3a line 15. (Henceforth, references to folio and line will be cited without explaining that the first number refers to folio and the second to line; thus, the above references would read M.1b24–3b2 and P. 2a2–3a15). Cf. also Aristotle *Categories* 1a 1–15.

20. In the introduction to his *Middle Commentary on Aristotle's Topics*, Averroës said: "This art has three parts. The first part sets forth the speeches from which dialectical conversation is composed—i.e., its parts, and the parts of its parts on to its simplest components. This part is found in the first treatise on Aristotle's book.

"The second part sets forth the topics from which syllogisms are drawn—syllogisms for affirming something or denying it with respect to every kind of problem occurring in this art. This is in the next six treatises of Aristotle's book.

"The third part sets forth how the questioner ought to question and the answerer answer. It also sets forth how many kinds of questions and answers there are. This is in the eighth treatise of Aristotle's book." Cf. Florence Laurenziano Manuscript CLXXX, 54, folio 88a, as cited by Fausto Lasinio in "Studi sopra Averroe, II" in *Annuari della Società Italiana per gli Studi Orientali* I (1873), pp. 140–142.

21. The title *On Sophistical Refutations* or, more literally, *On Sophistry* exists only in M.; P. has no title.

22. This is the title in M. In P., the title *Treatise on Assent* (*al-Qawl fī al-Taṣdīq*) is followed by the subtitle *Treatise on the Knowledge Preparing the Way to Assent* (*al-Qawl fī al-Ma'rifah al-muwaṭṭi'ah li al-Taṣdīq*).

23. As part of the title in P., the words "*and they are called Topics*" (*wa hiy al-musammāt Mawāḍi'*) are added. Although these words occur in M. as well, they are not placed in the title.

24. Cf. references to Alonso, Blumberg, and Davidson in n. 6, *supra*. Cf. also Gauther, *op. cit.*, p. 16. To date, insufficient attention has been given to the substantive divergences from Aristotle's text in all of the different kinds of commentaries by Averroës.

25. Although Aristotle wrote no book on dialectic as such, in this treatise Averroës discussed the theory of the nondemonstrative syllogism set forth in Book I of the *Topics* as though it had been a book on dialectic. He also emphasized the general rules for dialectical argument given in Book VIII of the *Topics*, the discussion of topics per se having been put into closer relation with the discussion of the demonstrative syllogism. As has been observed (cf. supra, n. 20), Averroës considered the *Topics* to be comprised of three distinct sections: Book I, Books II-VII, and Book VIII. A further indication of the extent to which he thought of these sections as distinct is that in his *Middle Commentary on Aristotle's Topics* he cited the date on which the second section was completed, something usually done only upon the completion of a whole work; cf. Florence Laurenziano Manuscript CLXXX, 54, folio 116a, as cited by Lasinio in "Il Commento Medio di Averroe alla *Poetica* di Aristotele," *op. cit.*, preface I, pp. xii–xiii, n. 2.

26. This title occurs only in M. and in the Hebrew translation of the Paris manuscript. In the Judaeo-Arabic version of the Paris manuscript, there is a blank space where the title ought to appear. However, that space is too small for the Munich title.

27. Cf. *Fī al-Qawānīn allatī ta'mal bihā al-Maqāyīs*, M. 38b19, P. 43a11. Cf. also infra, *Short Commentary on Aristotle's Topics*, para. 5, and infra, *Short Commentary on Aristotle's Rhetoric*, end. All of these references can only be to Averroës's own *Short Commentary on Aristotle's Prior Analytics*, for they refer to issues not occurring in Aristotle's text.

28. Cf. *Fī al-Qawānīn allatī ta'mal bihā al-Maqāyīs*, M. 41a3, P. 45a21.

29. Cf. Florence Laurenziano Manuscript CLXXX, 54, folio 88a, as cited by Fausto Lasinio in "Studi sopra Averroe, II," *op. cit.*, p. 140: "Among the multitude the term dialectic (*al-jadal*) signifies conversation between two people, each one of whom seeks victory over his fellow by any kind of speech whatever. That is why Aristotle assigned the term this meaning; it is the one which is closest in sense to what the multitude means and is the meaning we have defined. This book may also be called *Topics* (*Ṭubīqī*). What topics (*mawāḍi'*) are will be set forth later."

30. Cf. Prantl, *op. cit.*, Vol. II, p. 374, notes 289–290 and pp. 385–386, n. 346; also Steinschneider, *Alfarabi*, *op. cit.*, pp. 146–148 with p. 5, n. 7 and pp. 38–39.

While Prantl's particular arguments against the possibility of the collection being written by Averroës do merit serious attention, his general view of Averroës's writings on the *Organon* was badly confused. He was correct in stating that the medieval scholastic tradition spoke of three kinds of commentaries by Averröes on the *Posterior Analytics*: a short commentary, a middle commentary, and a long commentary. Similarly, he was correct in reporting that the scholastics thought Averroës had written two kinds of commentaries on the other books of the *Organon*: short commentaries and middle commentaries. However, in his discussion of Averroës's logical theory, he tried to correct the division set forth by the scholastics and their identification of the different commentaries. He thereby betrayed his own confusion about these works. For example, never citing the short commentaries, he identified the *Middle Commentary on Aristotle's Categories* as a short commentary. He further argued that the *Middle Commentary on Aristotle's Posterior Analytics* was a mixture between a short commentary and a middle commentary. Consequently, he tried to show that the *Epitome in Libros Logicae Aristotelis*, i.e., the *Short Commentaries on Aristotle's Organon* was still another kind of commentary, one which had to be rejected as spurious despite its acceptance by the scholastics. Cf. *ibid.*, pp. 374, 377–378, and 384–385. Gauthier demonstrated a similar kind of confusion about the differences between short commentaries and middle commentaries; cf. *Ibn Rochd*, *op. cit.*, pp. 12–14, 16, and 52, n. 1.

31. Cf. Lasinio, "Il Commento Medio di Averroe alla *Poetica* di Aristotele," *op. cit.*, preface I, pp. xvi–xvii. In a different context, Horten cited additional inconsistencies in the philosophical terminology of the Latin translations; cf. *Die Metaphysik des Averroes*, trans. Max Horten (Halle: Max Niemayer, 1912), pp. ix–xi. A major reason for this inconsistency in the Latin translations seems to be the heavy reliance of the translators upon Muslim or Jewish interpreters due to their own insufficient grasp of Arabic. Cf. R. de Vaux, "La Première Entrée d'Averroès chez les Latins," *op. cit.*, pp. 197, n. 2 and 199, notes 1–2; also Harry A. Wolfson, "The Twice-Revealed Averroes" in *Speculum* XXXVI (1961), pp. 373–392.

32. Cf. Prantl, *op. cit.*, Vol. II, p. 376, n. 294. Steinschneider sought to refute this objection by asserting that Averroës often altered in a subsequent work what he had set down in an earlier one. Consequently, inconsistencies in doctrine could be no proof of the spurious character of a work. In these terms, Steinschneider's argument is overstated and raises as many problems as it attempts to solve. Cf. Steinschneider, *Alfarabi*, *op. cit.*, pp. 149–150.

33. Cf. *Averroes Middle Commentary on Porphyry's Isagoge and on Aristotle's Categoriae*, *op. cit.*, p. 27: "This completes the subject matter of the *Isagoge*. I was led to comment upon it by friends in Murcia, men who are keen and eager for theoretical knowledge, may God show them mercy, and were it not for them, I would not have taken the trouble, for two reasons. One is that I do not consider the *Isagoge* necessary for beginning the art of logic, since its contents cannot belong to what is common to the entire art, as some imagine; for if what has been stated here in connection with the definitions of the predicables is demonstrable, it belongs to the *Posterior Analytics*, while if it is generally accepted opinion, it belongs to the *Topics*. In fact, Porphyry made these statements not as definitions, but rather as explanations of the meanings of the terms in question [so that they might be understood] whenever Aristotle uses them in his book. From this point of view, the *Isagoge* is not a part of logic. Alfarabi, however, implies that it is a part of logic. This is one thing that would have dissuaded me from commenting upon the book as part of my commentary on the books of Aristotle, and the second is that what this man says in the *Isagoge* is self-explanatory. Nevertheless, I wished to oblige the aforementioned scholars and assist them in everything that they, from their desire and love of science, considered to be to their benefit, and thus I was led to comment and dilate upon this book. In the few remarks I have made, I have alluded to most [of the things that should be discussed]. At some points there is room for speculation, but this is not the place for it." Cf. also *ibid.*, pp. xiii–xv, xvii–xviii, and xix–xx.

34. Averroës explained: "The purpose of this treatise is to present a Middle Commentary on the ideas contained in Aristotle's books on the art of logic, summarizing them according to our ability, as we have customarily done with his other books. We shall begin with the first of his books about this art, that is, the book about the *Categories*." Cf. *Averroès Talkhiç Kitab al-Maqoulat*, ed. Bouyges, *op. cit.*, p. 3.

It is possible that Averroës composed his *Middle Commentary on Porphyry's Isagoge* after the other Middle Commentaries, for the only mention of the Arabic text of this commentary was the description of the Florence Laurenziano manuscript CLXXX, 54 by J.B. Raimundus in about 1610. That description is not entirely trustworthy, however; cf. Lasinio, "Il Commento Medio di Averroe alla *Poetica* di Aristotele," *op. cit.*, preface I, pp. viii-x.

35. Cf. Prantl, *op. cit.*, Vol. II, pp. 390–392, n. 372 with pp. 384–385, n. 334 and pp. 360–361, n. 230. Cf. also supra, p. 7 . For Averroës's criticism of Avicenna, cf. *Magna Commentaria Posteriorum Resolutionarum* in *Aristotelis Omnia quae extant Opera... Averrois Cordubensis in ea... Omnes...*

Commentarii (Venice: apud Junctas, 1562), Vol. I, pars secunda, p. 7a: "Circa quod iam erravit Avicenna errore manifesto, cum putaret, praeponi Topicam arti Demonstrativae..." (trans. Abraham de Balmes); or "Et idea Manifeste erravit Avicenna circa hoc, cum existimet, dialecticam facultatem, seu topicam, debere precedere artem Demonstrativam..." (trans. Jacob Mantinus); cf. also 6a.

36. Cf. Averroës *Magna Commentaria Posteriorum Resolutionarum, op. cit.*, pp. 7b–8b.

37. Cf. *On the Rules by Which Syllogisms Are Made* (*Fī al-Qawānīn allatī ta'mal bihā al-Maqāyīs*), M 30a19–31a8, P 33a22–34a21. Steinschneider was so convinced Averroës had not spoken about dialectical reasoning in this section of the collection that he denied it should even be entitled *Topics*, reserving that title for the first treatise presented here; cf. *Alfarabi, op. cit.*, p. 148.

For some reason, none of the Latin editions presented the treatise on dialectic (*Short Commentary on Aristotle's Topics*) as a separate treatise. Instead, it was incorporated into the *Epitome in Libros Elenchorum* as chapter V and given the title *De Rationibus probabilibus et litigiosis.* Cf. *Aristotelis Omnia quae extant Opera... Averrois Cordubensis in ea Omnes... Commentarii, op. cit.*, Vol. I, pars prima, p. 72b; Vol. I, pars tertia, p. 72b; and Vol. II, p. 189b (in this volume, it is not set off as a separate chapter, and the title is in the margin). Cf. also *Aristotelis Omnia quae extant Opera... Averrois Cordubensis in ea Omnes... Commentarii* (Venice: apud Junctas, 1552), Vol. I, p. 357 (here it is not set off as a separate chapter). Cf. also *Aristotelis Omnia quae extant Opera... Averrois Cordubensis in ea Omnes... Commentarii* (Venice: apud Cominum de Tridino, 1560), Vol. I, p. 332b.

Similarly, there is confusion in these editions about the order of the treatises belonging to the collection. Despite Averroës's statement that his treatise *On the Rules by Which Syllogisms Are Made* (*Fī al-Qawānīn allatī ta'mal bihā al-Maqāyīs*) should precede the *Short Commentary on Aristotle's Posterior Analytics*, it is placed after the *Short Commentary on Aristotle's Posterior Analytics* in the Junctas 1562 edition. Moreover, only the Junctas 1552 edition presents the collection as a whole. The Junctas 1562 edition presents the *Short Commentary on Aristotle's Rhetoric* and the *Short Commentary on Aristotle's Poetics* in a separate volume, while the Tridino 1560 edition presents the *Short Commentary on Aristotle's Posterior Analytics* in a separate volume and the *Short Commentary on Aristotle's Rhetoric* and the *Short Commentary on Aristotle's Poetics* in yet another volume.

38. Cf. infra, *Short Commentary on Aristotle's Topics*, para. 1.

39. "There are two kinds of assent. One kind is for verifying the problem and dividing it into one of the two parts of the contradiction so that what is true is contained within one of them. The second kind is for verifying the composite argument bringing about assent; it is called syllogism. We shall begin with the first kind, since it is the one which ought first to be verified with regard to the problem, as it constitutes the knowledge preparing the way to assent." As has already been noted (supra, n. 22), the subtitle in the Paris Judaeo-Arabic manuscript is even more explicit: *Treatise on the Knowledge Preparing the Way to Assent* (*al-Qawl fī al-Maʿrifah al-muwaṭṭiʾah li al-Taṣdīq*). Cf. M. 10b19–11a2, P. 11a10–15.

40. Cf. *On the Rules by Which Syllogisms Are Made*, M. 30a19–30b3, P. 33a20–25: "We say: since the rules given in this art are of two types (a type which brings about and a type which makes known) and since the discussion which preceded has been about the things by which the species and classes of syllogisms are made known, we now ought to speak about the rules enabling us to make syllogisms." Cf. also M. 30b3–31a8, P. 33a25–34a18, and M. 1a4–8 (the corresponding folio in P. is missing).

41. The "Sections Which Are Necessary in the Art of Logic" were mentioned by Munk (*Mélanges*, *op. cit.*, pp. 351–352, n. 1) and Steinschneider (*Alfarabi*, *op. cit.*, pp. 15–16), but Professor H. Blumberg was the first to discuss them in any detail. Cf. "Alfarabi's Five Chapters on Logic" in *Proceedings of the American Academy for Jewish Research* VI (1934–1935), pp. 115–121. Although Blumberg promised a subsequent edition of the treatise, it never appeared. Only twenty years later when Professor D.M. Dunlop discovered the manuscript, apparently without ever having heard of Blumberg's article, were the "Sections" edited. Dunlop viewed the Paris manuscript as an inferior source and preferred to depend on the Istanbul Hamidiye Manuscript 182, folios 3a–5b. The treatise was edited and translated by Dunlop as "al-Fārābī's Introductory Sections on Logic" in *The Islamic Quarterly* II (1955), pp. 264–282. Professor Mubahat Türker edited the treatise again, using additional manuscripts, and translated it into Turkish; cf. "Fārābī'nin bazi Manṭiḳ Eseleri" in *Ankara Üniversitesi Dil ve Tarih-Coğrafya Fakültesi Dergisi* XVI (1958), pp. 165–181, 195–213.

Professor Türker has also edited "The Speech about the Conditions of Demonstration"; cf. "Fārābī'nin *Serāʾit ul-yakīnī*" in *Araṣtirma* I (1963); Felsefe Araṣtirmalari Enstitüsü, *Ankara Üniversitesi Dil ve Tarih-Coğrafya Fakültesi Dergisi*, pp. 173 ff.

42. This is the same scribe who made the copy of *Kitāb al-Ḥiss wa al-Maḥsūs* found in Modena (Bibliotèca Estensis Manuscript 13, I.D.

10); he claimed to have finished copying it in 1356 C.E., the same year he finished copying this manuscript. Cf. *Die Epitome der Parva Naturalia des Averroes*, ed. Helmut Gätje (Weisbaden: Otto Harrassowitz, 1961), pp. x–xi.

Some question about the identity of the Hebrew translator has arisen, because neither the colophon nor any other passage of the text provides specific evidence about his identity. In an extremely ambiguous footnote, Renan attributed the translation of the Paris manuscript to Jacob ben Abba-Maria ben Anatoli (cf. Renan, *op.cit.*, p. 188, n. 2). Munk later resorted to an equally ambiguous footnote in order to attribute the translation to Samuel ben Yehuda of Marseilles, but never explained why he disagreed with Renan (cf. *Mélanges*, *op. cit.*, p. 489, n. 3). Yet another candidate was suggested by Zotenberg, the compiler of the Paris catalogue. He identified Rabbi Jacob ben Makhir of Montpelier as the translator because of the closeness between the translation of the Paris manuscript and another translation of this work definitely attributed to Rabbi Jacob (cf. *Manuscrits Orientaux*, *op. cit.*, pp. 160, Ms. no. 917; 167–168, Ms. no. 956; and 182). Steinschneider and Lasinio accepted the identification of the Paris catalogue and rejected Renan's and Munk's conjectures without explaining the reasons for their decision (cf. *Alfarabi*, *op. cit.*, p. 147; *Die hebräische Übersetzungen*, *op. cit.*, pp. 54–56; and "Il Commento Medio di Averroe all *Poetica* di Aristotele," *op. cit.*, preface I, p. xvii). Father Bouyges did not reconsider the problem; like Steinschneider and Lasinio, he accepted the judgment of the Paris catalogue without question (cf. "Notes sur les Philosophes Arabes Connus des Latins du Moyen Age," *op. cit.*, p. 9).

Had Lasinio paid more attention to his own edition of the *Short Commentary on Aristotle's Poetics*, he might have come to a different conclusion: in the printed version of the Hebrew translation (which is definitely Rabbi Jacob's translation), there is a passage missing that is present in the Paris manuscript translation; and there is a passage in the printed translation that does not occur in the Paris manuscript translation. The problem is that the Paris manuscript is no more similar to the translation known to be by Rabbi Jacob than it is to another translation executed by Samuel. Zotenberg was clearly correct in his judgment that Samuel's translation differs little from Rabbi Jacob's, despite Samuel's allegation that he decided to do his own translation in order to correct the errors in Rabbi Jacob's version. However, the differences between these two identified translations are other than the differences between either one of them and the translation of the Paris manuscript.

43. For example, cf. infra, *Short Commentary on Aristotle's Topics*, para.

3, n. 3; *Short Commentary on Aristotle's Rhetoric*, para. 4, n. 12; and *Short Commentary on Aristotle's Poetics*, para. 2, n. 9.

44. For example, cf. infra, *Short Commentary on Aristotle's Topics*, para. 1, n. 3; *Short Commentary on Aristotle's Rhetoric*, para. 1, n. 4; and *Short Commentary on Aristotle's Poetics*, para. 2, n. 18.

45. Cf. infra, *Short Commentary on Aristotle's Topics*, para. 8, notes 5-6 and para. 16, note 3; also *Short Commentary on Aristotle's Rhetoric*, para. 23, note 4. Examples of passages where each manuscript differs from the best reading are: infra, *Short Commentary on Aristotle's Topics*, para. 9, n. 20; *Short Commentary on Aristotle's Rhetoric*, para. 2, n. 3; and *Short Commentary on Aristotle's Poetics*, para. 2, n. 10.

46. Cf. infra, *Short Commentary on Aristotle's Topics*, para. 1: "Since we have spoken about the things by means of which the certain assent and the complete concept are distinguished and subsequent to that have spoken about the things which lead to error concerning them, let us speak about dialectical and rhetorical assent and the extent each one provides." Cf. also, infra, *Short Commentary on Aristotle's Rhetoric*, para. 1. Although the art of poetics does not use syllogistic arguments, it persuades by means of imaginative representation; cf. infra, *Short Commentary on Aristotle's Poetics*, paras. 1 and 3.

The interpretation expressed here develops some ideas first expressed in an article entitled "Averroës: Politics and Opinion," *American Political Science Review* LXVI (1972), pp. 894–901.

47. The works in question are the *Kitāb Faṣl al-Maqāl wa Taqrīr mā bayn al-Sharī'ah wa al-Ḥikmah min al-Ittiṣāl* (*Book of the Decisive Treatise and Stipulation of the Relationship between Divine Law and Philosophy*), ed. by George F. Hourani (Leiden: E.J. Brill, 1959); the *Kitāb al-Kashf 'an Manāhij al-Adillah fī 'Aqā'id al-Millah* (*The Book of Uncovering the Clear Paths of the Signs about the Beliefs of the Religious Community*), ed. by Maḥmūd Kassem (Cairo: Maktabat al-Anglū al-Miṣrīyah, 1963); and the *Tahāfut al-Tahāfut* (*The Incoherence of the Incoherence*), ed. by Father Bouyges (Beirut: Imprimerie Catholique, 1930).

48. Cf. infra, *Short Commentary on Aristotle's Rhetoric*, paras. 38–40; and *Short Commentary on Aristotle's Poetics*, paras. 1–2.

49. Cf. *General Introduction*, M. 1a4–11: "The purpose of this treatise is to abstract the necessary speeches pertaining to each and every logical art by explaining the ranks of the kinds of concept and assent used in each and every one of the five arts—i.e., the demonstrative, the dialectical, the sophistical, the rhetorical, and the poetical. The reason is that this extent of this art is what is most necessary for learning the arts which have already been perfected. And in this time

of ours most of the arts, like medicine and others, are like this [i.e., perfected]." The corresponding folio in P. is missing.

50. Cf. infra, *Short Commentary on Aristotle's Poetics*, paras. 4–5. The prior judgment was made in the *Short Commentary on Aristotle's Posterior Analytics* where it was explained that man's ultimate perfection consisted in having certainty about the most remote causes of the beings and that philosophy provided such knowledge. It was also explained that a further development of the issue belonged in another work. Cf. M. 57a 17–19, P. 63a 2–4. The same sort of judgment applies to rhetoric, for the final definitions of rhetoric and of poetics are nearly identical; cf. infra, *Short Commentary on Aristotle's Rhetoric*, para. 45. Poetics, however, can only be spoken of in terms of what it allows one to make and do, because Averroës denied that it had any contribution to make towards understanding; cf. infra, *Short Commentary on Aristotle's Poetics*, paras. 1–2.

51. Cf. infra, *Short Commentary on Aristotle's Topics*, para. 21. Cf. also Averroës *Short Commentary on Aristotle's Posterior Analytics*, M. 56b 22–57a24, P. 62a 15–63a6; Averroës *Talkhīṣ Kitāb mā ba'd al-Ṭabī'ah* ed. by 'Uthmān Amīn (Cairo: Muṣṭafā al-Bābī al-Ḥalabī, 1958), pp. 1:10–2:8, 5:12–6:14; and Aristotle *Posterior Analytics* 77a29–35, 86a22–30.

52. Cf. infra, *Short Commentary on Aristotle's Topics*, paras. 1–4, 6, 8–11, 15–19.

53. Cf. *ibid.*, para. 21 and n. 3.

54. Cf. *The Incoherence of the Incoherence*, *op. cit.*, pp. 207–209, 356–358, 427-430, 514–515, 527-528. Concerning al-Ghazālī, cf. infra, *Short Commentary on Aristotle's Rhetoric*, para. 42, n. 2.

55. Cf. al-Fārābī *Iḥṣā' al-'Ulūm*, *op. cit.*, chapter 5, pp. 107–108: "The art of dialectical theology is a skill enabling a man to use arguments for defending the established opinions and actions declared by the Lawgiver and for refuting anything which contradicts them. This art [like jurisprudence] is divided into two parts: one concerning opinions and one concerning actions. It is unlike jurisprudence in that the jurist takes the opinions and actions declared by the Lawgiver as indisputable and considers them as principles from which he deduces their consequences, while the dialectical theologian defends the things used by the jurist as principles without deducing other things from them. If it happens that one man has a facility for both tasks, then he is a jurist and a dialectical theologian—a dialectical theologian insofar as he defends these [principles] and a jurist insofar as he deduces [other things] from them." The same role is assigned the dialectical

theologians by Louis Gardet in his article "Quelques Réflexions sur la Place du 'Ilm al-Kalām dans les 'Sciences Religieuses' Musulmanes" in *Arabic and Islamic Studies in Honor of Hamilton A.R. Gibb*, ed. by. G Makdisi (Leiden: E.J. Brill, 1965), pp. 258–259, 262–267.

56. Cf. infra, *Short Commentary on Aristotle's Rhetoric*, paras. 12, 31, 36, 42, and 43. Concerning Abū al-Ma'ālī, cf. *ibid.*, para. 12, n. 1.

57. *Ibid.*, paras. 12, 29–30, 31, 36, and 44. For a fuller discussion of this issue, cf. "Rhetoric and Islamic Political Philosophy" in *International Journal of Middle East Studies* III (1972), pp. 187–198.

58. Cf. infra, *Short Commentary on Aristotle's Rhetoric*, paras. 2, 3, 6, 8, 12, 13 (with paras. 7 and 10), 18–19, and 33.

59. Cf. infra, *Short Commentary on Aristotle's Topics*, para. 9; also *On the Rules by Which Syllogisms Are Made*, M. 37a24—37b10, P. 41a20—42a2, where rhetoric is substituted for sophistry as though they were identical. Cf. also infra, *Short Commentary on Aristotle's Rhetoric*, para. 17.

60. *Ibid.*, paras. 4–5, 6–7, 8–13, 14, 15, 16–22, 23–24, and 26–32.

61. *Ibid.*, paras. 1–5, 12, 29 and 31.

62. *Ibid.*, paras. 5, 15–17, and 23–24.

63. *Ibid.*, para. 43.

64. *Ibid.*, paras. 12 and 31.

65. *Ibid.*, paras. 33–44.

66. *Ibid.*, para. 34.

67. *Ibid.*, paras. 35–36.

68. *Ibid.*, paras 38–39 and cf. infra, *Short Commentary on Aristotle's Topics*, para. 11.

69. Cf. infra, *Short Commentary on Aristotle's Rhetoric*, para. 36.

70. *Ibid.*, paras. 37 and 40.

71. *Ibid.*, para. 42.

72. *Ibid.*, para. 43.

73. *Ibid.*, para. 44

74. Cf. infra, *Short Commentary on Aristotle's Poetics*, paras. 1 and 4.

75. *Ibid.*, paras. 1–3.

76. *Ibid.*, para. 1.

77. *Ibid.*, para. 2.

78. *Ibid.*

79. *Ibid.* "For the most part these representations cause error concerning the things which can be conceived of only by their representations or which can be conceived of only with difficulty; thus, there is much error about the latter..."

80. *Ibid.*

81. *Ibid.*, paras. 1 and 4.

82. Cf. al-Fārābī *Kitāb al-Millah* [*Book of Religion*], ed. by M. Mahdi (Beirut: Imprimerie Catholique, 1972), para. 1. "Religion is the opinions and actions which the first ruler prescribes to the collectivity. They are determined and restricted by qualifications as he seeks to obtain a specific goal with respect to the people or by means of them, through their practicing these opinions and actions... the craft of the virtuous first ruler is kingly and linked with revelation from God. Indeed, he determines the actions and the opinions which are in the virtuous religion by means of revelation..."

83. Cf. infra, *Short Commentary on Aristotle's Poetics*, para. 2.

84. *Ibid.*, para. 3.

85. Cf. Averroës *Talkhīṣ al-Khaṭābah*, Badawī edition, *op. cit.*, pp. 13–14.

86. Cf. infra, *Short Commentary on Aristotle's Poetics*, para. 4.

87. *Ibid.*, para. 5.

88. Cf. infra, *Short Commentary on Aristotle's Topics*, para. 13.

NOTES TO THE TRANSLATION OF THE *SHORT COMMENTARY ON ARISTOTLE'S TOPICS*

INVOCATION.

1. The clause "[I beseech] your succor, O Lord" was omitted from the Paris manuscript. In its place is the clause: "I have recourse to Him, and in Him I place my trust".

PARAGRAPH (1).

1. The word translated here as "assent" (*taṣdīq*) is one of two key terms for Averroës, the other being "concept"; cf. below, n. 2. At the very beginning of the collection of these Short Commentaries, Averroës explained that his whole analysis centered around these two terms since all the problems considered in the rational arts may be explained by means of them. "Assent is the firm assertion or denial of something, and it comes about in two ways: (a) either absolutely, like our saying 'does vacuum exist?' or (b) with qualification, like our saying 'is the world created?' Now this sort of seeking is always asked about by the particle 'does' [or 'is' (*hal*)]." Cf. M. 1b3–5; there is no corresponding folio in the Paris manuscript, as has been noted in the Introduction. Cf. also Harry A. Wolfson, "The Terms *taṣawwur* and *taṣdīq* in Arabic Philosophy and their Greek, Latin, and Hebrew Equivalents," *op. cit.*, pp. 114–128.

2. "Concept" (*taṣawwur*) is "the understanding of something in accordance with what gives an analogy of its essence or with what is supposed to give an analogy of its essence, and it is asked about—for the most part and primarily—by the particle 'what'; like our saying 'what is nature?' and 'what is the soul?' " Cf. M. 1a23–1b2.

Because the word "form" (*ṣūrah*) is derived from the same root, the term "concept" is used in a very strict sense; i.e., the mental image of the form of something.

3. The word translated here and in what follows as "arguments" could literally be translated as "speeches" (*aqāwīl*). Because the word means "arguments" in this context, because "speeches" are used as arguments in the art of dialectic, and because both here and in the following *Short Commentary on Aristotle's Rhetoric* the word is used to refer to those aspects of speech which produce assent rather than to the whole speech, this translation has been adopted.

PARAGRAPH (2).

1. The arabic word *ẓann* is translated here as "supposition." It is usually used to denote the thought someone holds about that in which he believes. For instance, al-Fārābī defined *ẓann* as: "believing that a thing is such or not such." He also explained: "Supposition and certainty have in common that both are opinion. Opinion (*ra'y*) is to believe that a thing is such or not such. It is like their genus, and they are like the two species." Cf. al-Fārābī *Kitāb al-Khaṭābah*, edited and translated by J. Langhade, in Langhade and Grignaschi, *Al-Fārābī: Deux Ouvrages Inédits sur la Rhétorique, op. cit.*, p. 31, lines 6–8; p. 33, lines 8-9.

Avicenna also defines supposition as a kind of opinion: "True supposition is an opinion about something being so, while it is possible for it not to be so." Cf. A.-M. Goichon, *Lexique de la Langue Philosophique d'Ibn Sina* (Paris: Desclée de Brouwer, 1938), para. 405.

Although some similarly does exist between *ẓann* and *ra'y*, there is a difference. These authors have tried to distinguish between the two words and apparently considered it possible for opinion, but not supposition, to reach the level of certainty.

2. The word translated here as "peculiar characteristic" is really the word for "property" (*khāṣṣah*); cf. infra, paras. 15 and 16, as well as para. 17, note 3.

PARAGRAPH (3).

1. According to Aristotle, "a premise is an affirmative or negative statement about some subject... [and] a syllogistic premise will be simply the affirmation or negation of some predicate of some subject... while the dialectical premise will be, for the interrogator, an answer to the question which of two contradictory statements is to be accepted, and for the one making the syllogism, an assumption of what is apparently true and generally accepted..." Cf. *Prior Analytics* 24a17–24b12; also *Topics* 104a2–37. Averroës said that the premise is the smallest statement which admits of truth or falsehood. "It is composed of a predicate and a subject, and insofar as it is a part of a syllogism, it is called a premise." Cf. *Short Commentary on Aristotle's Prior Analytics* M. 17a6–7; P. 18a8–9. A syllogism results from the combination of two or more premises.

PARAGRAPH (4).

1. Or "The same outside the soul as it is inside the soul" (*khārij al-nafs 'alā mā huw 'alaih fī al-nafs*).

2. Aristotle classified syllogisms as belonging to three different "figures" in accordance with the different manner in which the middle term (cf. infra, para. 6, note 3) might be arranged. This classification also served to distinguish the character of the different kinds of syllogisms; i.e., a syllogism occurring in the first figure was said to be perfect because "it requires nothing, apart from what is comprised in it, to make the necessary conclusion apparent," whereas a syllogism occurring in either one of the other two figures was imperfect because it "requires one or more propositions which, although they necessarily follow from the terms which have been laid down, are not comprised in the premises," and for this reason, such a syllogism was said to be merely valid. The superiority of the syllogisms occurring in the first figure is also apparent from Aristotle's contention that "it is possible to reduce all syllogisms to the universal syllogisms in the first figure" and that "all imperfect syllogisms are completed by means of the first figure." It is in this latter way that the syllogisms of the second and third figures ultimately become valid. Cf. *Prior Analytics* 24b23–27, 29b24–25, and 40b15–16. In the *Short Commentary on Aristotle's Prior Analytics*, Averroës followed Aristotle's schema and, after distinguishing the different kinds of premises and terms, explained that any problem which occurred to mind could be classified in one of three ways according to the different manner in which its subject and predicate might be related to the major term (cf. infra, para. 6, n. 4). By explaining the possible relations of the subject and predicate to the major term and the effects of each relation on the other two terms, Averroës was able to offer a plausible argument that there was no reason to adopt the fourth figure which Galen (cf. infra, *Short Commentary on Aristotle's Rhetoric*, para. 9, n. 1) had tried to impose upon Aristotle's classification. Cf. M. 17b16–18a2 and 19a3–24a8; P. 19a5–10 and 20a14–26a6. For examples of syllogisms occuring in each of the three figures, cf. infra, para. 6, n. 2.

PARAGRAPH (5).

1. Cf. supra, para. 2: "We say: the extent [of assent] they provide is supposition which approximates certainty." The meaning of this statement was explained in paras. 2–4.

2. All of the syllogisms which are divided into figures fall under the grouping "categorical syllogism" according to Averroës. Cf. *Short Commentary on Aristotle's Prior Analytics* M. 24a6–8, P. 26a5–6. Such a distinction does not occur in Aristotle's *Prior Analytics* because Aristotle insisted that all syllogisms are brought about by means of one of the three figures. Cf. *Prior Analytics* 40b22–23 and 41b1–5. Because

Aristotle made this statement subsequent to the long discussion of syllogisms based on modal attributions (*ibid.*, 29b29—40b16), he apparently did not intend to place them in a different class from the syllogisms which conclude immediately in one of the three figures (*ibid.*, 25b26–29b28).

3. Although Aristotle did not treat the conditional syllogism as a separate kind of syllogism, Averroës thought that arguments *ex hypothesi* (cf. *Prior Analytics* 40b17–41b7, 45b15–20, 50a16–50b4) should be understood as conditional syllogisms. In the *Short Commentary on Aristotle's Prior Analytics*, he explained that "the conditional syllogism is usually composed of two premises, a major and a minor. The major is composed of two categorical premises to which is attached a conditional particle (*ḥarf al-sharīṭah*). The minor is a part of this major and is that which is selected from one of the two categorical premises from which the major is composed." Cf. M. 24a8–27b6; P. 26a7–30a8. Conditional syllogisms are further divided into conjunctive and disjunctive (cf. infra, *Short Commentary on Aristotle's Rhetoric*, para. 8). One example of the conjunctive conditional syllogisms given by Averroës is: "If this entity is a human being, then he is an animal; but he is a human being, so he is necessarily an animal."

It appears that Averroës followed a well-established tradition by dividing the syllogisms into classes other than the three figures mentioned by Aristotle. Both Avicenna and al-Fārābī made the same kind of distinction. For Avicenna, cf. *al-Najāh* (Cairo: Maṭba'at al-Sa'ādah, 1938), pp. 32–52 and *al-Shifā'*: *Talkhīṣ Kitāb al-Qiyās* (Cairo: Wizārat al-Thaqāfah, 1964), pp. 231–426. For al-Fārābī, cf. *Kitāb al-Qiyās*, Hamidiye Manuscript no. 812 (Istanbul), folios 28b–42b. The tradition that all three followed seems to have had its origins in the theory of the hypothetical and disjunctive conclusions first presented by Theophrastus (371–288 B.C.E.) and later developed by Porphyry, both of whom were well-known to Arab thinkers. Cf. Prantl, *op. cit.*, Vol. I, pp. 294–295, 374–393, and 470–482; Vol. II, pp. 301–302, 309–311, 357–359, 368–370, and 379–384. Cf. also J. Tricot, *Traité de Logique Formelle* (Paris: Vrin, 1930), pp. 227–235.

4. Averroës defined the contradictory syllogism in the following manner: "The contradictory syllogism is composed from the categorical and the conditional [syllogisms]. It is used in this way: when we wish to explain the truth of a certain proposition, we take its opposite and we join to it a true premise whose truth is not doubted. From them one of the conclusive constructions is constructed, according to any of the categorical figures chanced upon. If a clear falsehood results, we know that the falsehood does not derive from the way the syllogism

is constructed—since it is a conclusive construction—nor from the true premise; so all that is left is that it is derived from the opposite of the common premise, and if its opposite is false, then it is true." Cf. *Short Commentary on Aristotle's Prior Analytics* M. 27b6–28a 23; P. 30a 8–31a8. This classification seems to be based on Aristotle's discussion of a particular kind of argument *ex hypothesi*, the *reductio ad impossible*; cf. *Prior Analytics* 45a23–45b15, 50a28–39, and 62b30–63b20.

PARAGRAPH (6).

1. The first figure, according to Aristotle, is the one in which the perfect syllogism occurs. A syllogism is perfect when its terms, i.e., the subject and predicate of the premises, are so arranged that "the last is wholly encompassed within the middle, and the middle is wholly encompassed within or excluded from the first." When he said that "one term is wholly encompassed within another," Aristotle meant that the latter may be "predicated of all of the former." Cf. *Prior Analytics* 24b27–31, 25b26–32. Averroës explained that the first figure occurs when the middle term is the subject of the major premise and the predicate of the minor premise. Cf. *Short Commentary on Aristotle's Prior Analytics* M. 17b18–23; P. 19a6–9.

Since a syllogism in the first figure is perfect, i.e., so formed that the necessary conclusion is readily apparent, it is very convincing; consequently, its force is very strong. The example given here is developed more fully in para. 8, infra.

2. Every syllogism has at least two premises and three terms. When a syllogism has more than two premises and three terms, there is always one term more than the number of premises. With respect to the first figure, Aristotle identified the minor term as "that which is subsumed under the middle term." By saying this, Aristotle meant that it is wholly encompassed within the middle term, i.e., that the middle term can be predicated of all of the minor term or that the middle term is more comprehensive than the minor term. In the second figure, as well as in the third figure, the minor term is most distant from the middle term. Cf. *Prior Analytics* 42a32–42b27, 24b28–30, 25b26–35, 26a23, 26b38, 28a14. Averroës expressed the idea somewhat differently: according to him, the minor term is the subject of the proposition resulting from the syllogism. Cf. *Short Commentary on Aristotle's Prior Analytics* M. 17b12–13; P. 19a3–4.

An example of a syllogism occurring in the first figure would be: "Every body is composed; every composed thing is created; thus, every body is created." In this example the terms are "body," "composed," and "created," and the minor term is "body." An example of a syllogism occurring in the second figure would be: "Every body is composed; no eternal entity is composed; thus, no body is eternal." In this example, the terms are "body," "eternal," and "composed," with "body" again being the minor term. Finally, an example of a syllogism occurring in the third figure would be: "Every theoretical science is learned [i.e., acquired by learning]; every theoretical science is a virtue; thus some virtues are learned [i.e., acquired by learning]." In this example, the terms are "theoretical science," "learned," and "virtue," with "virtue" being the minor term. Cf. Averroës, *ibid.*, M. 19b8, 21b23–22a2, 23a20–22; P. 21a5–6, 23a17–18, 25a9–10.

3. In the syllogisms occurring in the first figure, Aristotle identified the middle term as that term "which both is encompassed within another and encompasses another." In the syllogisms occurring in the second figure, the middle term is that term "which is predicated of both subjects." Finally, in the syllogisms occurring in the third figure, the middle term is that term "of which both predications are made." As a consequence, it literally occupies a middle position only in the syllogisms of the first figure. Cf. *Prior Analytics* 25b35–37, 26b36, 28a12–13. According to Averroës, the middle term is the part of the syllogism which is common to both of the other terms. Cf. *Short Commentary on Aristotle's Prior Analytics* M. 17b13; P. 19a4.

Taking the syllogism cited in the preceding note as an example of those syllogisms occurring in the first figure, "composed" is the middle term. With regard to the syllogism cited as an example of those syllogisms occurring in the second figure, "composed" is once again the middle term. In the syllogism cited as an example of those which occur in the third figure, "theoretical science" is the middle term.

4. With respect to the syllogisms occurring in the first figure, Aristotle identified the major term as "that within which the middle is encompassed." In syllogisms occurring in the second figure, the major term is "that which comes next to the middle." In syllogisms occurring in the third figure, he stated that the major term actually occupies the middle, but it is difficult to understand what he meant by such a definition. Cf. *Prior Analytics* 26a22, 26b38, 28a13–14. According to Averroës, the major term is the predicate of the proposition resulting from the syllogism. Cf. *Short Commentary on Aristotle's Prior Analytics* M. 17b13; P. 19a4.

Taking the syllogism cited in note 3 as an example of those syllogisms occurring in the first figure, the major term would be "created." In the syllogism cited as an example of those syllogisms occurring in the second figure, "eternal" would be the major term. With regard to the syllogism cited as an example of those syllogisms occurring in the third figure, "learned" would be the major term.

PARAGRAPH (7).

1. Although Aristotle discussed the major premise in the *Prior Analytics*, he does not appear to have presented a detailed explanation of what it is anywhere in that book. Apparently, the student of logic was expected to deduce the definition by reference to the previously presented analysis of the syllogisms. Accordingly, the major premise of the syllogism cited as an example of those occurring in the first figure would be the premise which has the middle term as its subject and the major term as its predicate, i.e., "every composed thing is created." For the syllogism which was cited as an example of those occurring in the second figure, the major premise would be the one having the major term as its subject and the middle term as its predicate, i.e., "no eternal entity is composed." Finally, the major term of the syllogism cited as indicative of those syllogisms occurring in the third figure would have the middle term as its subject and the major term as its predicate, i.e., "every theoretical science is learned [i.e., acquired by learning]." Cf. supra, para. 3, n. 1, para. 6, n. 2, and infra, para. 21, n. 1.

Averroës defined the major premise as "the premise whose predicate is the major term," a definition which can be valid only for the major premise of syllogisms occurring in the first and third figures. When he presented the example of the syllogism occurring in the second figure, he identified its major premise as being universal and negative, i.e., "no eternal entity is composed." However, when he presented the example of the syllogism occurring in the third figure, he explained that its minor premise could be converted to a particular and thus placed into the third type (mode) of syllogisms occurring in the first figure; by process of elimination, that means that the major premise of this syllogism must be "every theoretical science is learned [i.e., acquired by learning]." Cf. *Short Commentary on Aristotle's Prior Analytics* M. 17b16–17, 21b22–23, and 23a22–23 with 20a3–7; P. 19a5–6, 23a16, and 25a9–10 with 21a16–19.

2. Part of the syllogism, namely the minor premise, is left unstated. The complete syllogism would be: "Every man is an animal; every animal is sense-perceiving; thus, every man is sense-perceiving." The minor premise is "every man is an animal," and the major premise is "every animal is sense-perceiving." When the syllogism is fully stated, it is the kind of syllogism that would belong to the first figure.

3. The word translated here as "speaking being" (*nāṭiq*) is equivocal. It could be translated "rational being" with equal accuracy, because the verb root (*nṭq*) is as rich in meaning as the Greek word *logos*; in fact, one form of the verb root is the Arabic word for logic (*manṭiq*).

Here "speaking being" appeared to be more analogous to the idea of "laughing being" than "rational being."

Here, too, the syllogism is incomplete. However, this syllogism is incomplete only because the major premise is not stated in the beginning. The complete syllogism would be: "Every man is a speaking being; speaking is the same thing as laughing; thus every man is a laughing being." Given the qualifications established by Averroës, this syllogism could also be classified as falling within the first figure.

4. For a different perspective, cf. "Al-Fārābī's Introductory *Risālah* on Logic," ed. by D.M. Dunlop in *The Islamic Quarterly* III (1957), p. 229, lines 2–9. Actually, a better syllogism can be constructed if "laughing" is taken as encompassed within "speaking": "All laughing is speaking; every man is a speaking being; thus every man is a laughing being." This syllogism would be classified as falling within the second figure.

Paragraph (8).

1. The argument of the rest of the paragraph, as well as that of the following paragraph, will be much more easily understood once it is noted that the word "problem" (*maṭlūb*) is used here in the sense of the proposition which is the conclusion of some kind of syllogistic reasoning and that as a proposition it has a subject and predicate.

Paragraph (9).

1. In effect, with some more elaboration, the example of induction discussed in paras. 6 and 8 could be used to verify the major premise of the syllogism presented as an example of syllogisms occurring in the first figure, namely, "every composed thing is created" (cf. para. 6, n. 2). By reflecting on the difficulty of verifying that premise by induction, the reader will readily grasp the argument developed here and in the next two paragraphs by Averroës.

2. That is, the doubt raised in the last sentence of the preceding paragraph.

Paragraph (11).

1. The word translated here as "matter" (*māddah*) is to be understood in both a material and a qualitative sense. It refers to the materials which constitute the syllogism—i.e., to the premises—and to their quality—i.e., whether they are "necessary," "possible for the most part," or "equally possible."

PARAGRAPH (13).

1. Cf. supra, para. 3: "... the dialectical argument is a syllogism composed from widespread, generally accepted premises."

2. In the *Aphorisms*, Hippocrates said: "spontaneous weariness indicates disease." Cf. Hippocrates *Aphorisms*, Section II, no. 5, in *Hippocrates*, trans. by W. H. S. Jones (London: William Heinemann Ltd., 1931), Vol. IV, p. 109. Hippocrates lived from 460–370 B. C. E.

PARAGRAPH (14).

1. Cf. supra, paras. 3–4 and infra, *Short Commentary on Aristotle's Rhetoric*, para. 21. Although dialectical syllogisms may be partially false, that is not because the premises used in them are based on particulars. Rather, it is because the premises used in them are based on what is generally accepted and thus might not correspond to what is really true.

PARAGRAPH (15).

1. The discussion of the universal predicates was part of Averroës's *Short Commentary on Porphyry's Isagoge*; cf. *ibid.*, M. 4a15–6b4; P. 4a10–6a17. As has already been explained, this commentary served as a general introduction to the rest of the Short Commentaries on the logical arts.

Actually, Porphyry only discussed five universal predicates in the *Isagoge*: genus, species, differentia, property, and accident. In the *Short Commentary on Porphyry's Isagoge*, Averroës introduced the other three universal predicates (definition, description, and the statement which is neither definition nor description) as representative of the two types of meanings composed from those five original universal predicates; cf. *ibid.*, M. 6a7–6b3; P. 6a5–17. His explanation of the three additional universal predicates illustrated how the meaning which each of these could provide was identical to the meaning that could be provided by different combinations of two of the original five universal predicates. Cf. also "Al-Fārābī's Introductory *Risālah* on Logic," *op. cit.*, pp. 228–229.

Incidentally, it ought to be noted that when the word "predicate" occurs in the text with reference to one of these five or eight universal predicates, the reader might understand it as "predicable." However, since Averroës did not consider the distinction sufficiently important to warrant a change in terminology, it did not seem appropriate to correct his style.

2. According to Averroës, species (*naw'*) and genus (*jins*) are conceived of by analogy to each other, genus applying to what is more general and species to what is more particular. "When there is more than one universal distinguishing what a certain individual is and some are more general than others, then the more general is genus and the more particular is species" (cf. *ibid.*, M. 4a16–19; P. 4a12–13). "For example, body, the self-nourishing, animal, and man are all universals distinguishing what an individual man, who is pointed out, is. Now some of these [universals] are more general than others. There is nothing more general than the universal, 'body,' and nothing more particular than the particular, 'man' " (*ibid.*, M. 4a22–4b3; P. 4a 15–17).

3. Description (*rasm*), according to Averroës, is "a conditionally composed composite argument which illustrates the meaning alluded to, [but] not according to everything that is analogous to its essence. For the most part it is put together: (a) from genus and property, like our saying that man is an animal who educates his children in thought and deliberation; or (b) from genus and accident, like our saying that man is a writing animal" (*ibid.*, M. 6a13–19; P. 6a10–12).

4. According to Averroës, "The statement which is neither definition nor description is put together: (a) from species and accident, like our saying about Zayd that he is a white man; or (b) from accidents, like our saying about him that he is an excellent scribe. Now this is peculiar to the concept (*taṣawwur*) as employed in rhetoric" (*ibid.*, M. 6a19–22; P. 6a12–14).

5. In the *Topics*, Aristotle only discussed four universal predicates: definition, property, genus, and accident; cf. *Topics* 101b13–25, 101b35–102b26, and 103b20–21.

Paragraph (16).

1. Cf. Aristotle *Topics* 101b21, 101b35–102a16.

2. Cf. Aristotle *Topics* 102a30–102b3.

3. Cf. Aristotle *Topics* 101b17–18: "Since the differentia is of the same nature as the genus, it ought to be classed under it."

4. Cf. Aristotle *Topics* 101b19–22, 102a17–30.

5. Cf. Aristotle *Topics* 102b3–25.

Paragraph (17)

1. In the *Posterior Analytics*, Aristotle discussed the definition at great length in order to distinguish it from the thesis (cf. 72a 20–25)

and from the hypothesis (cf. 76b35–77a4), as well as to explain its relation to demonstration (cf. 89b23–100b17). In the course of explaining the relation of the definition to demonstration, Aristotle implicitly touched on matters pertaining to the other universal predicates; cf. *ibid.*, 91b27–33, 96b15–97b8 with 73a35–74b12; 99b9–14 with 73a7–8; and 96b35–100b1; (cf. also *Topics* 102b26–103a5 for the explanation of why all of the universal predicates are implicit in any discussion of definition). Averroës also stressed the importance of the definition in his *Short Commentary on Aristotle's Posterior Analytics.* However, he was much more explicit about the relation of the other universal predicates to the definition and structured his discussion in terms of the different relation each had to the definition. Cf. *ibid.*, M. 42a14–42b15, P. 47a9–22; M. 42b22–52a14 (especially 46a16–23 and 46b6–20), P. 48a2–57a21 (especially 51a19–22 and 52a2–9); and M. 52a15–56a27, P. 57a22–62a5.

2. At the end of the *Posterior Analytics,* Aristotle spoke of the ultimate genus of the genera as though it were a category; he developed this statement more thoroughly in the *Metaphysics.* Cf. *Posterior Analytics* 100a14–100b4; *Metaphysics* 1014a26–1014b15; and Hugh Tredennick's translation of the *Posterior Analytics* (London: William Heinemann Ltd., 1960), note e, p. 259. Although Averroës extensively developed the implications of the end of the *Posterior Analytics* in his short commentary on that work, I can find no discussion of this particular point.

3. The reasoning here would seem to be that the differentia risks looking too much like the genus, if it does not apply specifically to that which it differentiates; cf. Aristotle *Posterior Analytics* 91b27–33 and 96b15–97b8 with 73a35–74a4 and 100a14–100b4; also *Metaphysics* 1014b5–15.

PARAGRAPH (18).

1. In the Arabic text, this is the beginning of a long conditional sentence. Literally, the sentence begins "that is because if..." and the apodosis is not reached until the words "then if these syllogisms were enumerated in this manner..."

2. When he commented on Aristotle's *Posterior Analytics,* al-Farābī explained that there were really only three classes of demonstrative syllogisms: the demonstration *that* a thing is, i.e., the demonstration of its existence; the demonstration of *why* a thing is, i.e., the demonstration of its cause; and the demonstration that encompasses both of these. Although each of these classes could be subdivided into various types of demonstrative syllogisms, depending on the way the universal

predicates or predicables were used with them, al-Fārābī explicitly declared that many of the syllogisms resulting from such uses of the universal predicates were not demonstrative. Cf. *Kitāb al-Burhān*, Hamidiye Manuscript, *op. cit.*, folios 62b23–63a9 and 63a10–68b17; cf. also Prantl, *op. cit.*, Vol. II, pp. 318–325.

Paragraph (19).

1. Themistius was born in Paphlagonia, a province of the eastern Roman Empire in Asia Minor near the Black Sea (roughly the area between Ankara and Sinop of modern Turkey), circa 317 C.E. and died in Constantinople circa 388 C.E. He first gained recognition for his numerous commentaries on Aristotle's logical, physical, and philosophical writings. Although his interests turned more to practical matters later in life and he was raised to the post of prefect of Constantinople in 384 C.E. by the Roman Emperor Theodosius I, he did not abandon his philosophic activity. Unfortunately, few of his writings have survived until this day, and thus far nothing is known of the Arabic translations of his works to which Averroës might have had access.

It is said that Gerard of Cremona translated Themistius's *Commentary on Aristotle's Posterior Analytics* from Arabic into Latin some time in the latter half of the twelfth century, but no copy of that translation remains. Cf. Pauly-Wissowa *Real-Encyclopaedie* (Stuttgart: J.B. Metzlersche Verlagsbuchhandlung, 1934), Vol. VA, cols. 1642–1680.

For an indication of the notion to which Averroës referred, cf. Themistius *Analyticorum Posteriorum Paraphrasis*, I. vi, xxiv, and xxvii. Prantl, *op. cit.*, Vol. I, pp. 639–640 and 720–724, also gives adequate citations for identifying the idea.

2. Although Themistius is never mentioned by name in al-Fārābī's *Commentary on Aristotle's Topics*, there are at least three passages in which an argument is made that could have prompted such a statement by Averroës; cf. Hamidiye Ms., *op. cit.*, folios 90a2–4, 10–17; 91a22–91b16; and 104a15–105a12.

Paragraph (21).

1. Literally, "according to the argument." However, according to para. 12, supra, the discussion in paras. 5–11 was about the form of dialectical arguments. The discussion in paras. 13–19 was limited to the matters of dialectical arguments.

2. Cf. supra, para. 3, n. 1, para. 6, n. 2, and para. 7, n. 1. Aristotle was as laconic about the minor premise as he was about the major

premise. However, if the syllogism cited as an example of those occurring in the first figure is considered ("every body is composed; every composed thing is created; thus, every body is created"), the minor premise would be the premise which has the minor term as its subject and the middle term as its predicate, i.e., "every body is composed." For the syllogism which was cited as an example of those occurring in the second figure ("every body is composed; no eternal entity is composed; thus, no body is eternal"), the minor premise would be the premise which has the minor term as its subject and the middle term as its predicate, i.e., "every body is composed." Finally, for the syllogism which was cited as an example of those occurring in the third figure ("every theoretical science is learned [i.e., acquired by learning]; every theoretical science is a virtue; thus, some virtues are learned [i.e., acquired by learning]"), the minor premise would be the premise having the middle term as its subject and the minor term as its predicate, i.e., "every theoretical science is a virtue."

Averroës defined the minor premise as "the one whose subject is the minor term," a definition which can be valid only for the minor premise of syllogisms occurring in the first and second figures. For example, when he presented the example of the syllogism occurring in the second figure, he identified its minor premise as being universal and affirmative, i.e., "every body is composed." However, when Averroës presented the example of the syllogism occurring in the third figure, he explained that its minor premise could be converted to a particular and thus placed into the third type (mode) of syllogisms occurring in the first figure. If the example that Averroës gave of such a syllogism is considered, it becomes apparent that the minor premise of the previously cited syllogism would be "every theoretical science is a virtue." That this is an accurate interpretation of Averroës's explanation can be shown by converting this premise into a particular so as to make a syllogism representative of those occurring in the third type (mode) of syllogisms of the first figure, according to the necessary component. The new syllogism would be: "Some virtues are theoretical sciences; every theoretical science is learned [i.e., acquired by learning]; thus, some virtues are learned [i.e., acquired by learning]." Cf. *Short Commentary on Aristotle's Prior Analytics* M. 17b15–16, 21b23, and 23a22–23 with 20a3–6; P. 19a5, 23a17, and 25a9–10 with 21a16–19.

3. Because the problem is composed of a subject and a predicate, to solve a problem requires identifying the correct predicate for a given subject. The other idea is that some problems are pursued for their own sake, while others are pursued because they are related to another, more interesting, problem. Cf. Aristotle *Topics* 104b1–12 and 101b11–103a5.

4. In the *Topics*, Aristotle explained that in addition to mental training, the art of dialectic was useful for engaging in conversations, pursuing the philosophic sciences, and discovering the ultimate bases of each science. His reasoning was that the art of dialectic "is useful for conversations, because, having enumerated the opinions of the majority, we shall be dealing with people on the basis of their own opinions, not of those of others, changing the course of any argument which they appear to us to be using wrongly." Similarly, Aristotle deemed it useful for the philosophic sciences "because if we are able to raise difficulties on both sides, we shall more easily discern both truth and falsehood on every point." The art of dialectic was considered to be useful for discovering the ultimate bases or grounds of each science because of the impossibility of discussing those bases or grounds from the perspective of "the principles peculiar to the science in question, since the principles are primary in relation to everything else." The art of dialectic would permit one "to deal with them through the generally accepted opinions on each point." Cf. *Topics* 101a25–101b2.

Because Averroës's *Middle Commentary on Aristotle's Topics* was not completed until 1168 C.E., whereas this *Short Commentary on Aristotle's Topics* is thought to have been completed prior to 1159 C.E. (cf. Alonso, *op. cit.*, pp. 55–61 and 77–78), Averroës was clearly not referring to anything he had said in another commentary. What is significant, however, is his silence about the possible use of dialectic for conversations, as well as for the philosophical sciences, and above all his explicit denial of what Aristotle considered to be the fourth use of the art of dialectic, namely, its use with the ultimate bases of each science. Given al-Fārābī's emphasis on the uses that the art of dialectic had for both philosophy and demonstration (cf. *Commentary on Aristotle's Topics*, Hamidiye Ms., *op. cit.*, folios 88b19–22, 89a26–100a18) and given the emphasis that Averroës placed on the close relationship between dialectic and philosophy earlier in this collection of commentaries and in other writings, such a posture is most striking.

NOTES TO THE TRANSLATION OF THE *SHORT COMMENTARY ON ARISTOTLE'S RHETORIC*

INVOCATION

1. The clause "[I beseech] your succor, our Lord" was omitted in the Paris manuscript. Instead, it reads: "And in Him I place my trust; there is no Lord other than He."

TITLE

1. Cf. supra, *Short Commentary on Aristotle's Topics*, para. 1, n. 3.

PARAGRAPH (1)

1. Cf. *ibid.*, para. 2, n. 1. Cf. also Aristotle *Posterior Analytics* 88b30–89b9.

2. Cf. supra, *Short Commentary on Aristotle's Topics*, para. 2: "In general, supposition is believing that something exists in a particular kind of way, while it is possible for it to be different than it is believed to be." Cf. also n. 1 of the same paragraph.

PARAGRAPH (2)

1. The word translated here as "inductive investigation" is the term normally translated as "induction" (*istiqrā'*).

2. Literally, "things from outside." These are the things Aristotle called "non-technical" or "inartificial" (*atechnoi*); cf. *Rhetoric* I. ii. 1355b36–38, and I. xv. 1375a22–1377b12.

3. In Arabic the two words translated here as "public speaking" (*al-mukhāṭabah al-jumhūrīyah*) carry the connotation of speaking to the multitude, because *jumhūr* means multitude or the many, i.e., the *demos*. As will be made clear in the sequel, speaking in public usually means speaking to the large body of citizens; therefore, arguments used in such speech must not be too complicated.

4. Aristotle divided rhetoric into three general classes: deliberative, forensic, and epideictic. The use of deliberative rhetoric entails advising others, especially the ruler. Cf. *Rhetoric* I. iii–iv. 1358a 35–1360b3. Cf. also infra, para. 45, n. 3. With regard to the second example, cf. Aristotle *Metaphysics* 981a6–13.

PARAGRAPH (4)

1. Cf. supra, *Short Commentary On Aristotle's Topics*, para. 11. n. 1 and cf. also infra, paras. 16–25.

PARAGRAPH (5)

1. Cf. supra, *Short Commentary on Aristotle's Topics*, para. 5 and notes 2–4.

PARAGRAPH (6)

1. According to Aristotle, at least one of the premises must be universal for a syllogism to be possible. In syllogisms of the first figure, the major premise must be universal—either affirmative or negative. He defined a universal premise as "a statment which applies to all, or to none, of the subject." Cf. *Prior Analytics* 24a17, 26a16–20, 41a6–41b35. In the *Short Commentary on Aristotle's Prior Analytics*, Averroës explained that to say that something is universal means that it "exists as a predicate, either possibly or necessarily, for everything characteristic of its subject." Cf. M. 18b6–19a6; P. 20a3–16.

2. Cf. supra, *Short Commentary on Aristotle's Topics*, para. 6, n. 1.

3. In order to relate the two extreme terms of a syllogism, it is necessary to have a middle term. This is what is meant here by the conjunction. According to Aristotle: "We must take some middle term relating to both, which will link the predications together, if there is to be a syllogism proving the relation of one term to the other." Cf. *Prior Analytics* 40b37–41a12. Averroës explained that "if there is no conjunction at all between the two premises, then these two do not bring about any conjunction between the predicate and the subject of the problem and thus there is no syllogism at all." Cf. *Short Commentary on Aristotle's Prior Analytics* M. 17b2–5; P. 18a19–23. A little later, i.e., in the same passage cited in note 1 of this paragraph, he explained the need to have a universal major premise and an affirmative minor premise in order to effect the conjunction in a syllogism of the first figure. Cf. also Aristotle *Prior Analytics* 26a16–19, 26a37–26b25.

4. Cf. supra, *Short Commentary on Aristotle's Topics*, para. 21, n. 1.

5. Cf. *ibid.*, para. 6, n. 4.

6. The statement would not be accurate if the minor premise were also particular. Cf. *Prior Analytics* 26a3–26b30.

PARAGRAPH (7)

1. Literally, "the controlling premise with regard to the conclusion" (*al-muqaddamah al-mālikah fī al-intāj*), but it is obvious that Averroës

meant the premise which brings about the conclusion. This is usually the major premise; cf. infra, para. 16 "*al-muqaddamah... al-mālikah li al-intāj.*"

2. For Aristotle, the second figure occurs "when the same term applies to all of one subject and to none of the other, or to all or none of both," cf. *Prior Analytics* 26b34–36. Aristotle also said that in this figure the middle term is the one that is predicated of both subjects; cf. *ibid.*, 26b37. Averroës made this latter statement the basis of his definition of the second figure, saying that it is the one in which the middle term is the predicate of the major and the minor extremes. Cf. *Short Commentary on Aristotle's Prior Analytics* M. 17b23–18a1; P. 19a9. Cf. also *ibid.*, M. 21b21–23a11; P. 23a15–25a3.

3. Aristotle explained that the third figure is the one in which "one of the terms applies to all and the other to none of the same subject, or both terms apply to all or none of it"; cf. *Prior Analytics* 28a10–12. In this figure the middle term is "that of which both the predications are made"; cf. *ibid.*, 28a13. Averroës expressed this last idea in a slightly different way by saying that the third figure is the one in which the middle term "is a subject for the two extremes." Cf. *Short Commentary on Aristotle's Prior Analytics* M. 18a1–2; P. 19a9–10. Cf. also *ibid.* M. 23a11–24a8; 25a4–26a6. The conclusion of the third figure is not usually stated as a universal.

4. Cf. Aristotle *Prior Analytics* 27b10–39, 29a15–17.

Paragraph (8)

1. Cf. supra, *Short Commentary on Aristotle's Topics*, para. 5, n. 3. The explanation alluded to here occurs within Averroës's exposition of all of the different kinds of conjunctive syllogisms. Cf. *Short Commentary on Aristotle's Prior Analytics* M. 24a21–26b11, especially 25a11–15; P. 26a15–29a8, especially 27a15–18.

2. Cf. supra, *Short Commentary on Aristotle's Topics*, para. 5, n. 3. The selected term is the one which is selected as affirmative or negative and from which the affirmation or the negation of the term conditioned by it follows. Cf. Goichon, *op. cit.*, paras. 73, 76, 574, 586, and 611.

3. Cf. supra, *Short Commentary on Aristotle's Topics*, para. 5, n. 2.

4. According to Averroës, "the first part of the conditional syllogism, which is the cause of something resulting, is called the conditional term (*al-muqaddim*); the second part, which brings about the result, is called the conditioned term (*al-tāliy*)." Cf. *Short Commentary on Aristotle's Prior Analytics* M. 24a17 and margin; P. 26a12–13. The first, or conditional, term of a conditional syllogism would be "if the sun has risen,

it is daylight." The second, or conditioned, term is what restricts the conditional term and affirms or denies one part of it, e.g., "but the sun has risen." The conclusion of the syllogism is: "therefore, it is daylight." Cf. also Goichon, *op. cit.*, para. 573. Averroës sometimes used *muqaddim* to speak of the first half of the condition ("if the sun has risen"), while using the *tālin* to speak of the second half ("it is daylight").

5. Averroës was apparently thinking of the following kind of inaccurate conclusion: "Man exists because animals exist." The first, or conditional, term of this syllogism is: "if man exists." If the second, or conditioned, term ("then animals exist") is selected and the conditional term brought forth as a conclusion, the syllogism is not accurate, e.g., "but animals exist, therefore, man exists." The reason the syllogism must be inaccurate is that the conditioned term has a wider scope than the conditional term. Similarly, if the opposite of the conditional term is selected and the opposite of the conditioned term brought forth as a conclusion, the resulting syllogism is not accurate, e.g., "but man does not exist; therefore, animals do not exist." The inaccuracy of this syllogism is due to the same reason as in the first example: the conditioned term has a wider scope than the conditional term. The same problem occurs in a slightly different manner in the next paragraph.

Paragraph (9)

1. Galen (129-199) was born in Pergamum (now Bergama in western Turkey) and died in Rome. He has long been considered one of the greatest medical writers of Greek antiquity and was reputed among the Arabs as an anatomist, physiologist, practicing physician, and philosopher.

2. Cf. *Oeuvres Anatomiques Physiologiques et Médicales de Galien*, trans. by Ch. Daremberg (Paris: J.-B. Baillière, 1854–1856), Vol. I, pp. 498–508; Vol. II, pp. 167–171. Although it is not possible to find the direct quotation, many of Galen's remarks and proofs are similar to the way in which Averroës characterized him here.

3. Averroës refuted this very example on logical grounds, without naming Galen, in his explanation of the conjunctive syllogism. Cf. *Short Commentary on Aristotle's Prior Analytics* M. 24b7–17; P. 26a22–27a4.

Paragraph (11)

1. According to Averroës: "The disjunctive syllogism is the one to which particles of disjunction, like 'or' and 'either,' are attached."

He also explained that it is composed of opposing considerations and stated: "It is peculiar to the disjunctive syllogism that the conditional term in it is not a conditional term by nature and that the conditioned term is not a conditioned term by nature; rather, it may be possible for the conditional term to convert to a conditioned term and for the conditioned term to convert to a conditional term." Cf. *ibid.*, M. 24a19–20, 26b11–27b6; P. 26a14–15, 29a9–30a8. Thus, the disjunctive syllogism has an either/or quality. "Either this number is even, or it is odd." If the selected term "but it is not even" were omitted, the statement of the conclusion "thus, it is odd" would only raise the problem of how that conclusion might be proven.

PARAGRAPH (12)

1. Abū al-Ma'ālī 'Abd al-Malik ibn 'Abd Allah ibn Yūsuf al-Juwaynī, known as Imām al-Ḥaramayn, was born in Bushtanikān, a village near Nishapur, Iran in 419/1028 and died in the same village in 478/1085. During his lifetime, he taught in Baghdad, Mecca, and Medina. He was especially noted for his work in dialectical theology and for having been the teacher of al-Ghazālī (cf. infra, para. 42, n. 1), but he spent much time as well in the study of Islamic jurisprudence.

2. This book, *Kitāb al-Irshād ilā Qawāṭi' al-Adillah fī Uṣūl al-I'tiqād*, has been edited and partially translated by J.-D. Luciani (Paris: Imprimerie Nationale, 1938).

3. Cf. *ibid.*, Chapter XIX, Section XVII, pp. 215–216 of the translation and pp. 133-135 of the Arabic text. Although Averroës did not quote Abū al-Ma'ālī literally, he expressed the core of this author's thought very accurately. The divergence from literal quotation permitted Averroës to summarize Abū al-Ma'ālī's argument.

4. Oxymel (Arabic: *sakanjabīn*) is a mixture of honey and vinegar. The Arabic word is derived from the two Persian words which describe the elements of the compound: *sukar* (honey, sugar) and *jabīn* (vinegar).

Averroës was apparently referring to the fact that if these two liquids are cooked long enough, they will form a hard, chewy substance; thus, a new kind of existence arises from the mixture of the two ingredients.

PARAGRAPH (13)

1. Literally, "affirmative statement" (*al-mūjab*).

PARAGRAPH (14)

1. Cf. supra, *Short Commentary on Aristotle's Topics*, para. 5, n. 4.

2. This syllogism could be reordered so that it would be suitable for classification with syllogisms of the first figure: "Every man is an animal; every animal is sentient; thus, every man is sentient." However, if it were presented in that manner, it would no longer be a contradictory syllogism.

PARAGRAPH (17)

1. Cf. supra, para. 4. Note, however, that the earlier definition was actually the definition of "unexamined previously existing opinion." Averroës apparently considered the terms "unexamined opinion" (*bādi' al-ra'y*), "unexamined common opinion" (*bādi' al-ra'y al-mushtarak*), and "unexamined previously existing opinion" (*bādi' al-ra'y al-sābiq*) to be equivalent in meaning. Cf. infra, para. 23.

2. Cf. supra *Short Commentary on Aristotle's Topics*, paras. 3–4, 13–17, and 21.

PARAGRAPH (18)

1. Literally, "absolutely" (*'alā al-iṭlāq*).

2. This will be discussed more fully in para. 20, infra. It should be noted, however, that what is identified here as "proof" is the middle term of a syllogism occurring in the first figure; cf. supra, *Short Commentary on Aristotle's Topics*, para. 6, and Aristotle *Prior Analytics* 70a11–23. The way in which Averroës has used the term "proof" both here and in para. 20, below, indicates that he was thinking of the term Aristotle called *tekmerion*, not *pistis*; cf. *Rhetoric* I. ii. 14–17, 1357a23–1357b10, II. xx. 1393a20–1394a14, II. xxii. 1395b 27–1397a6; *Prior Analytics* 70b1–6.

3. This will be discussed more fully in paras. 21–22, infra. It should be noted, however, that what is identified here as "sign" is the middle term of a syllogism occurring in the second or third figure; cf. supra, *Short Commentary on Aristotle's Topics*, para. 6, n. 3. Cf. also *Prior Analytics* 70a4–29. The way Averroës has used the term "sign" here corresponds to Aristotle's use of the term *semeion*; cf. *Rhetoric* I. ii. 18, 1357b12–28.

PARAGRAPH (20)

1. To the best of my knowledge Aristotle never used the terms "specious proof" or "doubtful proof" in a technical sense. Averroës

may have been alluding, however, to some of the examples of fallacious signs cited by Aristotle in the *Rhetoric*; cf. II. xxiv. 5–11, 1401b7–1402a30.

PARAGRAPH (22)

1. In order to remain consistent with his previous terminology, Averroës ought to have spoken here of "signs in the third figure." Cf. supra, para. 18 and note the order of paras. 20–21. Nonetheless, the different terminology used here does not appear to suggest any significant change in the argument.

PARAGRAPH (23)

1. Cf. supra, para. 17: "Thus we say that the premises used in this class of arguments, especially the major premise, are taken here insofar as they are generally accepted according to unexamined common opinion... What is generally accepted according to unexamined previously existing opinion is divided into (a) generally received propositions... and into (b) sense perceptible things..."

PARAGRAPH (24)

1. Averroës used this example in his *Short Commentary on Aristotle's Prior Analytics*, but he did not mention Protagoras by name. Cf. *ibid.*, M. 26a14–15; P. 28a22.

The confutation of Protagoras to which Averroës alluded is not as stark as the example suggests. There is an exchange in the *Protagoras* where Socrates said something similar to what is reported here (cf. 331c–e), but the reference is much more suggestive of the way in which the doctrine of Protagoras is refuted in the *Theaetetus*. In the course of a discussion with Theodorus (a friend of Protagoras) and Theaetetus (a student of Theodorus), Socrates set out to examine the doctrine of Protagoras that "man is the measure of all things." The relativism to which the doctrine leads was clearly identified and harshly denounced, as were the doctrines which may have given rise to it. Even though Protagoras was dead when the conversation took place, Socrates resurrected him, so to speak, by addressing questions to Theodorus as though he were Protagoras—questions to which Theodorus replied without insisting on his own identity. Some of these exchanges come very close to the example given here. Cf. *Theaetetus* 167c, 169d–172c, 182c–183b, as well as the exchanges between Socrates and Theaetetus at 151e–154b, 157d–158a, 159c–160e, 164b-d, 165e–168c, 186e–187a. Cf. also Aristotle *Metaphysics* 999b1–15, 1007b18–

1011b23, and 1062b13–1063b18; Averroës *Tafsīr mā ba'd al-Ṭabī'ah*, ed. M. Bouyges (Beirut: Imprimerie Catholique, 1967), 238:17–241:13 and 382:10–454:11 (esp. 383:4–14 and 423:1–427:15); and *Alfarabi's Philosophy of Plato and Aristotle*, trans. Muhsin Mahdi (New York: The Free Press of Glencoe, 1962), p. 54.

PARAGRAPH (29)

1. Cf. Aristotle *Prior Analytics* 25b31–26a2, 26b22–33, 29b29–30a14, 32a7–14. Cf. also, Averroës *Short Commentary on Aristotle's Prior Analytics*, M. 18b6–19a7, 20b13–21b20; P. 20a3–16, 22a11–23a15.

2. Cf. supra, *Short Commentary on Aristotle's Topics*, para. 8, n. 1 and para. 6, notes 2, 4.

PARAGRAPH (30)

1. The notion that supposition (*ẓann*) is a species of opinion (*ra'y*) is evident here. Cf. supra, para. 1, notes 1 and 3. The term "ranks of supposition" refers to the different degrees of conviction an individual might have about the correctness of his supposition. Concerning the limits of sense perception for certainty about universal matters, cf. Aristotle *Posterior Analytics* 87b28–88a18, 99b15–100b17; *Metaphysics* 1009b13–17; and Averroës *Tafsīr mā ba'd al-Ṭabī'āh, op. cit.*, 417:14–418:9.

PARAGRAPH (31)

1. Although the term "dialectical theologian" (*mutakallim*) originally referred to any Muslim theologian, it later came to have a more specific connotation. Both the term for theology (*'ilm al-kalām*) and that for theologian were used to refer to scholastic theology with an atomistic basis, taking its roots from Democritus and Epicurus. It is to this distinction that Averroës was obviously alluding when he said that those authors who wrote about physics in verse could more properly be called dialectical theologians than poets. Just prior to this observation, Averroës had mentioned the name of Empedocles. Cf. Averroës *Talkhīṣ Kitāb Arisṭūṭālīs fī al-Shi'r*, Badawī edition, *op. cit.*, 204:1–10 and Aristotle *Poetics* 1447b9–23.

2. Partially because of textual difficulties, it is not easy to seize the precise nature of Averroës's criticism. All texts but one read: "The example only provides certainty as a means of guidance and scrutiny." Unfortunately, it has not been possible to locate anything resembling this statement in the few works of Abū al-Ma'ālī that are now available.

Averroës's criticism of Abū al-Ma'ālī seems to be based on the argument of the preceding paragraph about the inadequacy of the example for acquiring certainty about a universal (cf. also supra, paras. 27 and 29). Because Abū al-Ma'ālī only partially understood the limits of the example, he failed to account for the role of the syllogism in instruction and in scientific investigation. Averroës had already demonstrated the inadequacy of the induction for scientific investigation (cf. supra, *Short Commentary on Aristotle's Topics*, paras. 6–11, esp. para. 10) and carefully prepared the way for the role of the syllogism in that task (cf. *Short Commentary on Aristotle's Posterior Analytics*, end). The larger problem here is how to get at the fundamental principles of each science: since it is not possible to do that by means of the principles peculiar to the science, one must have recourse to reasoning based on probable opinion—the dialectical syllogism; but Abū al-Ma'ālī's statement has the consequence of eliminating that tool, since neither induction nor example can provide the needed premises. As Averroës pointed out here, that consequence is disastrous for learning—unless it is presupposed that the sciences already exist and one has only to select premises as one wishes. Abū al-Ma'ālī's other major error was forgetting that examples are based on sense perceptions and could not therefore be used to reason about a science whose subject is free from matter, a science like geometry. Cf. also Aristotle *Prior Analytics* 68b30–37, 69a12–18; and *Topics* 101a33–101b3.

3. The reference is to the *Almagest* of Ptolemy. Ptolemy, or Claudius Ptolemaeus, was an astronomer, geographer, and mathematician who lived during the 2nd century C.E. He was born in Greece but passed most of his life in Alexandria, and it was there that he composed his encyclopedic work on astronomy called *The Mathematical Collection*. This work was translated into Arabic in the 9th century C.E. and came to be known as the *Almagest* or "the Great." It was widely read and commented on by Arab thinkers.

Paragraph (33)

1. Averroës apparently considered the enthymeme and the example to be the first and second kinds of persuasive things. Since these have already been discussed, the other eleven are presented here. Cf. al-Fārābī *Kitāb al-Khaṭābah, op. cit.*, 69:7–81:11 for a similar enumeration.

Paragraph (35)

1. If Abū al-Ma'ālī can be trusted in such matters, Averroës has faithfully presented the traditional view concerning the report. Cf. *Kitāb al-Irshād, op. cit.*, pp. 345–351 of the translation and pp. 231–236 of the Arabic text.

PARAGRAPH (36)

1. The term is usually used to designate the more literal traditionalists, i.e., those scholars who specialized in gathering, perfecting, passing on, and studying the deeds and sayings traditionally attributed to the prophet Muḥammad. They influenced Islamic jurisprudence as much as they did Islamic theology. Averroës singled them out for criticism in some of his other writings because of the confusion to which their literalness sometimes led the people in matters of faith; cf. *Faṣl al-Maqāl*, *op. cit.*, 7:17–8:5 and *Kashf*, *op. cit.*, 133:4–19 (pagination of Müller edition: 27–28), 134:4–135:8 (Müller pagination: 28–29).

PARAGRAPH (37)

1. Abū al-Ma'ālī explained the continuous tradition in much the same way, but he also indicated that the reason for considering the number of people an essential element in making this kind of report more believable is that if it can be believed that these people knew what they were talking about, their number makes it unlikely that they have contrived a false tale. Because those making the report are presumed to have had no previous contact and to be ignorant of what others have reported about the particular event, the agreement of many people about something makes the truth of what they say more likely. Cf. *Kitāb al-Irshād*, *op. cit.*, pp. 346–350 of the translation and pp. 232–235 of the Arabic text; cf. also Muḥammad A'lā ibn 'Alī al-Tahānawī, *Kitāb Kashshāf Iṣṭilāḥāt al-Funūn* (*A Dictionary of the Technical Terms Used in the Sciences of the Musalmans*), ed. M. Wajīh, 'Abd al-Ḥaqq, and Gh. Qādir (2 vols.; Calcutta: W.N. Lees Press, 1862), Vol. II, pp. 1471–1473.

Throughout this section Averroës has used the term "report" as a general instance of the more specific term "tradition" (*ḥadīth*). The tradition was generally considered to be second in authority to the Qur'ān and was divided into two basic classes: the *ḥadīth nabawī* and the *ḥadīth qudsī*. The former is either an account of something the prophet Muḥammad said or did, or it affirms his tacit approval of something said or done in his presence. The latter is an account that expresses God's words, that is, not God's exact words, but words expressive of the meaning of His exact words. The continuous tradition would be one kind of *ḥadīth nabawī*. Neither of these classes of traditions is considered to fulfill the conditions permitting it to be accepted as revelation. Nonetheless, well-attested traditions should be accepted as explanations of ambiguous matters.

PARAGRAPH (38)

1. Literally, "as they are" (*'alā mā hiy 'alaih*).

PARAGRAPH (39)

1. Cf. supra, para. 38, n. 1.

2. Exhaustive reports are considered to be a little less compelling than the continuous tradition and a little more compelling than generally accepted reports (*mashhūrāt*). Cf. al-Tahānawī, *Kitāb Kashshāf Iṣṭilāḥāt al-Funūn, op. cit.*, Vol. I, pp. 748–749.

3. Literally, "supposed" from "*ẓann*," "supposition." Cf. supra, *Short Commentary on Aristotle's Topics*, para. 2, n. 1.

4. Literally, "caused things" (*al-musabbabāt*).

5. Cf. Aristotle *Metaphysics* 1025a14–34, 1026a33–1027b16, 1064b 15–1065b4; Averroës *Tafsīr mā ba'd al-Ṭabī'ah, op. cit.*, 693:7–696:10 and 716:10–736:8, esp. 719:15–18, 720:17–721:13, 725:14–17, 726:10–728:16, 734:1–4, and 736:5–8.

Cf. also Maimonides *Maqālah fī Ṣinā'at al-Manṭiq*, ed. by Mubahat Türker, "Mūsā ibn-i Meymūn'un al-Makala fī Sinā'at al-Manṭiḳ," in *Ankara Üniversitesi Dil ve Tarih-Coğrafya Fakültesi Dergisi*, XVIII (1960). p. 55, lines 14–16: "In general, all of the natural things that usually exist are essential; whenever they rarely exist, they are said to be accidental—like someone who digs a foundation and finds money. In general, all chance matters, whether they are things not intended by man or not intended by nonman, are said to be accidental whenever they occur."

PARAGRAPH (40)

1. According to the strictest teaching of the *Metaphysics*, there can be no accidental certainty (cf. supra, para. 39, n. 5). Nor did Aristotle ever speak of accidental certainty in *Sense and Sensible Objects*. To the contrary, he attacked his predecessors and contemporaries in that work for having confused accidental and essential causes; certainty could be attained only about essential causes (cf. *Sense and Sensible Objects* 437a18–438b16, 441a4–442b27, and 445a16–445b3).

The real issue, then, must be belief which is so strong as to be like certainty and which is due to accidental causes: how does it come about? There is a discussion of accidental causes in *On Prophecy in Sleep* (462b27–464b19), and it results in casting extensive doubt on the phenomenon of prophecy. Aristotle thought dreams were more often to be explained as coincidences than as signs or as causes of something. Since Averroës considered the treatise *On Prophecy in Sleep* to be part of the book *Kitāb al-Ḥiss wa al-Maḥsūs* (*Sense and Sensible Objects*), he may have been referring to that argument. When he later commented on that collection, he paid careful attention to the question of prophecy in dreams, denying that there was any basic mystery about it. He attributed the phenomenon to the kind of knowledge of causes that arises from a highly developed imaginative faculty. Cf. Averroës *Talkhīṣ Kitāb al-Ḥiss wa al-Maḥsūs li Arisṭū* in *Arisṭūṭālīs fī al-Nafs*, ed. by ʿAbd al-Raḥmān Badawī (Cairo: Maktabat al-Nahḍah al-Miṣrīyah, 1954), pp. 224–226.

If Alonso and Gätje are correct in their dating, the commentary on *Sense and Sensible Objects* was written eleven years after these commentaries (554/1159 versus 565/1170). Consequently, Averroës's reference here would be to Aristotle's work, not his own. Alonso, Gätje, and Wolfson also argue that despite the title of *Talkhīṣ* (Middle Commentary), Averroës's book on *Sense and Sensible Objects* is a Short Commentary (*Jawāmiʿ*). Cf. Alonso, *op. cit.*, pp. 55–82 and the corroborations from the secondary literature cited by him; Gätje, *Die Epitome der Parva Naturalia des Averroes*, *op. cit.*, p. v, n. 2 and pp. x–xi, and Wolfson, "Revised Plan for the Publication of a *Corpus Commentariorum Averrois in Aristotelem*," *op. cit.*, pp. 90–94.

Paragraph (42)

1. According to different traditions, the Prophet claimed that God would never let the nation of Islam agree about something that could lead them astray. It is in this sense that the Muslims are infallible. However, there is a problem about how to treat a member of the community who disagrees with the consensus which the others have supposedly reached. The problem arises from the difficulties of exactly identifying the consensus of the community on any given issue, particularly on theoretical issues. Averroës discussed this problem more fully in the *Decisive Treatise*; cf *op. cit.*, 8:15–10:18.

One tradition quotes the Prophet as saying: "Verily, God would not let my nation agree about an error." Another tradition reports a variant of that statement: "Verily, my nation would not agree about an error." In a different tradition, he is reported to have commanded Muslims: "Do not come to agreement about an error." Yet another version quotes the Prophet as praying: "Do not let them agree about an error." Cf. A.J. Wensinck et al., *Concordance et Indices de la Tradition Musulmane* (7 Vols.; Leiden: E.J. Brill, 1936–1969), Vol. I, pp. 97, 364, and 366; Vol. III, p. 517.

2. Abū Ḥāmid Muḥammad ibn Muḥammad al-Ṭūsī al-Ghazālī (450/1058–505/1111) was born at Ṭus, a small town in Khurāsān near the modern city of Meshed, Iran, and, after living in many other parts of the Middle East, returned there at the end of his life. He was a student of Abū al-Ma'ālī for many years and taught theology in Baghdad and later in Nishapur. The best source for a biographical and intellectual account of al-Ghazālī is his own *al-Munqidh Min al-Ḍalāl*, a book which is translated into English as *The Deliverance from Error*. Of al-Ghazālī's intellectual activities, the most important are his attacks on philosophy and his attempt to reform or renew religious belief and pratice. The attack on philosophy was brilliantly answered by Averroës: to al-Ghazālī's *Tahāfut al-Falāsifah* (*The Incoherence of the Philosophers*), Averroës replied with the *Tahāfut al-Tahāfut* (*Incoherence of the Incoherence*).

3. This work was written between 493/1099 and 499/1106 and provided a defense of al-Ghazālī's views. He examined the question of interpretation and the extent to which tradition and consensus could be used as a basis for knowledge about religious matters. The central theme in the book is indicated in the title: he wished to determine how atheism could be clearly defined.

The difficulties of identifying the precise date when the book was finished are presented by Father Bouyges. He did think, however, that the book was written after *The Balance* (cf. infra, para. 43, n. 2) and before the *Deliverance from Error*; cf. Maurice Bouyges, *Essai de Chronologie des Oeuvres de al-Ghazali*, edited by Michel Allard (Beirut: Imprimerie Catholique, 1959), pp. 50–51, 57–58, 70–71 and 4–6.

4. The quote is not exact, but Averroës caught the spirit of al-Ghazālī's thought. According to al-Ghazālī, one is not called a heretic for holding different opinions about the "branches" or side issues of Islam, except under special circumstances. The only clear case for deciding that someone is a heretic is his denial of the three roots of Islam, i.e., belief in Allah, his Messenger, and the Last Day—beliefs that Averroës accepted as crucial in the *Decisive Treatise*, cf. *op. cit.*, 14:13–15:8.

All other questions lead to the charge of heresy only under certain conditions, such as denying the religion passed on by Muḥammad or harming the belief of the common people. Consensus is a very obscure matter that al-Ghazālī preferred to leave for skilled jurists to settle; he even argued that the palpable error of Abū Bakr al-Fārisī about consensus did not warrant the charge of heresy. Cf. *Fayṣal al-Tafriqah* in *al-Quṣūr al-'Awālī Min Rasā'il al-Imām al-Ghazālī* (Cairo: Maktabat al-Jundī, no date), pp. 165:14–17; 166:5, 14–17; 166:18–167:6; 169:16–170:11.

The Munich manuscript has a sentence explaining this citation, but it has been bracketed as though if were not part of the text: "That is because the dialectical theologians disagree about the conditions to be set down about consensus." (Reading "*ijmā*'" [consensus] for "*iqnā*'" [persuasion]).

Paragraph (43)

1. The text reads *ḥusn al-ẓann*, i.e., literally, "good supposition."

2. This book was written between 493/1099 and 499/1106 but, at any rate, prior to *The Distinction between Islam and Atheism*; cf. supra, para. 42, note 2 and cf. also M. Bouyges, *op. cit.*, pp. 50–58, 70–71, and 4–6. *The Balance* is the last of five treatises written by al-Ghazālī against esoteric doctrines.

3. There is no remark in the book which corresponds to this quotation. Moreover, in this treatise, al-Ghazālī never used the term *al-jumhūr* to refer to the common people; instead he used the term *al-'awām*.

Averroës nevertheless summarized the main idea of the latter part of the book, for al-Ghazālī did make a distinction between the way the learned grasped religious notions and the way the common people did. The only mention of "miracle" occurred in a context which would make Averroës's statement appear to be a fair abridgement—but an abridgement, nevertheless. Cf. *al-Qisṭās al-Mustaqīm* in *al-Quṣūr al-'Awālī*, *op. cit.*, pp. 70:9–71:2. Cf. also pp. 59:1–60:9, 68:6–7, 69:11–15. Note the long digression on pp. 68:7–69:11 in which al-Ghazālī examined the question of the extent to which dialectic was of any scientific value.

Paragraph (45)

1. Epideictic rhetoric is concerned with praise or blame, is usually addressed to mere spectators, and has honor or disgrace as its end. Cf. Aristotle *Rhetoric* I. iii. 3–5. 1358b4–20 and I. ix. 1366a22–1368b1; cf. also Averroës *Talkhīṣ al-Khaṭābah*, Badawī edition, *op. cit.*, pp. 28–31, 71–82.

2. Forensic rhetoric is concerned with accusation or defense, is usually addressed to those who judge things that have taken place, and has justice or injustice as its end. Cf. Aristotle *Rhetoric* I. iii. 3–5. 1358b4–20 and I. x–xv. 1368b2–1377b10; cf. also Averroës *Talkhīṣ al-Khaṭābah*, Badawī edition, *op. cit.*, pp. 28–31, 83–130.

3. Deliberative rhetoric is concerned with exhorting or dissuading, is usually addressed to judges of things to come (like rulers), and has expediency or harm as its end. Cf. Aristotle *Rhetoric* I. iii. 3–5. 1358b4–20 and I. iv–viii. 1359a25–1366a21; cf. also Averroës, *Talkhīṣ al-Khaṭābah*, Badawī edition, *op. cit.*, pp. 28–31, 32–71.

4. In the Arabic text, this is the apodosis of the sentence beginning with the words: "When Aristotle became aware..."

NOTES TO THE TRANSLATION OF THE *SHORT COMMENTARY ON ARISTOTLE'S POETICS*

Invocation

1. In addition to this phrase, the Munich manuscript has the following phrase: "Praise be to God, Lord of both worlds." However, the Paris manuscript has the phrase, "I have recourse to Him and place my trust in Him," in addition to the phrase translated in the text.

Title

1. Although the word *aqāwīl* has often been translated as "arguments" (cf. supra, *Short Commentary on Aristotle's Topics*, para. 1, n. 3), it seemed more appropriate to translate it as "speeches" in this context.

Paragraph (2)

1. In the *Middle Commentary on Aristotle's Poetics*, Averroës gave examples of the particles of simile; cf. *Talkhīṣ Kitāb Arisṭūṭālīs fī al-Shi'r*, Badawī edition, *op. cit.*, pp. 201–202.

2. Substitution (*tabdīl*) is an Arabic grammatical and poetical term. When an author places a word or letter in place of another he is said to employ "substitution." Examples of substitution are: "the habits of the gentlemen and the gentlemen of habits"; "... the first house set down for mankind was at Bekkah," *Qur'ān* III. 97, where Bekkah is used in place of Mekkah; "... Oh, God, make me wealthy through need of You, but do not improverish me through belief in sufficient wealth to do without You." Cf. al-Tahānawī, *Kitāb Kashshāf Iṣṭilāḥāt al-Funūn*, *op. cit.*, Vol. I, pp. 145–146; Vol. II, pp. 978–989, 1171–1172. Note also the discussion of substitution in Averroës's *Middle Commentary on Aristotle's Rhetoric*, Badawi edition, *op. cit.*, pp. 204–209. Cf. also Abū 'Abd Allah Muḥammad al-Khuwārizmī, *Kitāb Mafatiḥ al-'Ulūm*, ed. G. Van Vloten (Leiden: E. J. Brill, 1895), p. 73.

In the *Middle Commentary on Aristotle's Poetics* (*op. cit.*, p. 202), Averroës gave two examples of substitution, one a clause from a Qur'ānic verse and the other the verse of poetry quoted in the next sentence of this text (cf. note 3, infra). The citation from the *Qur'ān*, occurring in surah XXXIII, verse 6 ("... his wives are their mothers..."), is part of a proof of how close the Prophet is to the believers—so close that his wives could be their mothers.

It is of some interest that Averroës considered the substitution used in the art of poetics to be more noble than the simile, just as he considered the syllogism used in dialectic to be more noble than the induction and the enthymeme used in rhetoric to be more noble than the example. Cf. *Middle Commentary on Aristotle's Topics*, Bibliotèca Laurenziana, Florence, *Codice Orientale Laurenziano*, Ms. CLXXX, 54, fol. 91a14–18.

3. This verse was cited by Averroës in the *Middle Commentary on Aristotle's Poetics* in exactly the same manner, and the editor of that work presented the complete verse in its correct version: "He is the sea from whichever direction you approach him / for his depth is the good deed, while generosity is his coastline" (*huw al-baḥr min 'ayy al-nawāḥī ataytah / falujjatuh al-ma'rūf wa al-jūd sāḥiluh*). According to the editor, the verse is from a poem by Abū Tammām, cf. *Middle Commentary on Aristotle's Poetics*, Badawī edition, *op. cit.*, p. 202 and note 2.

4. In the *Middle Commentary on Aristotle's Poetics*, Averroës also referred to Empedocles, identified him as a natural scientist, and explained that he was a poet only insofar as his arguments were set forth in meters. Averroës then suggested that those who made metered arguments about physical questions deserved to be called dialectical theologians more than they deserved to be called poets. Cf. supra, *Short Commentary on Aristotle's Rhetoric*, para. 31, note 1 and *Middle Commentary on Aristotle's Poetics*, Badawī edition, *op. cit.*, p. 204; cf. also *Poetics* 1447b18, 1457b24, 1461a24 for Aristotle's references to Empedocles. Empedocles (490–430 B.C.E.) thought that all the structures in the world arose from combinations of four primary substances—fire, air, water, and earth—by means of two forces: love and strife. Because he held that these primary substances are never destroyed, but only undergo alterations in their mixture, he denied generation and destruction.

Paragraph (5)

1. The word translated here as "treatises" is the same word which has been translated as "speeches" and as "arguments" (*aqāwil*). Because each of the commentaries in this collection has been spoken of in a speech or an argument about a certain subject, Averroës could conclude by speaking of all which preceded as so many speeches or arguments, i.e., *aqāwil.*

EPILOGUE

1. The scribe of the Hebrew translation added a colophon in which he stated: "It is finished and completed, praise be to the Lord of the world. The summary of the Art of Logic was completed, praise be to Him who dwells in a hidden, lofty place, on the third day of the month of Tishri in the year five thousand one hundred and seventeen since the period of creation. It was written for myself, as well as for anyone else who wishes [to read it]—Ezra bar Shlomo (may his memory live in the world to come), ben Gratnia of Saragossa (may the name protect them)." The Latin edition adds the following: "Verily, God is on high; it is God who aids and sustains; there is none other than God; praise be to God forever. Amen."

INDEX

The purpose of this index is two-fold. In the first place, it is designed to identify the proper names, titles, and technical terms which occur in these texts and the passages where they occur. Secondly, it is designed to serve as a glossary; for that reason, the Arabic equivalents of the technical terms are given. References are to the paragraphs of the texts presented here.

A. NAMES AND TITLES CITED BY AVERROËS

B. TECHNICAL TERMS USED BY AVERROËS

ARABIC TEXTS

جوامع لكتب أرسطوطاليس
في الجدل والخطابة والشعر

لأبي الوليد محمد بن احمد بن رشد

حقّقه وقدّم له وعلّق عليه

تشارلس بتروورث

الرموز

م — مخطوطة المكتبة الملكيّة بميونيخ ، رقم ٣٠٩ من المجموعة العبريّة .

ب — مخطوطة المكتبة القوميّة بباريس ، رقم ١٠٠٨ من المجموعة العبريّة .

ع — الترجمة العبريّة للمخطوطة « ب » .

ل — الترجمة اللاتينيّة « مجموعة كتب ارسطوطاليس مع شرح ابن رشد » (فينيسيا ١٥٦٠) .

[ ] — في المخطوطة أو المخطوطين ونقترح حذفه .

⟨ ⟩ — ليس في المخطوطة أو المخطوطين ونقترح إضافته .

جوامع كتاب الجدل

لأبي الوليد محمد بن احمد بن رشد

[1] بسم الله الرحمن الرحيم [1] [2] عونك يا ربّ [2]

كتاب الجدل

〈 التمهيد 〉

١. وإذ قلنا في الأشياء التي [1] بها يتميّز [1] التصديق اليقينيّ والتصوّر التامّ [2] وقلنا بعد ذلك في الأشياء التي [3] يغلط فيها [4] فلنقل [5] في التصديقات الجدليّة والبلاغيّة ومقدار ما يفيده [6] [م ٧٢ظ] واحد واحد منها . فأمّا القول فيما [ب ٨٠ و] تمّ به هذه الصنائع فغير ضروريّ في غرضنا . ولنبدأ [7] من ذلك بالأقاويل الجدليّة .

〈 مقدار التصديق الذي تفيده الأقاويل الجدلية 〉

٢. فنقول : « أمّا مقدار [1] ما تفيده ، فهو الظنّ المقارب لليقين » . فالظنّ [2] بالجملة هو أن يعتقد في الشيء أنّه بحال ما ويمكن ان يكون بخلاف ما اعتقد فيه . ولذلك خاصّته أنّه يمكن أن يزول بعناد [3] بخلاف ما

العنوان :

١) — ل .
٢) وبه استعيز وعليه أتوكل ب ؛ ובו לבדו אשען ועליו אבטח ع ؛ — ل .
٣) — ب .
٤) فيهما ب .
٥) فلنقول م .
٦) تفيده م .
٧) ولنبدئ م ، ب .

(١)

١) يتميّز بها ب .
٢) التمّ م .

(٢)

١) — ب .
٢) والظنّ م .

عليه البرهان فإنّ خاصّته أن لا يزول بعناد[٣]. وهذا[٤] قسمان، أحدهما ما لا يشعر بعناده[٥] وإن شُعر فيعسر وجوده وهذا هو الظنّ الجدليّ، والثاني وهو الذي يشعر بعناده[٥] وهو الخط‹١›بيّ.

٣. فأمّا أنّ[١] هذا المقدار من التصديق هو الذي تفيده هذه الصناعة فذلك[٢] ظاهر من حدّ الأقاويل المفيدة[٣] له، إذ كان القول[٤] الجدليّ إنّما هو قياس يؤلَّف عن مقدّمات مشهورة ذائعة[٥]. والمقدّمات[٦] المشهورة الذائعة[٧] إنّما يحصل التصديق بها من جهة شهادة الجميع أو الأكثر[٨] لا من جهة أنّ[٩] الأمر كذلك في[١٠] نفسه، بخلاف ما عليه الأمر في البرهان. فإنّ التصديق اليقيني إنّما يقع لنا فيه[١١] عن مقدّمات وقع لنا التصديق بها من[١٢] جهة ما هي في انفسنا[١٣] على ما هي عليه خارج النفس، لا من جهة أنّ ذلك رأى لغيرنا.

٤. وإذا كان ذلك كذلك، فكثيرًا ما تكون[١] هذه المقدّمات الجدليّة كاذبة[٢] بالجزء. وإن وُجدت صادقة بالكلّ فإنّما يوجد ذلك فيها بالعرض، أي من جهة ما عرض للمشهور أن كان في وجوده خارج النفس على ما هو عليه في النفس. إلّا[٣] أنّا لسنا[٤] نأخذه كما قلنا في هذه الأقيسة[٥] من هذه

---

٣) (غامضة، في الهامش) م.

٤) هذان م.

٥) — ب، ع؛ et haec est topica, altera autem est, quod non conjectetur eius contradictorium ل.

(٣)

١) (فوق السطر) م.

٢) فلذلك ب.

٣) المقيدة م؛ המחוברים ع؛ facientium... acquirere ل.

٤) — ب.

٥) — ب.

٦) — ع.

٧) — ب، ع، ل.

٨) الكثر م.

٩) — ب.

١٠) (فوق السطر) م.

١١) — ع.

١٢) ما م.

١٣) انفسها ب؛ in rebus ل.

(٤)

١) يكون ب.

٢) كاذبات ب.

٣) (فوق السطر) م.

٤) ليسنا م.

٥) الايقسة م.

الجهة ، بل من جهة الشهرة فقط . ولذلك يلزم ضرورة في [م ٧٣و] القياس الصحيح الشكل المؤلَّف من مثل هذه المقدّمات أن يفيد[٦] ظنّاً غالباً .

〈صور الأقاويل الفاعلة للتصديق〉

٥. وإذ قد تبيّن مقدار ما تفيده[١] هذه الصناعة من التصديق ، فنقول[٢] في أصناف الأقاويل الفاعلة له . فنقول: «أمّا الأقيسة التي يلزم عنها مثل هذا الظنّ المقارب لليقين فيلزم ضرورة أن تكون[٣] صحيحة الأشكال وإلاّ كانت أقاويل سوفسطائية[٤] مرائية[٥] ». ولذلك تكون أنواع الأقيسة المستعملة ههنا[٦] الثلاثة الأنواع المذكورة في كتاب القياس ، أعني الحمليّ والشرطيّ وقياس الخلف — البسيط منها والمركّب . فإنّه قد يمكن إثبات المطالب المركّبة[٧] وإبطالها بمثل هذه القياسات[٨] الجدليّة المركّبة إذ[٩] كان بأيدينا[١٠] في ذلك مقدّمات مشهورة تُفضي إلى المطلوب .

〈الاستقراء〉

٦. وقد تستعمل هذه الصناعة نوعاً آخر من التصديق خاصّاً بها وهـو الاستقراء . وهذا النوع من الأشياء الفاعلة للتصديق هو أن يقضى على أمر كلّيّ بحكم كلّيّ[١] موجب أو سالب لوجود ذلك الحكم في أكثر الجزئيّات[٢] التي تحت[٣] ذلك الأمر الكلّيّ . مثال ذلك أن نقضي أن كلّ جسم محدَث بأن نجد أكثر الأجسام على هذه الصفة . وهو قول قوّته قوّة قياس في الشكل

---

٦) نفيد م .

(٥)

١) (في الهامش) م .

٢) فلنقل ب .

٣) يكون ب .

٤) سوفسطانية م ، ب .

٥) مرابية ب .

٦) ها هنا (هنا وفيما بعد) ب .

٧) — ب ، ع ، ل .

٨) القياسة م .

٩) واذا ب .

١٠) بايدنا م .

(٦)

١) — ب .

٢) الجزيات م .

٣) — ب .

الأوّل ، إذ الطرف الأصغر [٤]هو ذلك الأمر[٤] الكلّيّ والأوسط هو الجزئيّات[٥] والأعظم هو الحكم ، إلاّ أنّ الأمر فيه بخلاف ما عليه الأمر في القياس[٦].

٧. وذلك أنّ القياس إنّما [١]نسير فيه[١] أبدّاً لتصحيح الأمر الجزئيّ[٢] المجهول من [ب ٨١ و] الكلّيّ[٣] الذي كان عندنا [م ٧٣ ظ] معلوماً أو[٤] من المساوي المعلوم الى المساوي المجهول ، على أنّ الكلّيّ المساوي المعلوم لسنا نأخذه ههنا مقدّمة كبرى[٥] من جهة ما هو[٦] مساوٍ[٧] بل من جهة[٨] ما هو[٨] كلّيّ سواء كان ذلك بالطبع أو بالوضع . أمّا ما نسير[٩] فيه لتصحيح الأمر الجزئيّ[١٠] من الكلّيّ الذي عندنا ، فمثل أن نبيّن أنّ كلّ إنسان حسّاس بأنّ كلّ حيوان حسّاس . فإنّ الإنسان الذي هو الطرف الأصغر ههنا داخل تحت المقدّمة الكبرى ومنطوٍ[١١] فيها . ومثال ما نسير فيه[١٢] من المساوي الى المساوي أن نبيّن أنّ كلّ إنسان ضاحك[١٣] بأنّ كلّ إنسان ناطق . فإنّ الناطق مساوٍ[١٤] للضاحك[١٥] ولكن الضاحك[١٥] أُخذ بالجملة منطوياً في الناطق وداخلاً تحته ، وإن كان مساوياً له ، إذ كان ذلك غير ضارّ . ولذلك قلنا في مثل هذا إنّه كلّيّ بالوضع .

٨. وأمّا الاستقراء ، فإنّما نسير فيه أبدّا من الجزئيّ[١] إلى الكلّيّ . ولذلك[٢] انّا[٣] إذا بيّنّا مثلاً بالاستقراء[٤] أنّ كلّ جسم محدَث بأن ألفينا بعض الأجسام

---

٤) — ب .
٥) الجزايات م .
٦) البرهان القيــاس ب ؛ בהקש המופת ع .

(٧)

١) نضربه ب .
٢) الجزاى م .
٣) الجزء كلّي ب .
٤) و ب ؛ ٦ ع ؛ et ل .
٥) نبدأ ب .
٦) (فوق السطر) م .
٧) مساوى م .
٨) (في الهامش) م .
٩) نشير ب .
١٠) الجزاى م ؛ الجزى ب .
١١) منطو ب .
١٢) — ب .
١٣) ضحاك ب .
١٤) مساوى م .
١٥) للضحاك ب .

(٨)

١) الاجزاء م ؛ الجزى ب .
٢) وذلك ب ؛ והנה ع .
٣) انه م .
٤) — ل .

محدَثاً ، فبيّن[5] انّا إنّما نسير إلى هذه[6] القضيّة[7] الكلّيّة وهي أنّ كلّ جسم محدَث بأن الفينا بعض الأجسام محدثة مثل الأرض[8] والماء[9] والهواء والنار وغير ذلك . فيأتي تأليف القول[10] الذي قوّته قوّة قياس في الشكل الأوّل هكذا : « الجسم منه[11] نار وهواء[12] وماء[13] وأرض ، وهذه محدَثة ، فالجسم محدَث » . إلاّ أنّه متى استعمل[14] الاستقراء مفردًا بذاته في بيان مطلوب مجهول لم يكن[15] قويّ الإقناع ، وذلك أنّه إذا ظهر بالاستقراء أن المحمول[16] في[17] الموضوع ، كان ذلك المطلوب مقدّمة بيّنة بنفسها ظهرت بالاستقراء ولم يكن[18] مجهولا .

٩. وهذه الصناعة[1] من جهة ما تستعمل القياس الصحيح[2] على[3] [م ٧٤و] مطلوب مجهول ليس[4] تأخذ المعلوم بنفسه على أنّه مطلوب بل مثل هذا أحرى بالطرق الخط ⟨ا⟩ بيّنة . ومن أجـل هذا صارت هذه[5] الصناعة إنّما تستعمل الاستقراء في الأكثر في تصحيح المقدّمة[6] الكبرى . لكن الاستقراء في مثل هذا أيضاً غير نافع . وذلك أنّا إن كنّا قد استقرينا أكثر الجزئيّات[7] الداخلة تحت المقدّمة الكبرى و[8] لم يكن[9] أحد ما[10] استقرينا في ذلك

---

٥) (كل ما يلي من «فبين» الى «محدثة») — ب ، ل .
٦) (كل ما يلي من «هذه» الى «مثل» غامض ، في الهامش) م .
٧) القضاية م .
٨) aqua ل .
٩) terra ل .
١٠) — م .
١١) منـا م .
١٢) ومـاء ب .
١٣) وهواء ب .
١٤) נעשה זה ع ؛ fecerimus per ل.
١٥) يكون م .
١٦) (في الهامش) م .
١٧) ذلك (فوق السطر) م .
١٨) يكون م .

(٩)

١) המלאכה מוסכלת ع .
٢) — ب ، ع ، ل .
٣) (مكررة) م .
٤) (فوق السطر) م ؛ لم ب .
٥) — ب ، ع .
٦) — ب .
٧) الحزايات م.
٨) او ب .
٩) يكون م .
١٠) أحدهما ب .

موضوع المطلوب[١١] ، فمن[١٢] أين حصل عندنا أنّ ذلك منطوٍ [ي] تحت المقدّمة الكبرى ؟ وبالجملة من أين حصل عندنا[١٣] اليقين بكلّيّة تلك المقدّمة ؟ وإن كنّا[١٤] قد استقرينا[١٥] موضوع المطلوب [١٦]في جملة ما استقرينا[١٦] ، عاد المطلوب بعينه مقدّمة بيّنة بالاستقراء وعاد الشكّ الأوّل . لكن صناعة الجدل ليس تتقصّى[١٧] الأمر[١٨] مثل[١٩] هذا التقصّي[٢٠] ، بل تقضي[٢١] بوجود الحكم للجميع من أجل وجوده[٢٢] للأكثر[٢٣] لأنّه من المشهور أنّ الأقلّ تابع للأكثر.

١٠. وأمّا الاستقراء [١]بما هو[١] استقراء فإنّه وإن استوفيت فيه جميع الجزئيّات[٢] فليس يعطي بذاته وأوّلا المحمول الضروريّ الذاتيّ ، إذ كان ليس يمتنع أن يكون ذلك الكلّيّ محمولا على جميع تلك الجزئيّات[٣] بالعرض ، مثل من رأى أنّ كلّ متكوّن إنّما يتكوّن عن موجود بالفعل . ولذلك كانت أمثال هذه مقدّمات [ب ٨٢و] مشهورة . وأمّا[٤] الاستقراء المستعمَل[٥] في البرهان ، فإنّما يُستعمَل[٦] للإرشاد إلى اليقين لا إلى إفادته[٧] أوّلا وبالذات . وفرق عظيم بين ما يستعمل[٨] مرشداً وبين ما يستعمل[٨] مفيداً[٩] بذاته . ولذلك

---

١١) (كل ما يلى من « المطلوب » الى « موضوع ») — ع .

١٢) (كل ما يلي من «فمن» الى «وبالجملة من» غامض، في الهامش) م .

١٣) لنـا ب .

١٤) fuerit ل .

١٥) — ل .

١٦) — ب .

١٧) تتقضى م؛ تنقضى ب؛ perficitur ل.

١٨) — ب .

١٩) (فوق السطر) م .

٢٠) التقضى م؛ النقضى ب؛ perfectione ل.

٢١) نقضى ب .

٢٢) وجود م .

٢٣) الاكثر م ؛ — ع ؛

(١٠)

١) — ب .

٢) الجزيايات م ؛ החלקים ع ؛

٣) الجزايات م.

٤) — م .

٥) הנעשה ع ؛ fit ل ؛

٦) יעשה ع ؛ fit ل .

٧) فائدته م؛ فادته ب؛ הקנותו ع .

٨) שנעשה ع ؛ fit ل ؛

٩) utile ل .

[10]لسنا نضطرّ[10] في المقدّمات التي يحصل[11] اليقين بها بالاستقراء إلى أن نتصفّح[12] جميع الجزئيّات[13] بل يكفي في ذلك بعضها .

١١. وإنّما يُضطَرّ[1] إلى استعمال[2] [م ٧٤ ظ] الاستقراء فيها لأحد أمرين : إمّا أنّ ذلك الجنس من المقدّمات لم يُتعرَّض بعد[3] لإحساس أشخاصها ، مثل من لم يحسّ قط أنّ السقمونيا تُسهل الصفراء . فإنّ مثل هذا يُحتاج[4] فيه إلى الاستقراء حتّى يحصل المحمول الذاتي . وهذه هي المعروفة[5] بالمقدّمات التجربيّة[6] ، وهذه[7] المقدّمات تتفاضل في مقدار ما يُحتاج[8] أن يُحَسّ من[9] أشخاصها ، وحينئذ[10] يقع اليقين بها . وذلك بحسب مادّة مادّة . فبعض[11] [12]يُحتاج فيها[12] أن يُحَسّ[13] منها شخص واحد فقط ككثير من المقدّمات العدديّة ، وبعض إلى أن يُحَسّ[13] فيه أكثر من واحد . وأمّا الأمر الآخَر الذي يضطرّ[14] فيه إلى استعمال[15] الاستقراء في البرهان فهو أنّ كثيرًا من الناس ليس يعترف بكلّيّة كثير من المقدّمات بل يعترف بأحد جزئيّاتها[16] ، كمن يعترف أنّ معرفة الصحّة والمرض[17] لعلم واحد وهو علم الطبّ ، فإن قيل[18] له أنّ الأضداد[19] علمها واحد ، لم

---

١٠) non oportet ل .
١١) تحصل ب .
١٢) تتصفح م ؛ يتصفح ب ؛ שיתבארו ع .
١٣) الجزيات م .

(١١)
١) نضطر ب ؛ נצטרך ع ؛ indigebimus ل .
٢) עשיית ع ؛ facere ل .
٣) — ع .
٤) יצטרך ع ؛ indiget ل .
٥) المعرفة م .
٦) الجزئية ب .
٧) وهذا م .
٨) שיצטרך ع ؛ oportet ل .
٩) عن ب .
١٠) ut ل .
١١) بفعضى م .
١٢) יצטרך ع ؛ oportet ل .
١٣) sentiamus ل .
١٤) indigemus ل .
١٥) עשיית ع ؛ facere ل .
١٦) جزاياتها م ؛ מחלקין ع .
١٧) — ع .
١٨) قل م ؛ נאמר ع ؛ diceremus ل .
١٩) اضداد ب .

يعترف بهذه الكلّيّة[٢٠] حتّى تستقرئ[٢١] له فحينئذ يقع له [٢٢]اليقين بكلّيّتها[٢٢].

١٢. فهذه صورة الأقاويل الجدليّة التصديقيّة[١].

⟨ موادّ الأقاويل الجدليّة التصديقيّة ⟩

١٣. فأمّا موادّها، فهي المقدّمات المشهورة كما تقدّم. وهذه[١] أصناف:

⟨١⟩ منها ما هي مشهورة عند الجميع، [٢]وهذا الصنف أشرفها[٢]، وبهذا[٣] يمكن أن تتلاقي[٤] جميع الأمم[٥] المختلفة مع تباين نحلها[٦] وفطرها[٧]، مثل [٨]أنّ شكر المنعم[٨] حسن وبرّ الوالدين[٩] واجب.

⟨٢⟩ ومنها ما هي مشهورة عند الأكثر من غير أن يكون عند الباقين[١٠] في ذلك خلاف، مثل أنّ الله واحد[١١].

⟨٣⟩ ومنها المشهورة

⟨أ⟩ عند [١٢]العلماء والحكماء[١٢] أو[١٣] عند أكثرهم[١٤] من غير أن يخالفهم الباقون[١٥]، مثل أنّ [م ٧٥و] المعرفة فاضلة لذاتها، أو

---

٢٠) الكليات ب.

٢١) يستقرى م؛ تستقرا ب؛ inquirat ل.

٢٢) illius universalitas ل.

(١٢)

١) — ل.

(١٣)

١) هذا م.

٢) וזה החלק יותר מהחלק שקדם ع.

٣) بهذه م.

٤) يتلاقى ب.

٥) الامام ب.

٦) بحلها م؛ — ع؛ regionarum ل.

٧) ועניניהם ع.

٨) ששבח החסידים ع؛ commendatio studiosorum ل.

٩) الوالذين ب.

١٠) البقايين م؛ الباقيين ب.

١١) واحدا م، ب.

١٢) החכמים הראשונים והיודעים ع.

١٣) و ب؛ — ع.

١٤) (كل ما يلى من «اكثرهم» الى «لذاتها او عند») — ب، ع، ل.

١٥) الباقين م.

⟨ب⟩ عند أكثرهم مثل أنّ السماء كريّة .

⟨٤⟩ ومنها ما هي مشهورة

⟨أ⟩ عند[١٦] أهل الصنائع من غير أن يخالفهم في ذلك الجمهور ، مثل ما في[١٧] صناعة الطبّ أنّ[١٨] السقمونيا[١٩] تسهّل[٢٠] الصفراء وشحم الحنظل[٢١] البلغم . أو

⟨ب⟩ عند المشهورين بالحذق[٢٢] في الصنائع من غير أن يخالفهم أهل الصناعة ، مثل قول ابوقراط[٢٣] إنّ الإعياء[٢٤] الحادث[٢٥] من غير سبب متقدّم منذر[٢٦] بمرض ، أو

⟨ج⟩ عند أكثرهم .

⟨٥⟩ وأيضاً[٢٧] الشبيه[٢٨] بالمشهور مشهور ، مثل أنّه إن كان[٢٩] من المشهور[٢٩] أنّ العلم بالمتضادّات واحد بعينه فالحسّ بالمتضادّات[٣٠] واحد بعينه .

⟨٦⟩ وأيضاً المضادّ للمشهور[٣١] مشهور ، مثل إن كان من المشهور أنّ الأصدقاء[٣٢] ينبغي أن يُحسَن[٣٣] إليهم ، فالأعداء[٣٤] ينبغي أن يُساء إليهم .

وأشرف هذه كلّها[٣٥] ما شهد به الجميع أو الأكثر ، وإنّما صار[٣٦]

---

١٦) אבל אצל ع .
١٧) — ب .
١٨) — ب .
١٩) السقمنيا م .
٢٠) تصحل م .
٢١) الحنطل م .
٢٢) بالحدق ب .
٢٣) ابقراط ب .
٢٤) الانويا م ؛ labores ل .
٢٥) الحادت م ، ب .
٢٦) منذر م ، ب .
٢٧) فايضا ب .
٢٨) النسبة ب .
٢٩) — ل .
٣٠) — ع .
٣١) المشهور م .
٣٢) الاصدفاء ب ؛ שהאוהב ع ؛ amico ل .
٣٣) يحسين ب .
٣٤) فالعـداء م ؛ השונא ع ؛ inimico ل .
٣٥) — ع .
٣٦) ضار ب .

ما[٣٧] دونها[٣٨] مشهوراً[٣٩] لشهادة الجميع لها أو الأكثر[٤٠] فإنّ آراء العلماء إنّما صارت[٤١] مشهورة لأنّ الجميع أو الأكثر يرون أنّ آراءهم ينبغي أن [ب ٨٣و] تُقبَل، وكذلك الآراء التي تخصّ الصناعات، وكذلك في سائرها.

١٤. وهذه المقدّمات المشهورة هي ضرورة[١] كلّيّات، إذ كانت الجزئيّات[٢] متبدّلة[٣] وليست مشتركة الإحساس للجميع. وإن كانت، إنّما تؤخذ في هذه المقاييس[٤] مهمَلة وليس[٥] يبلغ من التحفّظ بها أن يُصرَّح فيها بالإضمار[٦]. ولذلك ما[٧] تكذب بالجزء[٨].

١٥. والكلّيّات كما تقدّم المفردة منها والمركّبة ثمانية أصناف: [١]الجنس والنوع[١] والفصل والخاصّة والعرض والحدّ والرسم والقول الذي ليس بحدّ ولا رسم. وإذا كان كذلك فالمحمولات الجدليّة ضرورة [م ٧٥ ظ] تكون أحد هذه الأصناف. لكن لمّا كان النوع لا يُحمَل إلاّ على شخص، والقضيّة[٢] التي محمولها شخص ليست[٣] تُستعمَل في هذه الصناعة، لم يعد ههنا[٤] محمولاً. وأمّا الرسم فهو داخل في الخاصّة إذ كانت قوّتها[٥] واحدة. وكذلك القول الذي ليس بحدّ ولا رسم داخل في العرض أيضاً[٦]. فتكون المحمولات الجدليّة إذاً خمسة أصناف: حدّ وجنس وفصل وخاصّة وعرض.

---

٣٧) من ب.
٣٨) — ل.
٣٩) مشهور م.
٤٠) (كل ما يلى من «الاكثر» الى «الجميع او») — ب.
٤١) ضارت م.

(١٤)

١) ضرورية م.
٢) الجزايات ب.
٣) latentes ل.
٤) المقايس (هنا وفيما بعد) م، ب.
٥) وليست م.
٦) الاسوار م، ب؛ באומות ع؛ signis ل.
٧) — ل.
٨) בחלק ع.

(١٥)

١) הסוג המין ع.
٢) in enuntiatione ل.
٣) ليس ب.
٤) يعدها هنا م؛ تعد ب.
٥) قوتها م.
٦) — ل.

١٦. أمّا الحدّ ، فيُكتفى[١] من رسمه ههنا[٢] أنّه قول يدلّ على معنى الشيء الذي به بيّن[٣] قوامه ووجوده . وأمّا الجنس، فإنّه يُحدّ[٤] ههنا[٥] بأنّه المحمول[٦] على كثيرين مختلفين بالنوع من طريق ما هو . وأمّا الفصل ، فإنّه المحمول أيضاً[٧] على كثيرين مختلفين بالنوع من طريق أيّ شيء هو . والخاصّة هي[٨] المحمول[٩] الذي[١٠] [١١]لا يدلّ[١١] على ما هو الشيء ويوجد[١٢] لجميعه ووحده ودائماً . وأمّا العرض، فإنّه يُرسَم[١٣] ههنا برسمين : أحدهما أنّه الذي يوجد للشيء وليس بجنس ولا فصل ولا خاصّة ولا حدّ ، والثاني هو الذي يمكن أن يوجد لشيء واحد بعينه وأن[١٤] لا يوجد له . وإنّما رُسم[١٥] ههنا برسمين لأنّ بمجموعها يحصل تصوّر العرض على الإطلاق[١٦] . وذلك أن الرسم الأوّل[١٧] منهما يخصّ[١٨] من العرض ما لا يفارق ، والثاني المفارق .

١٧. وبيّن أنّ هذه[١] الرسوم ههنا ليست بكافية[٢] في تصوّر واحد واحد[٣] من هذه[٤] التصوّر التامّ ، لكن[٥] هذا هو التصوّر[٦] الكافي في أمرها[٧] ههنا ، [٨]وذلك أنّ[٨] تصوّر الأشياء[٩] التي منها تلتئم الحدود كماله[١٠] في كتاب

---

(١٦)

١) يكفى ب .
٢) — ل .
٣) (في الهامش) م ؛ — ب ، ع ، ل.
٤) يحدها ب .
٥) — ل .
٦) المحمول أيضاً م ، ب ؛ הנשוא גם כן ع .
٧) — ل .
٨) هو م.
٩) — ل .
١٠) الدى ب ؛ — ع .
١١) — ع .
١٢) توجد ب .
١٣) يرسم أيضاً م ، ب ؛ יורשם גם כן ع .
١٤) — ب ، ع ، ل .
١٥) رشم م .
١٦) اطلاق م .
١٧) una ل .
١٨) attribuitur ل .

(١٧)

١) هذا م .
٢) كافية ب .
٣) — ل .
٤) هذا م .
٥) لاكن ب .
٦) — ب ، ع ، ل .
٧) significato ل .
٨) perfectio enim ل .
٩) הדבר ع .
١٠) كمالة م ؛ — ل .

البرهان . وكذلك الذي أُخذ[11] ههنا في حدّ الجنس بيّن[12] أنّه من الأجناس الجنس الأخير . وكذلك الفصل ليس يكفي فيه أن يكون [م ٧٦و] محمولا[13] من طريق أيّ شيء هو دون أن يكون خاصّاً بالشيء الذي هو فصل له .

١٨. وإذا كانت المحمولات في المقدّمات[1] الجدليّة أحد هذه الأصناف الخمس ، وجب أن تكون ضروب المقاييس الجدليّة بحسب ما يأتلف من هذه الخمسة من جهة ما هي متصوَّرة بهذا[2] النحو من التصوّر . وذلك أنّه[3] اذا أُخذت محمولة على المجرى[4] الطبيعيّ ومعكوسة وجُعلت الحدود الثلاثة في المقاييس منسوبة بعضها إلى بعض إمّا[5] بواحدة واحدة من هذه النسب الخمس مثل نسبة الحدّ[6] أو غيرها من النسب ، وإمّا مركّبة مثل أن تكون نسبة[7] أحد الحدود نسبة الفصل والثاني نسبة العرض أو [ب ٨٤و] غيرها من النسب ، أو أُخذت أيضاً[8] على جهة أخرى[9] وهو أن تنسب فيها أبدا حدّين[10] إلى الثالث[11] : إمّا الطرف الأعظم والأوسط للأصغر ، وإمّا الأصغر والأوسط للأعظم من غير أن يكون بين الطرفين المنسوبين نسبة من هذه النسب ، بل يكون حملها ‹ عليهما › بالعرض ، وذلك أيضاً على وجهين إمّا ان تجعل[12] نسبتهما[13] إلى الطرف الواحد[14] نسبة واحدة ، مثل أن تكون[15] نسبة [16]الطرف الأعظم[16] والأوسط إلى الأصغر نسبة الحدّ فقط[17] أو [18]واحدة واحدة[18]

---

١١) أخذ ب ؛ accepimus ل .
١٢) (فوق السطر) م .
١٣) (مكرّرة) م .

(١٨)

١) propositionibus ل .
٢) بهذه م .
٣) — م .
٤) المجرا ب .
٥) (مكرّرة) م .
٦) الحدود م .
٧) — ع ، ل .
٨) semper ل .
٩) uno ل .
١٠) حدان ب .
١١) الثاث م .
١٢) نجعل م ؛ ponamus ل .
١٣) יחסם ع ؛ amborarum illorarum ل .
١٤) — ل .
١٥) يكون ب .
١٦) termini ل .
١٧) (كل ما يلى من « او » الى « بهذه النسبة » غامض ، في الهامش) م .
١٨) واحد م ؛ unius ل .

من النسب[١٩] الخمس ، أو بعكس[٢٠] ذلك[٢١] — أعني أنّ نسبة[٢٢] الأصغر و[٢٣] الأوسط إلى الأعظم بهذه النسبة أو [٢٤]واحدة واحدة منهـا[٢٤] ، وإمّا أن تجعل[٢٥] نسبتها[٢٦] إلى الطرف الواحد نسبتين مثل أن يكون نسبة الطرف الأعظم إلى الأصغر نسبة الحدّ والأوسط[٢٧] إلى الأصغر نسبة الفصل أو[٢٨] غيرها من النسب ، أو[٢٩] عكس ذلك — أعني أن تكون نسبـة الأصغر إلى الأعظم[٣٠] نسبة الحدّ[٣١] والأوسط إلى الأعظم[٣٢] نسبة الفصل أو غيرها[٣٣] من النسب فإذا[٣٤] سُلك[٣٥] في إحصاء[٣٦] هذه[٣٧] المقاييس هذا[٣٨] المسلك[٣٩] كانت ضروب المقاييس الجدليّة أضعاف[٤٠] المقاييس البرهانيّة. وإنّما [م ٧٦ ظ] كان ذلك لأنّه لا تحتفظ[٤١] فيها بالحمل على المجرى[٤٢] الطبيعيّ ولا بالحمل الذاتي. ولشدّة شبهها[٤٣] وقربها [٤٤]من ضروب المقاييس البرهانيّة[٤٤] ظنّ كثير من الناس أنّه سقط في[٤٥] كتاب أبي نصر كثير من ضروب[٤٦] المقاييس البرهانيّة. وهي[٤٧] في الحقيقة مقاييس جدليّة.

---

١٩) النسوب م .
٢٠) بالعكس ب .
٢١) — ب ، ع .
٢٢) ينسب ب ؛ שיורחס ع ؛ proportionetur ل .
٢٣) او م .
٢٤) alterius illorum ل .
٢٥) يجعل ب ؛ ponamus ل .
٢٦) نسبتها ب ؛ יחסר ع .
٢٧) (كل ما يلى من « الاوسط » الى « نسبة الحد ») — ل .
٢٨) و ب .
٢٩) (مكرّرة) م .
٣٠) الاعظم أيضاً م .
٣١) (كل ما يلى من « الحد » الى « الاعظم نسبة » غامض ، في الهامش) م .
٣٢) الاعظم ايضاً ب ؛ הגדול גם כן ع .
٣٣) غيره م .
٣٤) וכאשר ع .
٣٥) كذلك م ؛ הלכנו ع ؛ processerimus ل .
٣٦) combinationibus ل .
٣٧) — ع .
٣٨) هذه م ؛ בזאת ع .
٣٩) المسلق م ؛ הדבר ع .
٤٠) اصعاف م .
٤١) يتحفظ م ، ب ؛ servant ل .
٤٢) المجرا ب .
٤٣) assimilationis ل .
٤٤) — م .
٤٥) من ب .
٤٦) — ل .
٤٧) وهو ب .

١٩. وههنا صنف آخر من أصناف الأقاويل التصديقيّة وهي المعروفة بالأقاويل المنطقية. وهو الصنف ‹ الذي › يأتلف من المقدّمات الصادقة التي ليست بذاتيّة بل هي أعمّ من الجنس التي تُستعمَل فيه[١]. فمن جهة ما هو صادق يُظَنّ به أنّه معدود في أصناف البراهين[٢]. ومن جهة ما هو غير ذاتيّ يُظَنّ به أنّه جدليّ. أمّا تامسطيوس[٣] فيصرّح في هذا الصنف أنّه ليس بجدليّ. وأمّا أبو نصر فالذي يظهر من قوّة قوله[٤] أنّه جدليّ. وأنا أقول[٥]: إنّه إذا لم يكن[٦] سبب وقوع التصديق بمطلوب [٧]مشهور اليقين[٧] أنّ المحمول في[٨] جوهر الموضوع أو[٩] الموضوع في جوهر المحمول، فليس يفعل التصديق في ذلك شيء[١٠] غير الشهرة أو الاستقراء. وما هذه سبيله فهو ضرورة جدليّ. لكن أمثال هذه المقاييس هي[١١] أرفع[١٢] رتبة من المقاييس الجدليّة إذ كانت ليست كاذبة ولا بالجزء.

٢٠. فهذا المقدار الذي قلناه بحسب غرضنا[١] ههنا كافٍ[٢].

‹ الانتهاء ›

٢١. وأمّا أرسطو فإنّه لمّا تميّزت[١] له هذه الأقاويل الجدليّة من البرهانيّة لا في المواد فقط بل وبالقول، رأى[٢] أنّ مثل هذه الأقيسة[٣] و[٤] إن لم

---

(١٩)

١) — ب.

٢) البرهانية م.

٣) تامسطاس م.

٤) قيله م؛ verborum ل.

٥) ראנחנו נאמר ع؛ nos autem dicimus ل.

٦) يكون م، ب؛ — ع.

٧) ما شعره (ويمكن أن تكون «ما تشعر به») النفس ب؛ מה שישער הנפש ع؛ quod putatur in anima ل.

٨) فمن (و «ف» فوق السطر) م.

٩) ا ع.

١٠) — م.

١١) — م.

١٢) اربعة ب.

(٢٠)

١) غرذنا م.

٢) كافي م.

(٢١)

١) تميز م.

٢) השב ع.

٣) الاقيسية م؛ — ل.

٤) — م.

تكن[٥] برهانيّة[٦] فإنّ لها منافع[٧] من أشهرها الارتياض[٨]. وذلك أنّه لمّا كان كثير من المقدّمات المشهورة متقابلات[٩] أمكن أن يُثبَت الشيء الواحد بعينه من هذه المقدّمات[١٠] [م ٧٧و] ويُبطَل ، وذلك إذا أضيف إلى المقدّمة الصغرى المقدّمتان[١١] المتقابلتان[١٢] [١٣]رأي أنّ[١٣] استعمال المتناظرين[١٤] أمثال هذه الأقيسة في إثبات الشيء وإبطاله على أن يكون أحدهما [ب ٨٥و] يروم حفظه والآخر إبطاله يحصل[١٥] عنه ارتياض عظيم على جهة ما يحصل في الصنائع التي هي معدّة نحو غيرها كصناعة المثاقفة[١٦] وغيرها . و[١٧] من أجل هذا جُعلت هذه الصناعة بين سائل ومجيب . وجعل السائل سبيله[١٨] أن يتسلّم من المجيب ما يُبطَل عليه وضعه[١٩] . وسبيل[٢٠] المجيب ألاّ يسلّم شيئاً يبطل عليه وضعه . وأعطى لذلك جميع المواضع التي منها يستنبط[٢١] المقاييس في جميع المطالب ، سواء[٢٢] كان المطلوب ممّا يُطلَب في الموضوع بإطلاق أو كان يُطلَب باشتراك[٢٣] ، مثل أن يُطلَب هل هو جنس[٢٤] [٢٥]أو حدّ أو واحد[٢٥] من النسب الخمس . ثمّ أعطى مع هذا[٢٦] كيف يسأل[٢٧] السائل ويجيب[٢٨] المجيب . وأعطى مع ذلك الوصايا التي تخصّ

---

٥) تكون م .
٦) برهانيات م .
٧) شافع ب ؛ exercitium ل .
٨) (غامضة ولكن كانت « الارتباط » أولا) م ، — ل .
٩) (هكذا ولكن فوق السطر « يقينية ») م .
١٠) المقدّمات مقدّمات م .
١١) والمقدّمتان ب ؛ וההקדמות ع .
١٢) المتقابلان ب ؛ המקבילות ع .
١٣) שתי דעות ع .
١٤) المتناظرين ب .
١٥) et eveniet ل .
١٦) المتاقفة م ؛ المتافكة ب ؛ העמידה ع ؛ dialectica ل.
١٧) — م .
١٨) سيبله ب ؛ שאלתו בדרך ع .
١٩) (كل ما يلى من « وضعه » الى « يبطل عليه ») — ب .
٢٠) modum instituit ل .
٢١) تستنبط م .
٢٢) sicut ل .
٢٣) باشتراط م .
٢٤) جنساً ب .
٢٥) اوحدا او واحدا م ؛ واحد وواحد ب .
٢٦) ذا م ، ب .
٢٧) يسئل م ؛ يسل ب .
٢٨) (هذه فوق السطر ولكن « وبحسب » على السطر) م .

[٢٩]السائل والوصايا التي تخص[٢٩] المجيب . ولذلك ما حُدِّت[٣٠] هذه الصناعة بأنّها ملكة يقدر السائل بها أن يعمل من مقدّمات[٣١] مشهورة قياساً في إبطال أيّ طرفي النقيض[٣٢] تسلّمه السائل من المجيب . ويقدر المجيب أن لا يسلّم للسائل شيئاً يلزمه عنه نقيض ما وضع . ولهذه[٣٣] الصناعة منافع أُخَر قد عدّدت في كتاب الجدل . إلاّ أنّ مثل هذا الارتياض يشبه ألاّ يكون ضرورياً عند كمال الصنائع البرهانيّة بل إن كان ولا بدّ فمن جهة الأفضل[٣٤]

[٣٥]فرغ الجدل بحمد الله وعونه[٣٥]

---

٢٩) — ب .

٣٠) يحدث ب .

٣١) propositionibus ل .

٣٢) النقوض م .

٣٣) (مكرّرة) ب .

٣٤) manifestioris ل .

٣٥) — ب ، ع ، ل .

جوامع كتاب الخطابة

لأبي الوليد محمد بن احمد بن رشد

بسم الله الرحمن الرحيم [1]عونك يا ربّنا[1]

[2]القول في الأقاويل الخط⟨ا⟩بيّة[2]

⟨التمهيد⟩

١. وإذ قد فرغنا من القول في المقاييس[1] الجدليّة وفي مقدار ما تفيده من التصديق ، فلنقل في الأشياء المقنعة وفي[2] مقدار[3] ما تفيده أيضاً [4]من التصديق[4] . وهو ظاهر أنّ القناعة ظنّ ما غالب تسكن إليه النفس مع شعورها بمعاندة . وقد حدّدنا فيما سلف ما هو الظنّ .

٢. وأمّا الأشياء الفاعلة للقناعة ، فيظهر بالتصفّح والاستقراء[1] أنّها تنقسم أوّلا إلى صنفين : أحدهما أقاويل[2] ، والثاني أشياء من خارج ليست بأقاويل كالإيمان[3] والشهادات[4] [5]وغير ذلك ممّا سنعدّده[5] . وكذلك أيضاً يظهر بالتصفّح أنّ الأقاويل التي تُستعمَل في[6] هذه المخاطبة الجمهوريّة صنفان :

عنوان

١) وعليه أتوكل لا رب غيره ب ؛ ועליו אשען אזן ⟨אין⟩ גדול זולתו ع ؛ — ل .

٢) —ب ؛ in librum Rhetorices ل .

(١)

١) المقايس (هنا وفيما بعد) م .

٢) وفيما م .

٣) مقادر م .

٤) — ب ، ع .

(٢)

١) الاسترقاء م .

٢) الأقاويل م .

٣) كالالسان م ؛ كالايمار ب ؛ באמונות ع .

٤) الشهدات م .

٥) — ل .

٦) (مكرّرة) م .

مثال وحجّة[٧] ، وهو المسمّى في هذه الصناعة ضميراً . وذلك أنّه ، إذا[٨] أشار واحد منهم على آخر بأخذ[٩] دواء[١٠] ما ، يقول له : « استعمله لأنّ فلاناً[١١] استعمله فانتفع به » ، فيقنعه بالتمثيل ، أو يقول له[١٢] : « بك علّة كذا وكذا »[١٣] ، وكذلك في شيء شيء ممّا يتخاطبون به .

٣. وإذ قد ظهر أنّ هذا [ب ٨٦و] النحو من المخاطبة يستعمل[١] هذين الصنفين من الأقاويل ، فلنقل فيهما أوّلا . ثمّ نصير بعد ذلك إلى القول في المقنعات الأخَر ، إذ كانت هذه هي أحقّ[٢] أن تكون مقنعة من تلك ، وهي أكثر تقدّماً بالطبع .

〈الضمير〉

٤. فنقول إنّ الضمير هو قياس[١] [م ٧٨و] منتج بحسب بادئ الرأي السابق[٢] للجميع أو للأكثر[٣] . وبادئ الرأي السابق هو الرأي الذي إذا فاجأ[٤] الإنسان ، وقع[٥] له به ظنّ ما[٦] غالب وسكون نفس إليه من قبل أن يتعقّبه . والمقاييس إنّما تصير منتجة[٧] بحسب بادئ الرأي السابق إمّا من قبل صورها[٨] وإمّا من قبل موادّها . أمّا من قبل صورها[٨] ، فان تكون منتجة بحسب بادئ الرأي وأمّا[٩] من قبل موادّها[١٠] ، فأن[١١] تكون مقدّماتها[١٢] صادقة أيضاً بحسب بادئ الرأي .

---

٧) טענות ع ؛ argumentationes ل .
٨) متى ب .
٩) يأخذ ب .
١٠) ذوا م ، ب ؛ תורה ع ؛ nominis ل .
١١) فلان م .
١٢) له لانّ ب ، quando sic est, concluditur sic ل .
١٣) — ب .

(٣)
١) تستعمل م
٢) احرى (فوق السطر) م .

(٤)
١) (مكرّرة) م .
٢) سابق م .
٣) أكثر للأكثر ب .
٤) — ب .
٥) ووقع م .
٦) — ب .
٧) منتجا م ؛ concludunt ل .
٨) — م .
٩) sed ل .
١٠) suam materiam ل .
١١) (مكرّرة) م .
١٢) مقاماتها م .

⟨صور المقاييس⟩

٥. وصور[١] المقاييس إنّما تكون منتجة[٢] بحسب[٣] بادئ الرأي بأن يُسامَح[٤] فيها ويُحذَف[٥] منها الشيء الذي به ضروريّة اللزوم، على ما شأن الجمهور أن[٦] يجتزوا[٧] به[٨] في مخاطبة بعضهم بعضاً. ولذلك[٩] ينبغي أن نتأمل هذا المعنى في نوع نوع من أنواع[١٠] المقاييس التي أحصيناها، فإنّ بإحصاء ذلك يحصل[١١] لنا ضروب جميع المقاييس المقنعة[١٢] من جهة صورها.

٦. فنقول: إنّه[١] بيّن، ممّا تقدّم[٢] أنّ التي[٣] تفعل ضروريّة[٤] اللزوم في الشكل الأوّل هي المقدّمة[٥] الكليّة وأنّ الذي يفعل الاتّصال هو أن تكون المقدّمة الصغرى موجبة. وإذا كان ذلك كذلك فإذا يحذف المقدّمة الكبرى يصير[٦] الشكل الأوّل[٧] مقنعاً أو[٨] يأخذها[٩] مهملة. لكنّ حذفها أكثر إقناعاً[١٠] لأنّه قد يُوهم حذفها أنّها إنّما حُذفت لأنّه[١١] ليس فيها موضع عناد وأنّها بيّنة الظهور جدّاً، على جهة ما يفعل ذلك المبرهنون. وكذلك قد يصير أيضاً مقنعاً في بعض المواضع[١٢] بحذف[١٣] الصغرى أو[١٤] بأخذها[١٥] سالبة.

---

(٥) ١) صورة ب.
٢) concludunt ل.
٣) (فوق السطر) م.
٤) — ب؛ בשקלרע؛ negligunt ل.
٥) ויחסרוע.
٦) — م، ع.
٧) يجتزو م؛ — ب؛ שיעברוע؛ observunt ل.
٨) — م.
٩) ولذلك ما م.
١٠) انوع م.
١١) تحصل م.
١٢) rhetoricorum ل.

(٦) ١) انام.
٢) exacta sunt ل.
٣) الذي ب.
٤) ضرورة ب.
٥) المقدّمات م.
٦) (والكلمات «يصير الشكل الاول مقنعاً» مكرّرة) م.
٧) — ب، ع، ل.
٨) aut similiter ل.
٩) بأخذها م؛ כשתלקח ع.
١٠) اقنعا ب.
١١) لا نا م.
١٢) الماوضع م.
١٣) يحذف ب.
١٤) و ب.
١٥) يأخذها ب.

٧. وأمّا الشكل الثاني والثالث ، [م ٧٨ ظ] فلمّا لم تكن[١] فيهما[٢] المقدّمة[٣] المالكة [٤]في الانتاج[٤] بيّنة من أوّل الأمر بل[٥] قد تكون الصغرى وقد تكون الكبرى ، وكذلك المقدّمة الفاعلة للاتّصال ، لم يكن[٦] ضارّاً أن يصرّح فيهما بالمقدّمتين جميعاً. لكن ينبغي متى فعل ذلك ولم يحذف أحدهما[٧] أن توخذا[٨] مهملتين ، وإلاّ لم يبق[٩] فيهما[١٠] موضع للعناد أصلاً. وأيضاً من أنواع التأليفات الغير منتجة ما يُظنّ به في بادئ[١١] الرأي أنّه منتج[١٢] من غير [١٣]أن يكون كذلك في الحقيقة. وهذه الأنواع أيضاً من الأقاويل هي مقنعة[١٤] بحسب صورها . مثال ذلك ما يأتلف من موجبتين في الشكل الثاني والضروب المنتجة التي في الشكل الثالث ، إذا أُخذت [١٥]نتائجها كلّيّة[١٥] كانت من هذا النوع . لكن ينبغي مع ذلك ألاّ يُصرَّح فيها بالإضمار[١٦] وتؤخذ مهملة ليكون موضع العناد فيها أخفى .

[١]وأمّا المقاييس الشرطيّة[١] :

٨. فإنّ منها منفصلاً — [٢]كما تقدّم[٢] [ب ٨٧و] — ومتّصلاً . أمّا المتّصل فإنّما[٣] يكون[٤] ضميراً بأن يبقى فيه[٥] أيضاً موضع للعناد. وقد تبيّن في كتاب

(٧)

١) تكون م ، ب .

٢) فيها ب .

٣) المقدّمات م .

٤) لأمر الانتاج م ؛ בתולדה ع ؛ rem in conclusione ل .

٥) — ب .

٦) يكون م .

٧) احداهما ب .

٨) يوخذ م ؛ توخذ ب .

٩) يتّفق م .

١٠) فيها ب .

١١) مبادئ م .

١٢) (والكلمات « منتج من غير ان يكون ») — ل .

١٣) — ب .

١٤) غير مقنعة ب ؛ בלתי הלציים ع .

١٥) نتائجها كلّها كلّيه م ؛ sunt duae conclusiones universales ل .

١٦) بالأسوار م ، ب ؛ בחומות ع ؛ signa ل .

(٨)

١) (كتبت هذه الجملة كعنوان في المخطوطات) .

٢) — ل .

٣) فسنما م .

٤) — ب .

٥) فيها م .

القياس أنّه إنّما يكون منتجاً بأن يكون صحيح اللزوم ويكون المستثنى فيه [6] بيّنا بقياس حمليّ . وإن كان المستثنى فيه[6] بيّنا بنفسه ، فيكون ⟨إذن⟩ اللزوم[7] ضرورة ممّا يُحتاج إلى أن يُبيَّن . وتبيّن أيضاً هناك[8] أنّه ليس أيّ شيء اتّفق من مقدّم أو تال[9] هو المستثنى فيه ولا أيّ شيء[10] اتّفق منهما[10] هو المنتج . وإذا كان ذلك كذلك ، فإذن[11] إنّما يصير[12] هذا النوع من القياس ضميرًا بأن يخلّفه[13] ببعض هذه الشروط[14] . و[15] لكن أوّل[16] ما يصير[17] به مقنعاً هو حذف المستثنى منه . وقد يصير مقنعاً بأن ينتج فيه أيّهما اتّفق من مقدّم أو تال[18] أو مقابلهما . لكن ينبغي مع هذا فيما لم يكن[19] صحيح الإنتاج ألاّ يصرّح في الأكثر بالمستثنى الذي[20] [م ٧٩ و] [21]لزم عنه[21] مخافة[22] أن يشعر[23] الخصم[24] ⟨به⟩ كمن يستثنى[25] التالي بعينه فينتج المقدّم أو[26] يستثني مقابل المقدّم فينتج مقابل التالي . وقد يُصرّح بالمستثنى في مثل هذا ، فيكون القول مقنعاً ، كقول بعض القدماء : « إن كان الموجود تكوّن ، فله مبدأ ، لكنّه لم[27] يتكوّن ، فليس[28] له[29] مبدأ » .

٩. وجالينوس وكثير من المشرّحين يستعملون هذا النوع من القياس في استنباط ما جُهل أسبابه من أفعال[1] الحيوان . مثال ذلك أنّه يقول : « متى

---

٦) (غامضة ، في الهامش) م .
٧) coniunctio ل .
٨) هنالك ب .
٩) تالى م .
١٠) منهما اتّفق ب .
١١) فإذًا (هنا وفيما بعد) م ، ب .
١٢) (وكل مـــا يلى من «يصير» الى «اول ما» غامض ، في الهامش) م.
١٣) يكلّفه م ؛ בשיעזוב בו ع ؛ subtrahemus ل .
١٤) الشرائط ب .
١٥) — ب .
١٦) اولى م .
١٧) (مكرّرة) م .
١٨) تالي م .
١٩) يكون م .
٢٠) (مكرّرة) م ؛ — ل .
٢١) — ل .
٢٢) محافة ب .
٢٣) putet ل .
٢٤) الحكم ب ، המריבה ع .
٢٥) שירושנה (⟨שישנה⟩) ع .
٢٦) و ب .
٢٧) ليس ب .
٢٨) — ب .
٢٩) فله ب .

(٩)

١) افعل م .

ارتفع العصب[2] [3]الراجع ، ارتفع الصوت ، فإذن متى وجد العصب[3] الراجع وجد الصوت » . وليس يلزم كما قيل ، فإنّه متى [4]ارتفـع الحيوان ، ارتفع الإنسان[4] ، وليس يلزم عن وجود الحيوان وجود الإنسان .

١٠. وأمّا إذا كان المنتج صحيحاً ، مثل أن يكون مقابل التالي أو المقدّم بعينه ، فيجب ألاّ يُصرَّح فيه بالمستثنى ، وإلاّ لم يبقَ[1] في القول موضع عناد إلاّ أن يُضمَر[2] الاتّصال[3] ولا يُصرَّح به[4] .

١١. وأمّا المنفصل ، فإنّه إنّما يصير مقنعاً بأن لا يستوفى جميع المتعاندات فيه متى كانت أكثر من إثنين وألاّ يستوفى فيها أيضاً جميع[1] المستثنيات . فأمّا حذف[2] المستثنى في هذا القياس ، فليس يصير به مقنعاً ، بل متى فعل ذلك بقي[3] في صورة ما يطلب به[4] بيان أحد النقيضين[5] اللذين[6] ينقسم إليهما[7] الطلب[8] .

١٢. مثال ما لم يستوف[1] جميع المتعاندات فيه قول [2]أبي المعالي[2] في كتابه الملقّب بالإرشاد حين أراد[3] أن يبطل التكوّن عن الاسطقسات . فإنّه قال : « إن كان يوجد متكوّن عن الاسطقسات الأربع ، فلا يخلو أن يكون ذلك إمّا على جهة أنّ الأجسام تتداخل بعضها في بعض حتّى يجتمع الجسمان

---

٢) العرب ب .
٣) (غامضة ، في الهامش) م .
٤) ارتفع الحيوان (وبعد هذا كلمتان غامضتان فوق السطر) الانسان م.
(١٠)
١) يبقى م .
٢) يصير ب ؛ שיסתמך ع ؛ insinuetur ل .
٣) الاتّصل م .
٤) — ع .
(١١)
١) — ب .
٢) אם חוסר ع .
٣) بقا م .
٤) فيه م .
٥) النقصين ب .
٦) الذين م .
٧) إليها ب .
٨) — ل .
(١٢)
١) يستوفى م ، ب .
٢) אבו מאלמעאלי (هنا وفيما بعد) ع ؛ Abualmaphal (هنا وفيما بعد) ل .
٣) اداد م .

معاً في مكان واحد أو يكون على أن كلّ [م ٧٩ ظ] واحد منها[٤] قائم في المركّب بنفسه متميّز[٥] ، وكلا[٦] هذين الصنفين محال . فأن يكون ههنا[٧] اسطقسات أكثر من واحد يتكوّن[٨] منها موجود واحد محال » . وهذا القول قد أسقط منه أحد ما كان ينبغي أن يجعل معانداً في القياس ، وذلك أن يكون الكون على وجه الاختلاط كما يُرى[٩] ذلك في السَّكَنْجَبِين[١٠] وفي غير ذلك من الأشياء [ب ٨٨ و] الصناعيّة[١٠] .

١٣. وأمّا الضرب الذي يبتدئ فيه من سالب وينتهي إلى سالب ، فإنّما يصير مقنعاً فقط[١] بأن يُحذَف[٢] المستثنى[٣] ويُصرَّح[٤] بالنتيجة . فإنّه[٥] متى حُذف المستثنى والنتيجة معاً ، لم يدر[٦] السامع أيّ شيء قصدت[٧] انتاجه . وليس يمكن أن يكون المستثنى ههنا أن يصرّح[٨] به أيّ شيء اتّفق ولا في بادئ الرأي ، بل انّما يستثنى فيه أبداً الموجب ، فينتج السالب . لكن[٩] متى فعل ذلك ، لم يبق[١٠] فيه موضع اقناع .

في قياس الخلف :

١٤. و[١] أمّا قياس الخلف ، فإنّه ينبغي إذا أردنا أن يصير مقنعاً أن يُصرَّح بالموضع المشكوك فيه والمحال اللازم ويُضمَر[٢] المقدّمة التي يلزم عنها

---

٤) منهما م ، ب .
٥) متحيز م ؛ — ب .
٦) كلي م؛ Accipiamus itaque ambas ل .
٧) ها هنا (هنا وفيما بعد) ب .
٨) (كلمة غامضة فوق «يتكوّن») م .
٩) يرا ب .
١٠) — ل .

(١٣)
١) — ب ، ع ، ل .
٢) subtrahemus ل .
٣) (وكل ما يلى من « المستثنى » الى «حُذف» غامض ، في الهامش) م:
٤) ostendemus ل .
٥) فإنّها م .
٦) يدري م .
٧) فضرب ب ؛ כוונך ع .
٨) صرح م ؛ نصرح ب .
٩) لاكن ب .
١٠) يبقى م ، ب .

(١٤)
١) — ب.
٢) تضمر ب؛ Notemus ل .

المحال. وقد يُصرَّح بها متى لم يكن[3] اللزوم ظاهراً، مثل قولنا: «إن لم يكن[3] كلّ إنسان حساساً[4]، فليس [5]كلّ حيوان[5] حساساً[6] إذ كلّ إنسان حيوان». فإنّ هذا اللزوم هو في الشكل الثالث.

١٥. فهذه هي[1] أصناف الضمائر من جهة صورها. وهي معادة لأصناف المقاييس بإطلاق.

⟨موادّ المقاييس⟩

١٦. وأمّا قسمة أصنافها من جهة الموادّ، فيجب أن تؤخذ[1] من جهة ما تنقسم إليه المقدّمات[2] أنفسها، وبخاصّة المقدّمة الكبرى[3]، إذ كانت هي المالكة للإنتاج[4]. وأمّا الصغرى[5]، فقد يمكن أن تؤخذ كيف ما اتّفق من كونها مقنعة[6] أو مشهورة أو غير ذلك.

١٧. [م ٨٠ و] فنقول[1] إنّ المقدّمات[2] المستعملة[3] في هذا الصنف من الأقاويل، وبخاصّة الكبرى[4]، إنّما تؤخذ ههنا من حيث هي مشهورة في بادئ الرأي المشترك. وقد حدّدنا فيما[5] سلف[6] ما هو بادئ الرأي كما أنّ المقدّمات الجدليّة إنّما تستعمَل من حيث هي مشهورة في الحقيقة. وكما أنّ المشهورات قد يتّفق فيها أن تكون[7] صادقة وألاّ[8] تكون، كذلك المقدّمات

---

٣) يكون م.
٤) حساس م.
٥) omne est animal ل.
٦) حساس م.

(١٥)

١) — ب.

(١٦)

١) توكد م؛ توجد ب.
٢) المقادّمات م.
٣) الكبرا ب.
٤) للاتناج م.
٥) الصغرا ب.
٦) Rhetorica ل.

(١٧)

١) فكذلك فنقول م.
٢) المقدّمة م؛ הקדמות ع؛ praemissa ل.
٣) المستعملات م؛ facta ل.
٤) الكبرا ب.
٥) فيوما م.
٦) exactis ل.
٧) يكون ب.
٨) والتكون ب؛ et quae non sint ل.

التي في بادئ الرأي قد يتّفق لها بالعرض أن تكون مشهورة أو صادقة وقد لا يتّفق ، إلاّ أنّها بالجملة إنّما تؤخذ ههنا من حيث هي مشهورة في بادئ الرأي ، كما أنّ المقدّمات[٩] الجدليّة إنّما تؤخذ من حيث هي مشهورة في الحقيقة فقط . والمشهورة التي في بادئ الرأي السابق تنقسم إلى قضايا مقبولات ، وهي مقدّمات تؤخذ كلّيّة في بادئ الرأي السابق[١٠] ، وإلى[١١] أشياء[١٢] محسوسة[١٣] تؤخذ دلائل على أشياء أخر في بادئ الرأي أيضاً .

١٨. وهذه[١] الدلائل منها ما تؤخذ دلائل على وجود الشيء على الإطلاق[٢] ، كأخذنا[٣] الإناء[٤] الفارغ[٥] دليلاً[٦] على وجود الخلاء ، ومنها ما تؤخذ دلائل على وجود المحمول للموضوع . وهذه ، متى كانت أعمّ من الموضوع وأخصّ من المحمول أو مساوية له ، ائتلف<ت> في الشكل الأوّل ، وخُصّت عند القدماء باسم الدليل . وإن كانت أعمّ من الطرفين ، ائتلف<ت> في الشكل الثاني . وإن كانت أخصّ منهما[٧] ائتلفت في الثالث . وهذان يُخصّان عند القدماء باسم [ب ٨٩ و] العلامة[٨] . وهذه الدلائل التي[٩] تؤخذ[١٠] ههنا ، قد تكون[١١] أمورًا متأخّرة[١٢] عن المدلول — كلواحقه[١٣] — وقد[١٤] تكون متقدّمة[١٥] كأسبابه .

---

٩) مقدّمات م .
١٠) (فوق السطر) م .
١١) (وبقية الجملة غامضة ، في الهامش ويمكن ان نقرأ : « وإلى أشياء مح<سوسة> توخذ دلائل على أشياء <أخر في> بادئ الرأي) م .
١٢) الأشياء ب ؛ הדברים ع .
١٣) המותשים (<המוחשים>) ع .

(١٨)

١) هذا م .
٢) إطلاق ب .
٣) فأخذنا ب .
٤) الانه م .
٥) القارج ب ؛ הרק ع .
٦) دلائل م .
٧) منها ب ؛ — ل .
٨) العلامات ب ؛ האותות ع ؛ Signorum ل .
٩) اا ب .
١٠) تيخذ م .
١١) تكن م .
١٢) متأخرًا ب .
١٣) Sicut passiones ل .
١٤) (مكرّرة) م .
١٥) مقدّمة م ؛ متقدّما كليّات ب .

١٩. وكلّ واحد من صنفي المقدّمات – المقبولات والدلائل – قد تكون في المادّة [م ٨٠ ظ] الضروريّة ، والممكنة على الأكثر ، والممكنة على التساوي. أمّا[١] المقبولات التي تكون في المادّة الضروريّة[٢] ، فمثل[٣] أنّ كلّ [٤]مفعول له فاعل[٤]. وأمّا التي[٥] في المادّة الممكنة على الأكثر ، فمثل أنّ كلّ عليل يطيع شهواته ولا يصغي إلى أقوال الأطبّاء فليس يبرأ[٦]. وأمّا التي[٧] في الممكنة على التساوي ، فمثل[٨] أنّ كلّ ما هو أكثر مؤاتاة[٩] وأسهل فهو آثر[١٠]. فإنّ هذا بعينه قد يمكن أن يُحتَجّ[١١] به على أنّ الأمر ليس[١٢] بأثر.

وأمّا الدلائل :

٢٠. أمّا ما كان منها[١] في الشكل الأوّل ، وهو الذي يُخَصّ باسم الدليل في المادّة الضروريّة ، فمثل قولنا : « القمر[٢] ينمو[٣] ضوؤه[٤] قليلاً قليلاً[٥] ، فهو كرّي. » وأمّا ما كان منها في المادّة الممكنة على الأكثر ، فمثل قولنا[٦] : « فلان يجمع الرجال[٧] ، ويعدّ[٨] السلاح[٩] ، ويحصّن[١٠] بلاده[١١] ،

---

(١٩)
١) – م .
٢) الضرورة م .
٣) مثعل م .
٤) Patienti sit agens ل .
٥) الذي ب .
٦) يبرى م ؛ يبرو‌أ ب .
٧) الذي ب .
٨) הנה המשל בו ع .
٩) (مؤاتاة لكنّ « مؤاتاها » في الهامش) م ؛ מוסכם ع .
١٠) اكثر ب .
١١) ينتج م .
١٢) –ل .

(٢٠)
١) – م .
٢) (وترجمت هذه الجملة « القمر ... كرى » بمعنى غير صحيح : Luna auget suum lumen paulatim secundum lunarem figuram ipsa itaque est spherica) ل.
٣) بنمو ب .
٤) ضوة م ؛ صورة ب .
٥) (في الهامش) م .
٦) D.cere ل .
٧) الراجل م .
٨) بعد ب .
٩) חרבות והמייף ع ؛ enses et arma ل .
١٠) يحضر ب .
١١) חומות ארצו ع ؛ moenia suae terrae ل .

وليس قربه[١٢] عدو[١٣] ، فهو إذن مزمع[١٤] أن يعصي[١٥] السلطان . » وهذا كان يُعرَف عند القدماء بالدليل الأشبه[١٦] . وأمّا التي في المادّة[١٧] الممكنة على التساوي ، فمثل قولنا[١٨] : « فلان لم يرم[١٩] عن موضعه ، [٢٠]وقد انهزم أصحابه حتّى أُصيب[٢٠] ، فهو إذن شجاع . » فإنّ هذا أيضاً بعينه قد يستعمل دليلاً على الجبن[٢١] الذي لا يستطيع الإنسان معه [على] الفرار[٢٢] . وهذا الدليل أيضاً كان القدماء[٢٣] يعرفونه بالدليل المشتبه .

وأمّا العلامات :

٢١. أمّا ما كان منها في المادّة الضروريّة في الشكل الثاني فمثل قولنا[١] : « إنّ العصب نبت[٢] من الدماغ لأنّه مغروز فيه . » وأمّا[٣] ما كان منها في المادّة الممكنة الأكثريّة ، فمثل قولنا[٤] : « فلان دلّ[٥] العدو على عورة[٦] البلد لأنّه صعد على السور وتطلّع[٧] إلى[٨] العدو ، [م ٨١ و] والدالّ[٩] على العورة[٩] يفعل هذا . » وأمّا التي من هذه في[١٠] المادّة الممكنة على التساوي ،

---

١٢) ﻟﻐ ع ؛ — ل .
١٣) عدوه م .
١٤) עושה תחבולה ع ؛ utitur versutia ل .
١٥) — ب .
١٦) والأشبه ب .
١٧) (مكرّرة) ب .
١٨) exemplum ل .
١٩) يزم م ؛ ישתדל ع ؛ recessit ل .
٢٠) וכבר הכניע חביהעד שמצאתהו התלאה ع ؛ et superavit suum rivalem et adeo quo successit illi lassitudo ل.
٢١) الحين م ؛ الحبن ب .
٢٢) الفراد م .
٢٣) primi ل .

(٢١)

١) — م ؛ ut dicendo ل .
٢) ينبت م ؛ نبزت ب .
٣) وإنّما م .
٤) dicendo ل .
٥) percussit ل .
٦) العورة هذا م .
٧) (وترجمت بقية هذه الجملة من «وتطلع» الى «هذا» بمعنى غير صحيح : et obviam factus est ei ipse inimicus: significans autem injuriam est hic actus) ل.
٨) على (ولكن « إلى » فوق السطر) م.
٩) عورة (ولكن « على ال » فوق السطر) م .
١٠) — م .

فقوّتها قوة الدلائل التي في هذه المادّة، إذ كانت الكلّيّات فيها قوّتها قوّة الجزئيّات[11]، والجزئيّات[12] تنعكس وترجع إلى الشكل الأوّل، فإذا أُخذت كلّيّة[13]، لم يكن[14] كذبها بأكثر من كذب الجزئيّات[15] ولذلك أسقط القدماء هذا الضرب من العلامات التي في هذه المادّة.

وأمّا الدلائل التي في الشكل الثالث:

٢٢. أمّا ما كان منها في المادّة الضروريّة، فمثل قولنا: «إنّ الزمان هو كرّة الفلك لأنّ الأشياء كلّها في الزمان[1] والأشياء كلّها في[2] كرّة الفلك[3].» وأمّا التي في المادّة الأكثريّة، [4]فمثل قولنا[4]: «الحكماء[5] فاضلون[6] لأنّ سقراط حكيم[7] فاضل[8].» وأمّا التي من هذه في الممكنة على التساوي، فالعلّة في إسقاطها هي العلّة بعينها[9] في إسقاطها في الشكل [ب ٩٠ و] الثاني.

٢٣. وينبغي أن تعلم[1] أنّ هذه القسمة ليست ذاتيّة لمقدّمات الضمائر بما هي مقدّمات ضمائر — أعني قسمتها إلى الضروريّ والممكن. وذلك أنّ مقدّمات الضمائر إنّما تؤخذ من حيث هي مقبولة[2] في بادئ الرأي[3] كما قلنا أو من حيث هي علامات ودلائل في بادئ الرأي[3]، لا من حيث أنّها في مادّة ضروريّة أو ممكنة، لأنّ الأشياء[4] التي تؤخذ المقدّمات فيها بهذه

---

١١) الجز (ولكن يمكن انها كانت «الجزايت» إلاّ أنّ زاوية هذه الصفحة ممزوقة) م ؛ الجزييت ب.
١٢) الجزايت م ؛ الجزييت ب.
١٣) — م.
١٤) يكون م.
١٥) الجزايت م ؛ الجزييت ب.

(٢٢)
١) زمان ب.
٢) — ع، ل.
٣) العالم م.
٤) sicut, exempli gratia
dicere ل.
٥) philosophi ل.
٦) فاضلين ب ؛ studiosi ل.
٧) philosophus ل.
٨) studiosus ل.
٩) ببعينها م.

(٢٣)
١) sciamus ل.
٢) مقولة ب.
٣) — ب.
٤) (غامضة، في الهامش) م ؛ — ب، ع، ل.

الصفة هي المقاييس[٥] البرهانيّة — أعني أنّها التي تأخذ المقدّمات من حيث هي ضروريّة أو ممكنة أكثريّة. وأمّا[٦] الممكنة على التساوي، وهي التي يُظَنّ ‹بها› أنّها أخصّ بهذه الأقاويل [٧]إذ كانت ليست تستعملها[٧] [٨]صناعة برهانيّة، فإنّ هذه الصناعة أيضاً — أعني صناعة الخطابة — ليست تستعملها[٨] من جهة ما هي على التساوي لأنّها لو استعملتها[٩] بهذه الجهة لم يكن[١٠] أن يلزم عنها الشيء أحرى[١١] من[١٢] أن يلزم نقيضه، بل[١٣] إنّما تستعملها[١٤] من حيث يترجّح[١٥] أحدهما ولو أدنى ترجيح[١٦] [م ٨١ ظ] في بادئ الرأي. وذلك إمّا في وقت مّا أو حال مّا. ولمّا جهل هذا المعنى قوم، أنكروا[١٧] أن تستعمل[١٨] هذه[١٩] الصناعة دليلاً في المادّة على[٢٠] التساوي لأنّهم[٢١] زعموا أنّ ما هو على التساوي ليس يقع به إقناع.

٢٤. وهذه الصناعة، كما قيل، ليس لها موضوع خاصّ كما ليس لصناعة[١] الجدل موضوع خاصّ، إذ كانت هاتان[٢] الصناعتان[٣] ليست[٤] تأخذ المقدّمات المستعملة فيها[٥] في النفس على الجهة التي هي عليها خارج النفس، بل إنّما يُحكم[٦] أبداً أنّ المحمول في الموضوع [٧]من أجل الشهرة،

---

٥) المقايس ب.
٦) وإنّما م.
٧) כיהיו ארץ שמושם ع.
٨) (غامضة، في الهامش) م.
٩) استعملها ب.
١٠) يكون م.
١١) احدى م.
١٢) מי״ ع.
١٣) (وترجمت بقية هذه الجملة من «بل» الى «بادئ الرأي» بمعنى غير صحيح: Sed utitur illis ex parte qua cognoscitur unum illorum medica judicii inclinatione in initio opinionis) ل.
١٤) ישתמשו ع.
١٥) تترجح م؛ يترجع ب.
١٦) ترجع ب.
١٧) abjecerunt ل.
١٨) תעשה ع.
١٩) هذا م.
٢٠) عـل ب.
٢١) — ل.

(٢٤)

١) صاعة ب.
٢) هاتين م.
٣) الصناعتين م.
٤) ليس م، ب.
٥) فيها م.
٦) judicant ل.

إمّا في بادئ الرأي وإمّا في الحقيقة ، لا[٧] من أجل أنّ المحمول في طباعه[٨] أن يوجد[٩] للموضوع أو في طباع[١٠] الموضوع أن يوجد[١١] له المحمول . وليس فقط تأخذ[١٢] هذه الصناعة المقدّمات من حيث هي[١٣] شائعة[١٤] في بادئ الرأي من غير أن يُشترَط فيها جهة وجود ، بل قد تأخذ[١٥] الضروريّ على أنّه ممكن بحسب بادئ[١٦] الرأي وكذلك الممكن على أنّه ضروريّ . أمّا أخذ الضروريّ على أنّه ممكن ، فمثل من يتوهّم أن السماء ممكن أن تكون[١٧] بشكل آخر[١٨] وأنّه[١٩] ممكن أن[١٩] يتكوّن كلّ شيء من أيّ شيء اتّفق . وأمّا أن[٢٠] يتخيّل أنّه ممتنع وهو ممكن ، فأشياء كثيرة ليس يعسر وجودها عند[٢١] تأمّل اعتقادات الجمهور فيها ، وإن كان النحو الذي ملنا[٢٢] اليه من التصديق منذ الصباء[٢٣] هو أنّ الأشياء كلّها ممكنة وأنّه لا شيء ههنا ممتنع حتّى أنّه يلزم من قال بذلك ألاّ[٢٤] يكون قوله هذا ضروريّاً[٢٥] ، كما قيل في مناقضة[٢٦] أفلاطون أفراطغوروش[٢٧] حيث قال له أفراطغوروش[٢٧] : « ولا شيء ما مدرك »[٢٨] ، فقال له أفلاطون[٢٩] : « فشيء ما مدرك »[٣٠] ، يعني حكمه بهذا[٣١] الحكم .

---

٧) (غامضة ، في الهامش) م .
٨) صناعة طباعة م .
٩) يوخذ ب .
١٠) طابع م .
١١) يوخذ ب .
١٢) يأخذ ب .
١٣) (غامضة ، فوق السطر) م .
١٤) شابعة ب ؛ מבוארות מתפשטות ع ؛ notae divulgatae ل .
١٥) يأخذ ب .
١٦) في بادئ ب .
١٧) يكون ب .
١٨) أخرا ب .
١٩) — ب .
٢٠) ما م .
٢١) qui vero ل .
٢٢) ميلنا ب .
٢٣) السباب ب .
٢٤) (كل ما يلى من « الا » الى « قيل فى ») — ع .
٢٥) ضروري م .
٢٦) — ب .
٢٧) افراطا عوريش ب ؛ Socrates ل .
٢٨) Scitur ل .
٢٩) أفلطون م .
٣٠) Scitam ل .
٣١) بهذه م .

٢٥. وقد فرغنا ممّا[١] كنّا بسبيله فلنرجع إلى حيث كنّا ، فنقول [٢] انـــه يشبـّه[٢] أن يكون الأمر الذي اضطرّ القدماء إلى تقسيم مقدّمات الضمائر بحسب الموادّ أنـّه [م ٨٢ و] يعرض[٣] للمقدّمات الشائعة[٤] في بادئ الرأي ضعف وقوّة بحسب مادّة مادّة . ولذلك تكون المقدّمات التي في بادئ الرأي إذا عرض لها أن تكون من المادّة الممكنة على الأكثر [ب ٩١ و] أشدّ إقناعاً منها[٥] إذا كانت في[٦] التي على التساوي . فقد تبيّن من هذا القول كم[٧] أصناف الضمائر من جهة الصورة والمادّة .

المثـــال

٢٦. [١]وينبغي أن نقول في المثال[١] . والمثال أصناف : منها أن يُحكَم[٢] على وجود محمول في موضوع أو سلبه عنه من أجل وجود ذلك المحمول في شبيه ذلك الموضوع أو سلبه عنه[٣] ، إذا[٤] كان وجوده في الشبيه أو سلبه عنه أعرف ، مثل قولنا : « السماء مكوّنة لأنّ الحائط مكوّن . » ومنها[٥] أن نحكم[٦] بوجود محمول في موضوع أو سلبه عنه من أجل وجود شبيه ذلك المحمول في ذلك الموضوع أو سلبه عنه ، إذا كان وجود الشبيه أو سلبه أعرف ، مثال ذلك أن نحكم[٦] على السماء أنـّها مستحيلة من أنـّها منتقلة[٧] . ومنهـــا أن نحكم[٨] بوجود محمول لموضوع[٩] أو [١٠] سلبه عنه لوجود شبيه ذلك المحمول[١١] في شبيه

---

(٢٥)

١) عن ما م ؛ عما ب .

٢) ـــ ل .

٣) (مكرّرة) م .

٤) السابقة (فوق السطر) م .

٥) ـــ ب .

٦) ـــ ب ، ع .

٧) quod sunt ل .

(٢٦)

١) (كتبت هذه الجملة كعنوان في كلّ واحدة من المخطوطات إلاّ اللتينية) .

٢) נשפוט ع ، enuntiemus ل .

٣) عنه اعرف م .

٤) اذ م .

٥) منها ب .

٦) يحكم م .

٧) متقلبة ب .

٨) يحكم م .

٩) للموضوع ب .

١٠) (مكرّرة) م .

١١) الموضوع م ، ب ؛ הנושא ع .

ذلك الموضوع[١٢] أو سلبه عنه ، إذا كان وجود شبيه المحمول في شبيه الموضوع أعرف أو كان سلبه عنه أعرف ، مثال ذلك : « العسل مقطّع لأنّ السكّر[١٣] محلّل[١٤] . »

٢٧. وقد يكون الحكم كلّيًّا والشبيه جزئيًّا[١] كقولنا : « الملذّات شرّ لأنّ الخمر شرّ . » والفرق بين هذا وبين الاستقراء أنّ[٢] الاستقراء إنّما صحّحنا فيه الكلّيّ بالجزئيّ[٣] وهنا إنّما صحّحنا الواحد بالآخر من حيث هو[٤] شبيه ، لا من حيث [م ٨٢ ظ] أحدهما [٥]جزئيّ والآخر كلّيّ[٥] .

٢٨. والشبيه صنفان : إمّا شبيه بأمر[١] مشترك وإمّا شبيه في المناسبة . مثال[٢] الشبيه في أمر مشترك ما تقدّم . ومثال الشبيه بالمناسبة قولنا : « الملك في[٣] المدينة كالإله في العالم ، وكما[٤] أنّ الإله واحد ، كذلك ينبغي أن يكون الملك . »

٢٩. فالمثال[١] بالجملة ، كيف ما كان ، ليس فيه حكم بكلّيّ على[٢] جزئيّ[٣] ، لأنّ المتشابهين ليس أحدهما[٤] أعمّ من الآخر ولا يوجدان متشابهين من هذه الجهة . وبيّن ممّا تقدّم في كتاب القياس أنّ القول المنتج بالضرورة

---

١٢) المحمول م ، ب ؛ הנושא ع .
١٣) السوكر م .
١٤) محللى م ؛ محل ب .
(٢٧
١) جزيا م .
٢) لأنّ م ؛ quia ل .
٣) الجزاى ب .
٤) — م .
٥) في الآخر ب ؛ באחר ع ؛ sit in altero ل .
(٢٨
١) (ينقص كل ما يلى من « بأمر » الى « فى امر » ولكن يمكن أنّ هذا قد صُحّح في الهامش إلاّ أنّ زاوية هذه الصفحة ممزوقة) م.
٢) مثل ب ، כדמיון ع .
٣) (فوق السطر) م .
٤) أمّا ب .
(٢٩
١) بالمثال ب .
٢) — م .
٣) جزاى م ؛ جزى ب .
٤) أحدهم ب .

إنّما هو ما يُبيَّن[٥] فيه الجزئيّ[٦] بالكلّيّ . وإذا[٧] كان ذلك كذلك[٨] ، فالمثال ليس يلزم عنه بالضرورة قول آخر اضطرارًا ولا هو منتج بالذات . ومثال ذلك أنّا ، متى حكمنا[٩] على[١٠] السماء أنّها مكوّنة لمشابهتها للأجسام المكوّنة في التحيّز[١١] والتغيّر[١٢] والاتّصال[١٣] وغير ذلك ، فالسماء في هذا القول هي الطرف الأصغر في القياس إذ كانت هي موضوع المطلوب ، والمكوّن[١٤] هو الطرف الأعظم إذ كان هو محمول المطلوب ، والحدّ الأوسط هو التحيّز[١٥] و[١٦] التغيّر[١٧] . فمتى ألّفنا[١٨] القياس[١٩] ، قلنا هكذا : « السماء متحيّزة[٢٠] والمتحيّز[٢١] مكوّن ، فالسماء مكوّنة » .

٣٠. لكنّ[١] قولنا[٢] « إنّ المتحيّز[٣] مكوّن[٤] ليس يكفي فيه أن يؤخذ[٥] مهملاً إن أردنا أن تنطوي[٦] السماء بالضرورة[٧] تحته بل حتّى نأخذه[٨] كلّيًّا ، وهو « إنّ كلّ متحيّز[٩] مكوّن[١٠] » . فإن كانت حصلت هذه الكلّيّة

---

٥) بين ب .
٦) الجزاى م ؛ الجزى ب .
٧) وإذ م .
٨) — ب .
٩) (غامضة) م .
١٠) — ب .
١١) التحييز م ؛ التخير ب ؛ אחיזת מקים ع ؛ solidatem ل .
١٢) ההשתנות ع ؛ equalitatem ل ؛
١٣) الا تصل م ؛ הדבקות ع ؛ contrarietatem ل .
١٤) المدري (أو يمكن أنها «المبرى») ب
١٥) — ب ؛ אחיזת מקום ع ؛ soliditas ل .
١٦) — ب .
١٧) ההשתנות ع ؛ equalitas et caetera ل.
١٨) القينا (وكتبت « ف » فوق القاف) م ؛ الفينا ب .
١٩) القاس م .
٢٠) متحيرة ب ؛ משתנים ع ؛ solidum ل .
٢١) المتحير ب ؛ המשתנה ع ؛ solidum ل .

(٣٠)
١) لاكن ب .
٢) dicenti ل .
٣) المتحيرة ب ؛ המשתנה ع ؛ solidum ل .
٤) متكوّن ب .
٥) sit ل .
٦) ننطوي ب ؛ concludere ل .
٧) فالضرورة ب .
٨) ياخذه ب .
٩) متحيّر ب ؛ משתנה ع ؛ solidum ل .
١٠) متكوّن ب .

عندما تصفّحنا بعض المتحيّزات[١١] [ب ٩٢و] على ما شأنه أن تحصل[١٢] المقدّمات الجزئيّة[١٣] ، فالتصريح[١٤] بالمثال [١٥]في ذلك فضل[١٥] ، إلاّ أن يؤخذ على جهة التفهيم[١٦] والإرشاد لوقوع اليقين[١٧] بالكلّيّة . وإن كان لم يقع لنا [١٨]يقين كلّيّ[١٨] عندما[١٩] أحسسنا[٢٠] بعض المتحيّزات[٢١] [م ٨٣و] متكوّنة[٢٢] وبقيت عندنا هـذه المقدّمة مهملة ، لم[٢٣] يلزم عن إحساسنا[٢٤] ذلك شيء باضطرار ، بل في بادئ الرأي . ومن هنا يظهر أنّ حصول اليقين[٢٥] بالكلّيّة في أمثال هذه المقدّمات ليس[٢٦] عن الحسّ بل عن قوّة أخرى[٢٧] ، إذ كان الحسّ إنّما يدرك منها أشخاصاً محدودة العدد ؛ وأنّ مراتب الظنّ إنّما هي بحسب قربها من هذا الحكم الكلّيّ وبُعدها . والظنّ بالجملة هو القضيّة[٢٨] الكلّيّة[٢٩] من الحسّ فقط .

٣١. ولمّا [١]لم يشعر[١] بهذا[٢] بعض متأخّري المتكلّمين ، وهو الملقّب بأبي المعالي ، قال : « إنّما يفيد المثال اليقين[٣] على جهة الإرشاد [٤]لا على جهة القياس[٤] والتصفّح[٥] فقط . » لكنّ[٦] لـمّا كان لا يقول بالقياس الصحيح

---

١١) المتحيّرات ب ؛ המשתנים ع ؛ solida ل .

١٢) يحصل م .

١٣) التجربيّة م ؛ — ب ؛ expertae ل.

١٤) بيينّة بالتصريح ب ؛ בבאור ع .

١٥) — ع .

١٦) praevii apparatus ل .

١٧) veritatis ل .

١٨) كلّيّ يقين ب ؛ veritatis de universalitate ل.

١٩) (كل ما يلى من « عندما » الى « لم يلزم ») — ل .

٢٠) حسسنا ب .

٢١) المتحيّرات ب ؛ המשתנים ع .

٢٢) متحيزات متكوّنة م .

٢٣) فلم م .

٢٤) احسسنا ب .

٢٥) veritatis ل .

٢٦) أنّه ليس م .

٢٧) أخرا ب .

٢٨) القضايا م ؛ الفصل ب .

٢٩) بالكلّيّة ب .

(٣١)

١) شعر ب ؛ ובעסד ששערו ع ؛ imaginati sunt ل .

٢) بهذا ب .

٣) האמתי ع .

٤) — ب ، ع ، ل .

٥) וההתבוניות והגלוי ع ؛ advertentiae ل .

٦) لاكن ب .

الشكل ، لزمه أن تكون[7] العلوم كلّها أوّليّة فلا يكون هناك معلوم[8] بقياس ، حتّى يكون مثلاً كتاب المجسطي يمكن أن يقرأه من لم ينظر قطّ في شيء من الهندسة ، ويكون حدوث العالم معلوماً بنفسه .

٣٢. فقد تبيّن ما مرتبة المثال في التصديق ، و[1] هو في هذه الصناعة نظير[2] الاستقراء في الجدل ، كما أنّ الضمير[3] ههنا نظير[4] القياس في الجدل .

⟨المقنعات التي ليست بأقاويل⟩

٣٣. وقد ينبغي بعد هذا أن نصير إلى القول [1] في المقنعات[1] التي ليست بأقاويل وفي مقدار ما تعطيه[2] من التصديق . وهذه المقنعات هي في الجملة[3] ثلاثة عشر جنساً :

⟨١⟩ منها فضيلة القائل ونقيصة[4] خصمه[5] فإنّه من البيّن أنّها تكسب[6] الإنسان حسن ظنّ به وقبول لما يقوله[7] .

⟨٢⟩ ومنها استدراج[8] السامعين[9] بالانفعالات[10] نحو[11] التصديق ، مثل[12] أن يمكّن في نفس السامع انفعالات[13] فيوجب تصديقه

---

٧) يكون ب .
٨) aliquod quod doceatur ل.
(٣٢)
١) (مكرّرة) م .
٢) simile et conforme ل .
٣) الظمير م ؛ שההסתר ع .
٤) simile et conforme ل .
(٣٣)
١) مقنعات (و « في ال » فوق السطر) م .
٢) يعطيه م .
٣) فالجملة م .
٤) نقيضه ب .
٥) حصمه ب .
٦) يكسب ب .
٧) بقواله ب .
٨) praevius apparatus ل .
٩) السامغير ب .
١٠) affectum ل .
١١) (كل ما يلي من « نحو » الى « فيوجب » في الهامش) م .
١٢) (كل ما يلي من«مثل»الى«تصديقه») مثل أن يمكن في يقين انفعلات يوجب تصديقه ب ؛ כמו השומע הפעולות יחוייב האמנתו ع ؛ Prout possible est in verificatione audientis affectus, cogens eius verificationem ل.
١٣) انفعالا م .

من عصبيّة[١٤] أو رحمة[١٥] أو خوف أو غضب. وهذا[١٦] [م ٨٣ ظ] أيضاً ظاهر أنّه يميّل[١٧] الإنسان الى التصديق.

⟨٣⟩ ومنها ما يميّل السامعين[١٨] بالأقاويل الخلقيّة[١٩]، وذلك بأن يخيّل[٢٠] لهم أنّ قولهم إنّما يقبله الأزكياء[٢١] و[٢٢]أهل الفطر الفائقة[٢٢] ومَن[٢٣] لم يتدنّس[٢٤] برأي فاسد ولا كان مقلّداً[٢٥]، [٢٦]كما يفعل جالينوس[٢٦].

⟨٤⟩ ومنها تعظيم[٢٧] الأمر الذي فيه القول وتصغيره[٢٨]، فأنّ[٢٩] القول، متى عُظِّم[٣٠]، كانت النفس أميَل[٣١] إليه. وبالضدّ، متى[٣٢] خُسِّس[٣٣]، نفرت[٣٤] عنه النفس ولم يقع لها إليه ميْل.

⟨٥⟩ [٣٥]ومنها الإجماع[٣٥].

⟨٦⟩ ومنها الشهادات[٣٦].

⟨٧⟩ ومنها الترغيب[٣٧] والترهيب[٣٨].

⟨٨⟩ ومنها التحدّي[٣٩] والمراهنة[٤٠].

---

١٤) عصيانه م ؛ عصبيه ب ؛ מדוהר ع ؛ dolore ل .
١٥) رحمه ب ؛ מקרובר ع .
١٦) هذه ب .
١٧) declinare faciat ل .
١٨) السامغير ب .
١٩) بالخلقية م ؛ الخليقية ب .
٢٠) يخل ب .
٢١) الأذكية م ؛ الأزكي ب ؛ החשובים ع ؛ proclari intellecto ل .
٢٢) أهل الفطن الفائقة ب ؛ אנשי היצירה המשובה ع ؛ viri nobilis educationis ل.
٢٣) متى ب .
٢٤) הדגיל ع ؛ utitur ل .
٢٥) חגור ع ؛ perversus ل .
٢٦) — ب ، ع ، ل .
٢٧) הגדלה ع .
٢٨) purificatio ل .
٢٩) بان ب .
٣٠) גדל ع .
٣١) declivis ل .
٣٢) (فوق السطر) م .
٣٣) خخسس م ؛ — ع .
٣٤) بقرت ب .
٣٥) الاجماع م ؛ — ب ؛ וממנו הקבוץ ع ؛ et de illis sunt conciones ل .
٣٦) المشاهدات ب .
٣٧) הרעב ع ؛ supplicatio ل .
٣٨) — ب ، ع ، ل .
٣٩) النحدي ب ؛ הייחוד במדברות ع ؛ fideiussio ل .
٤٠) וסבול התלאות (ويمكن ان تكون هذه العبارة ترجمة للكلمة «الترهيب» التي سلفت) ع ؛ pignoratio ل.

〈 ٩ 〉 [٤١]ومنها الأيمان[٤١] .

〈 ١٠ 〉 ومنها أن تكون[٤٢] كيفيّة القول والصوت والنغمة[٤٣] بحال[٤٤] تخيّل[٤٥] وجود الأمر الذي يروم إثباته ، مثل مَن[٤٦] يخبر عن أمر مخوف وقد أصفر[٤٧] وجهه[٤٨] وعلا[٤٩] صوته .

〈 ١١ 〉 ومنها [٥٠]تحريف الأقاويل[٥٠] وإسقاط كثير منها وتصييرها بصورة ما تظهر[٥١] شنعته وتسهل معاندته ، وهذه في السفسطة أدخل منها في الخطابة .

فهذه جميع [ب ٩٣ و] المقنعات التي من خارج .

٣٤. وهو بيّن من أوّل[١] الأمر في كثير منها أنّها إنّما تفيد[٢] إقناعاً فقط[٣] ، وفي بعضها قد يخفى ذلك بعض خفاء . ونحن نقول في هذه .

〈الشهادة〉

٣٥. ومن[١] أقواها مرتبة هو[٢] الشهادة . والشهادة بالجملة هي خبر ما . والخبر ، إمّا أن يكون المخبرون به واحداً[٣] أو أكثر من واحد ، والأكثر من

---

٤١) — ب ، ع ؛ Et de illis est solitude in eremo et tollerantio laborum et vita monastica ل .

٤٢) يكون ب .

٤٣) التغمة (ويمكن أنّها « التجمة ») ب .

٤٤) بحل ب .

٤٥) يحيل ب .

٤٦) ان ب .

٤٧) pallescit et erubescit ل .

٤٨) وجهة م ، ب .

٤٩) على م .

٥٠) depravatio sermonum et ipsorum declinatio ل .

٥١) يظهر ب ؛ לא יראר ع ؛ detegat ل :

(٣٤)

١) اويل م .

٢) يفيد ب .

٣) يفقط ب .

(٣٥)

١) (هــذه الجملة من « ومن » الى «الشهادة» غير صحيحة فى الترجمات) ומהיותר הזק מדרגה מהם ענין העדות ع ؛ vehementiore gradu istorum, qui est ipsa attestatio ل .

٢) معنى ب .

٣) واحد م .

واحد قد يكون[4] جماعة[5] يمكن حصرهم وقد يكون[6] جماعة لا يمكن حصرهم . والأشياء المخبَر عنها إمّا محسوسة وإمّا معقولة . والمخبرون عن الأشياء المحسوسة إمّا[7] أن يكونوا هم الذين أحسّوها[8] [م ٨٤و] وإمّا[9] أن يكونوا مخبرين عن آخر⟨ين⟩ مثلهم أو أقلّ او أكثر . والأشياء المحسوسة المخبر عنها إمّا أن تكون[10] أمورًا ماضيةً[11] لم نحسّ نحن بها وإمّا أن تكون في الزمان الحاضر لكن[12] تكون[13] غائبة[14] عنّا[15] .

٣٦. وأمّا الأشياء التي أحسسناها ، فلا غناء[1] للأخبار فيها ولا فائدة . وكذلك يشبه [2]أن يكون[2] الأمر في المعقولات عند أهل[3] الصنائع الذين شأنهم أن يُستنبَط في صناعتهم تلك المعقولات . وأمّا عند الجمهور فقد يمكن أن تفعل الشهادة فيها إقناعاً . ولهذه العلّة تجد[4] الطائفة التي تُعرَف بالمتكلّمين من أهل ملّتنا لم يقتصروا في[5] معرفة حدوث العالم ووجود البارئ وغير ذلك على [6]شهادة الشارع[6] فقط بل استعملوا في معرفة ذلك المقاييس . وأمّا الطائفة[7] التي تُعرَف بالحشويّة[8]، فرفضوا[9] ذلك .

---

٤) تكون م .
٥) universitas ل .
٦) يكونون ب .
٧) (وترجمة كل ما يلى من « اما » الى « عن آخرين » غير صحيحة). aut narrant illas quas viderint, aut narrant quae audiverint ab aliis ل .
٨) احشواها ب .
٩) (مكررة) م .
١٠) يكون ب .
١١) مضية ب .
١٢) لاكن ب .
١٣) يكون ب .
١٤) غايته م ، ب ؛ lateant ل .
١٥) غما م .

(٣٦)

١) ימפיק ع ؛ immorandum ل.
٢) — م .
٣) اقل م .
٤) نجد م ؛ invenimus ل .
٥) من م .
٦) עדות התורה ع ؛ radicibus legis super attestione legis ل .
٧) الطابقة ب .
٨) אלחשריה ع ؛ secta autem, quae Deum cognoscit ل .
٩) افرضوا م .

٣٧. [١]والشهادات والأخبار[١] عن الأمور المحسوسة التي[٢] لم تشاهــد[٣] يقوى[٤] التصديق بها ويضعف بحسب عدد[٥] المخبرين وغير ذلك من القرائن التي تقترن[٦] لهم. فأقوى التصديقات[٧] الحاصلة [٨]عن الأخبار[٨] ما أخبرت به جماعة لا[٩] يمكن حصرهم أنّهم أحسّوه [١٠]أو ما[١٠] أخبرت به جماعة[١١] عن جماعة أخرى[١٢] لا يمكن حصرها أنّهم أحسّوه. وكذلك [١٣]ما زادت الجماعة على واحد فصاعداً بالغاً ما بلغت[١٣] إذا استوا[١٤] أوّلها ووسطها وآخرها في أنّهم لا يمكن حصرهم [١٥]أو يعسر[١٥]. وهذا الصنف من الأخبار هو الذي يسمّى المتواتر[١٦].

٣٨. وهذا قد يحصل[١] به اليقين [٢]في أمور ما[٢] كبعث النبيّ[٣] ووجــود [م ٨٤ ظ] مكّة[٤] والمدينة[٥] وغير ذلك. وقد ينبغي أن ننظر على أيّ جهة

(٣٧)

١) והעדות והספור ع ؛ in narratione autem et attestione ل .

٢) — ل .

٣) نشاهد م؛ يشاهد ب؛ נראה ع ؛ videmus ل .

٤) يقوم ب ؛ quod fortificetur ل .

٥) عند ب ؛ כפי ع .

٦) يقترن م .

٧) fidei sunt quae ل .

٨) — ع .

٩) لم ب .

١٠) إنّما ب .

١١) جماعة لا يمكن حصرها م ؛ جماعة حصرها ب ؛ קהל רב עד כי חזל לספור ع ؛ innumerabilis universitas ل .

١٢) اخرا ب .

١٣) כלמה שנוסף הכליל הנה תהיה הפלגה מה שהפליגו ع ؛ quando excedit una universitas aliam, et magis sunt adepti excellentium illius, quod attingerunt ل .

١٤) استور م ؛ הסכימו ع .

١٥) — م ؛ aut difficile foret illos confundere ل .

١٦) المتواثم ب ؛ התורה ع ؛ rora in scriptura sacra ل .

(٣٨)

١) يأصل م .

٢) aliquo modo ل .

٣) محمد ب ؛ משה הנביא עליו השלום ع ؛ Moses principis prophetarum, supra ipsum sit pax ل .

٤) — م ، ب ؛ סיני ع ؛ Sinai ل .

٥) חורב ع ؛ Horeb ل .

يحصل ذلك ؛ فإنّ الصادق منه بالذات ومنه بالعرض . وهو بيّن أنّ التصديق بوجود [6] الأمور المحسوسة[6] إنّما تحصل أوّلا[7] بالذات عن[8] الحسّ . ولذلك من فقد[9] حاسّة ما فقد[10] محسوساً ما . وليس ‹التصديق ب›وجود المحسوسات يحصل بالذات فقط عن الحسّ بل وتخيّلها[11] أيضاً على ما هي عليه . وقد يحصل اليقين أيضاً بوجود المحسوسات بالذات عن القياس ؛ [12]مثال ذلك[12] أنّ هذا حائط مبنيّ ، فله بانٍ[13] ، إلاّ انّه لا يحصل عنه صورة البـاني الخاصّ بالذات .

٣٩. وأمّا الأمور المحسوسة التي لم تُحَسّ قطّ ولا [ب ٩٤و] كان لنا سبيل إلى إدراك وجودها بقياس ، فإنّه[1] قد يحصل اليقين بوجودها لكن[2] على الأقلّ كما أنّه قد يحصل لنا تصوّرها على ما هي[3] عليه على[4] الأقلّ . لكنّ أمثال هذه وإن لم تمرّ[5] بالحسّ أشخاصها فلا بدّ أن تمرّ[6] به أسماؤها أو ما يدلّ عليها[7] . وفاعل هذا التصديق عند الأكثر من الناس هو[8] عـن التواتر[9] والأخبار[10] المستفيضة[11] . لكن من البيّن أنّ ذلك فعل لها بالعرض

---

٦) העניין המוחש ع ؛ rem sensatam ل .
٧) ولا ب ؛ תחלה יגיעת מה ع .
٨) (ينقص كل ما يلى من «عن الحس» الى « يحصل بالذات » ولكن « ‹م›حسوسات ... ذات » في الهامش وزاوية هـذه الصفحة ممزوقة) م .
٩) שנפקד ממנו ع .
١٠) הנה נפקד ממנו ع .
١١) يحيلها ب ؛ per imaginationem ل .
١٢) مثل م .
١٣) بانى م .
(٣٩)
١) — ع ، ل .
٢) — م ؛ لاكن ب .
٣) هرا (أو يمكن أنّها ترا) م؛ بني ب ؛ שהוא נבנה ع ؛ fabricatum ل .
٤) — ب .
٥) يمر (والكلمة التي فوق السطر غامضة)م؛ تمرا ب؛ penetret ل.
٦) تمو م ؛ يمر ب ؛ penetrat ل .
٧) عليه ب .
٨) (غامضة) م .
٩) التراتر ب ؛ התורות ع ؛ legibus ل .
١٠) الا خبر م؛ הספורים ع ؛ historiis ل .
١١) — ب ، ع ، ل .

لأنّ الصدق فيها يتبع ما يُظَنّ أنّه سبب له وهو[١٢] الأخبار[١٣] على الأقل على[١٤] جهة ما تتبع[١٥] المسبّبات [١٦]أسبابها العرضيّة[١٦] .

٤٠. وأمّا السبب في حصول هذا اليقين[١] الذي بالعرض وكيف يحصل[٢] فليس ممّا يلزم الوقوف عليه في[٣] هذا العلم ، فقد قيل في كتاب الحسّ[٤] والمحسوس . ولمّا[٥] شعر بهذا[٦] قوم، راموا أن يشترطوا في الأخبار[٧] عدداً يحصل عنه اليقين بالذات . فلمّا[٨] لم يتحصّل لهم ، قالوا : « إنّه محصّل في نفسه ، وإن لم يكن[٩] عندنا . » وهذه مغالطة بيّنة ، فإنّه لو كان ههنا[١٠] عدد ما [م ٨٥ و] بالذات[١١] يحصل عنه اليقين[١٢] لم تتفاضل[١٣] الأشياء المتواترة[١٤] في عدد[١٥] المخبرين ، ولكان[١٦] هذا العدد ممكن أن يُحَسّ ويوقف[١٧] عليه ، بل الكثرة والقلّة قريبة من القرائن . ولذلك لمّا رام[١٨] بعضهم أن يشترط

---

١٢) (مكرّرة) م .
١٣) ההגדה ع ؛ historia ل .
١٤) لا على ب ؛ לא על ع .
١٥) يتبع ب .
١٦) סבתם המקרית ع ؛ suam causam accidentalem ل .

(٤٠)

١) (غامضة) م .
٢) גיניע הנה ع .
٣) من ب ؛ מן ع .
٤) بالحسّ ب .
٥) ובעבור ع .
٦) بهاذا ب .
٧) הגדה ع ؛ historia ل .
٨) ولمّا ب ؛ וכאשר ع .
٩) يكون م .
١٠) ما بينا ب ؛ מה שבארנו ع ؛ si esset aliquis numerus ل .
١١) بال (مكرّرة) م ؛ — ل .
١٢) veritas essentialiter ل .
١٣) يتفاضل ب ؛ יהיה מעלת ع ؛ se excederunt ل .
١٤) المتساترة ب ؛ התוריים ع ؛ res divulgate ل .
١٥) عند ب .
١٦) (ترجمت هذه الجملة من « ولكان » الى « القرائن » بمعنى غير صحيح : Et possibile esset quod hic numerus esset proportionatus et constaret multitudo veri et paucitas sunt compositae ex combinationibus) ل .
١٧) — ع .
١٨) رسم م ؛ שהשתדלו ع ؛ innituntur ل .

في التواتر[١٩] شروطاً يحصل عنها اليقين[٢٠] فلم[٢١] يتحصّل[٢٢] لهم[٢٣] ، قالوا : « و[٢٤] من شروطه[٢٥] أن يحصل عنه اليقين[٢٦] . » وإذا[٢٧] كان ذلك ، فليس[٢٨] فيها شرط أصلاً يشترط[٢٩] ولا جهة يحصل عنها اليقين بالذات . وهذه الصناعة إنّما تستعمل الأخبار[٣٠] والشهادات من جهة ما [٣١]يؤخذ عنها[٣١] [٣٢]أكثريّا ، وهو الظنّ . فإنّما[٣٢] يؤخذ[٣٣] على الأقلّ لشيء ما لا تستعمله[٣٤] صناعة أصلاً .

〈السنن المكتوبة〉

٤١. وأمّا الاستشهاد بالسنن[١] المكتوبة فالأمر أيضاً[٢] في ذلك واضح ، لكن[٣] [٤]ما يحصل من التصديق بها من أجل النشء عليها[٤] والاعتياد[٥] قويّ جدّاً[٦] . ولذلك ترى[٧] كثيراً[٧] ممن[٨] ينشأ[٩] في السير[١٠] الجاهلية يعتقدون[١١] خرافات لا [١٢]نقدر نصرفهم[١٢] عنها .

---

١٩) תורות ع ؛ legibus ل .
٢٠) veritas quae non sint necessariae ل .
٢١) — ل .
٢٢) ينحصر م ؛ يتحصر ب ؛ — ل .
٢٣) — م ، ل .
٢٤) — م .
٢٥) (غامضة) م ، شروطهم ب ؛ תנאיהם ع .
٢٦) veritas essentialiter ل .
٢٧) (هذه الجملة كلها من « واذا » الى « بالذات ») — ل .
٢٨) (فوق السطر) م .
٢٩) تشترط ب .
٣٠) ההגדה ع ؛ historia ل .
٣١) يوجد فيها (فوق السطر) م .
٣٢) — ع .
٣٣) يوجد (فوق السطر) م .
٣٤) يستعمله ب .

(٤١)

١) — ب ؛ Statuorum ل .
٢) — ع ، ل .
٣) لاكن ب .
٤) quo evenit de illis verificatio, est ipsorum consuetus usus ل .
٥) الاعتاد (وفوق السطر « ق » : يعني الاعتقاد) م .
٦) سدا ب .
٧) يرا م ؛ ترا ب .
٨) مما م ؛ מי ع .
٩) يتسمى ب .
١٠) السيار م ؛ السبار ب ؛ מנהג ع ؛ consuetudine ل .
١١) تعتقدون ب .
١٢) تقدر أن تصرفهم ب ؛ יהיו נושעים בעבורם ع .

⟨الإجماع⟩

٤٢. وأمّا[١] الإجماع[٢] الذي هو اتّفاق[٣] أهل الملّة وتواطؤهم[٤] على أمر في الملّة فستنده أيضاً في الإقناع شهادة الشرع لهم بالعصمة . ولـمّا[٥] شعر قوم بهذا ، قالوا : « إنّ خارق[٦] الإجماع[٧] ليس[٨] بكافر[٩] . » [١٠]وأبو حامد[١٠] قد صرّح بهذا المعنى في الإجماع في أوّل كتابه[١١] الملقّب بالتفرقة[١٢] بين[١٣] الاسلام[١٤] والزندقة[١٥] . قال[١٦] : « إنّه[١٧] لم يُجمَع بعدُ[١٨] على ما هو الإجماع . »

---

(٤٢)

١) (ترجمت هذه الجملة كلها من «واما» الى « بالعصمة » بمعنى غير صحيح : Convenimus etiam persuasioni attestionis legis, decori, et conventioni virorum legalium de aliqua re ipsius legis) ل .

٢) הקבוץ ع .

٣) اتفق م ؛ اتقاق ب .

٤) تواطيهم م ؛ تواطى بهم ب ؛ שהאמינו ع .

٥) ובעבור ש.. ع .

٦) حارن ب ؛ שמשכילו ع .

٧) הקהל ع .

٨) (كل ما يلى من «ليس» الى «الاجماع» في الهامش) م ؛ (وفي ع « الإجماع » مترجمة بكلمة הקבוץ كما في الحاشية رقم ٢) ع .

٩) يكافر ب ؛ יכפור ع .

١٠) ابن حمد م ؛ ابو حمد ب ؛ אבו חמד ع ؛ Abulhamadh autem Algazel ل .

١١) ספר ع .

١٢) في التفرقة ب .

١٣) بن م .

١٤) اسلام م ؛ הישמעאלים ع ؛ Mauros ل .

١٥) الريدقة ب ؛ ואלזנדקה ع ؛ Amazonides ل .

١٦) (هذه الجملة كلها من « قال » الى « الاجماع » في الهامش وبعد هذه الجملة في النص ولكن بين هلالين : « وذلك أنّ المتكلـّمين قد اختلفوا في الشروط التي يقع بها نحــو الإقناع ») م ؛ (وفي ع «الإجماع» مترجمة بكلمة ההסכמה وينبغي أن تكون بعكس הקבוץ أو הקהל كما سنف) .

١٧) أنـّها م .

١٨) — ع .

〈التحدي〉

٤٣. وأمّا التحدّي[١]، فقد يكون بأشياء[٢]. إلاّ أنّ أقنعه التحدّي[٣] الذي يكون بالمعجز[٤] الخارق[٥] للعوائد[٦]، وهي الأمور التي تُرى[٧] أنّها ممتنعة على البشر. لكن[٨] من البيّن أنّه، وإن كان الفعل[٩] في[١٠] نهاية الغرابة[١١]، فإنّه [م ٨٥ ظ] لا يفيد شيئاً غير حسن الظنّ بفاعله[١٢] والثقة به وفضيلته، إذا كان الأمر إلاهيّاً[١٣]. وقد صرّح أبو حامد[١٤] في كتابه[١٥] [١٦]الملقّب بالقسطاس بهذا[١٦] وقال: «الإيمان بالرسل[١٧] بطريق المعجز[١٨] على ما رسمه[١٩] المتكلّمون[٢٠] هو طريق جمهوريّ، وإنّ طريق الخواصّ هو غير [ب ٩٥ و] هذا.»

٤٤. فهذه التي عدّدناها[١] من الأمور الخارجة هي[٢] التي يُظَنّ بها أنها يحصل[٣] عنها يقين[٤]. [٥]وأمّا سائر ذلك، فبيّن بنفسه إقناعه[٥]. وإنّما كانت الضمائر[٦] أشرف من هذه وأشدّ تقدّماً لأنّها قد تستعمل في إثبات ما

---

(٤٣)

١) הייחוד ع ؛ contentiones ل.

٢) in differentiis verborum ل.

٣) הייחוד ع ؛ contentiones ل.

٤) المحجز ب ؛ בכל זה ع ؛ de lasso ل.

٥) יעורר ع ؛ scindente ل.

٦) התשובות ع ؛ promisiones legis ل.

٧) يرا ب.

٨) لاكن ب.

٩) agens ل.

١٠) — م.

١١) العزابة ب ؛ המתינות ع ؛ maxime enormis ل.

١٢) בפעולתו ع.

١٣) الاهية ب.

١٤) אבו חמד ع ؛ Abuhamadh Algazel ل.

١٥) ספר ع.

١٦) inscripta circa haec ل.

١٧) simpliciter ل.

١٨) المحجز ب ؛ הפלאה ع ؛ lassi ل.

١٩) رسموه م.

٢٠) المتكلّمين م ؛ המדברים ع ؛ loquentes ل.

(٤٤)

١) عدّدنها م.

٢) معنى ب.

٣) محصل م.

٤) אמת ع ؛ veritas ل :

٥) Rhetorica autem residui huius est nota ل.

٦) הסמנים ع ؛ signa ل.

كان من هذه [٧]غير بيّنة الوجود[٧] أو [٨]غير بيّنة الإقناع[٨]. مثال ذلك أنّه، متى لم تكن[٩] فضيلة[١٠] القائل[١١] بيّنة ولا مشهورة، استُعملت[١٢] في تبيين ذلك؛ وكذلك[١٣] متى ظنّ ظانّ بالذي[١٤] زعم[١٥] أنّه معجز[١٦] أنّه ليس بمعجز[١٦]، أستُعملت[١٧] معـه في بيان ذلك أنّه معجز[١٨]. وكذلك في الشهادات[١٩] وفي السنن[٢٠] وغيرها متى [٢١]نازع فيها الخصم[٢١]. وجميع هذه الأشياء المقنعة، سواء[٢٢] كانت أقاويل أو أموراً[٢٣] خارجة، قـد يمكن أن تُستَعمل[٢٤] في جميع الصنائع الفكريّة على طريق[٢٥] ما كان يستعملها[٢٦] من سلف من القدماء، لأنـّهم كانوا يظنّون بها أنـّها طرق[٢٧] اليقين[٢٨].

〈الانتهاء〉

٤٥. وأمّا أرسطو، فلـمّا[١] تبيّنت له مرتبتها[٢] في التصديق[٣] و[٤] رأى[٥] أنّ غناء[٦] هذه التصديقات إنّما هي في[٧] استعمال الجمهور اياها[٨] بينهم في

---

٧) ignotis esse ل.

٨) غير بيّنة الاقنع م؛ ignotum esse ل.

٩) تكون م؛ يكون ب.

١٠) חשיבות ع؛ prestantia ل.

١١) loquentis ل.

١٢) ישתמשו ع.

١٣) ו זה ع.

١٤) فالذي م.

١٥) שחשב ع.

١٦) נלאה ع.

١٧) ישתמשו ع.

١٨) נלאה ع.

١٩) شهادات ب.

٢٠) דינים ع؛ judiciis ل.

٢١) יקרה בהם חזיכות ع؛ accidit disputatio de illis ل.

٢٢) (كل مـا يلي من «سواء» الى «خارجة») — ل.

٢٣) أمور م.

٢٤) يستعمل م، ب.

٢٥) — ب، ع، ل.

٢٦) שישתמשו בהם ع؛ usi sunt ل.

٢٧) طريق ب؛ דרך ع؛ via ل.

٢٨) האמת ع؛ veritatis ل.

(٤٥)

١) הנה בעבור ש.. ع؛ ex quo ل.

٢) مرتبها م؛ מדרגתם ع.

٣) veritate ل.

٤) — ل.

٥) را ب.

٦) عناء م؛ שצרך ع؛ opportunitas ل.

٧) — ع.

٨) אותם בדברים ع.

الأشياء الجزئيّة[٩] الإراديّة التي[١٠] يحكم بها الحكّام[١١] أنّها خيرات[١٢] أو شرور ، ولمّا كانت الأشياء الإراديّة التي يحكم بها الحكّام[١٣] أنّها خيرات أو شرور ‹ ١ › منها ما يوجد للإنسان في ذاته وفي[١٤] الزمان الحاضر وتلك هي الفضائل والرذائل[١٥] ، — ‹ ٢ › ومنها ما يوجد في الزمان الحاضر في غيره وذلك هو الجور[١٦] والعدل[١٧] ، — ‹ ٣ › ومنها ما يوجد[١٨] له في المستقبل و[١٩] تلك هي الأمور النافعة والضارّة — أمّا الأولى[٢٠] فتسمّى[٢١] المخاطبة[٢٢] المنافريّة[٢٣] ، وأمّا[٢٤] [م ٨٦ و] الثانيّة[٢٥] فتسمّى المشاجرة[٢٦] ، وأمّا الثالثة فتسمّى المشاوريّة[٢٧] — وكان الإنسان[٢٨] من طريق ما هو[٢٨] مشارك ومدنيّ[٢٩] بالضرورة[٣٠] ما يستعمل[٣٠] الأقاويل[٣١] الخط‹ا›بيّة في هـذه الأجناس الثلاثة ، شرع[٣٢] أرسطو في إعطاء[٣٣] القوانين[٣٤] و[٣٥] الأشياء التي بها يمكن الإنسان أن يقنع[٣٦] في شيء شيء من هذه[٣٧] على أتمّ ما يمكن في ذلك الشيء . ولذلك ما حدّ هذه[٣٧] الصناعة ، بأنّها سبيل يقدر[٣٨] الإنسان[٣٩]

---

٩) الجزاية م . ل .

١٠) ألذي م .

١١) המשפט ع ؛ judicium ل .

١٢) (كل ما يلى من « خيرات » الى « انها خيرات ») — م .

١٣) המשפט ع ؛ decernit ل .

١٤) (كل ما يلى من « وفي » الى « ما يوجد ») — م .

١٥) והפחתיות ع .

١٦) היושר ع ؛ equitas ل.

١٧) והעול ع ؛ et iniquitas ل .

١٨) توجد م .

١٩) ف ب .

٢٠) الأوّل م .

٢١) فيسمّى م .

٢٢) הגדה ع .

٢٣) המרחקת ع ؛ demonstrativa

٢٤) وأمّا منافريّة وأمّا م .

٢٥) الثناية ب .

٢٦) הסודיות ع ؛ judicialis ل .

٢٧) المشورية ب ؛ העצות ع .

٢٨) quomodo ل .

٢٩) החמרי ع .

٣٠) Quod autem fiant ل .

٣١) الاقايل ب .

٣٢) באר ع ؛ exposuit ل .

٣٣) tradendo ل .

٣٤) הסדרים ع .

٣٥) في ب .

٣٦) تقنع م ؛ שיליץ האדם ع .

٣٧) — م .

٣٨) بقدر ب .

٣٩) האנושות ع .

بها أن يفعل الإقناع[٤٠] في شيء شيء من الأمور الجزئيّة[٤١] على أتمّ ما يمكن في ذلك الشيء بحسب صناعة[٤٢].

٤٦. والذي قلناه بحسب غرضنا [١]في هذا[١] كافٍ[٢].

[١]وتمّ جميع كتاب الخطابة والحمد لله تعالى[١].

---

٤٠) الأقنع م.

٤١) الجزاية م.

٤٢) טבעך ع؛ suam naturam ل:

٤٦)

١) — ع.

٢) كافي م.

خاتمة

١) (تعالى كتبت «تعلى») م؛ — ب، ع، ل؛

جوامع كتاب الشعر

لأبي الوليد محمد بن احمد بن رشد

[١]بسم الله الرحمن الرحيم[١] [٢]والحمد لله ربّ العالمين[٢]

[٣]في الأقاويل الشعريّة[٣]

١. وأمّا[١] الأقاويل الشعريّة، فهي أقاويل موزونة يُلتمَس[٢] بها تخييل[٣] الشيء بالقول وتمثيله إمّا لتحريك[٤] النفس[٥] [٦]نحو الهرب عن الشيء[٦] أو [ب ٩٦ و] الإيثار له أو الغرابة[٧] فقط للإلتذاذ[٨] الذي في التخييل. وإنّما جُعلت موزونة لأنّ بذلك تكون[٩] أتمّ تخييلاً[١٠]. وكما أنّ ما[١١] تخيّل كثير[١٢] من الصناعات من الأمور المحسوسة كصناعة الزواقة[١٣] وغيرها ليست هي في الحقيقة الأمور [م ٨٦ ظ] [١٤]المحسوسة، كذلك الأقاويل[١٤] التي تخيّل الشيء ليست هي الأقاويل التي[١٥] تفهّم[١٦] ذاته.

العنوان :

١) — ل .

٢) وبه استعين وعليه أتوكل ب ؛ ובו לבדו אשעין ״ ع ؛ — ل .

٣) במאמרים ה<שיר>יים ع .

(١)

١) ואלו ع .

٢) التمس (هكذا في النصّ الذي حقّقه فوستو لاسينيو ، راجع التمهيد ص ١ ، وسوف نذكر هذا النصّ بالرمز « فل » بعد هذا).

٣) تخيل م ، فل.

٤) بتحريك ب ؛ בתכועת ع .

٥) الشيء ب ؛ הדבר ع ؛ rem ل.

٦) aut fugens enormitatem ل .

٧) القرايـة م ؛ القرابة فل ؛ ההתקרבות ع .

٨) للالذاذ م ، ب ؛ للا لذات فل؛ ללא ערבות ع .

٩) يكون م .

١٠) تخيلا م .

١١) من ب .

١٢) in maiore parte ل .

١٣) המשקולות ع ؛ picturae ل .

١٤) ال م .

١٥) (« التي تفهم ذاته ») — م .

١٦) يفهم بها فل ؛ intelligitur ل .

٢. والخيالات[١] صنفان[٢] ، إمّا صنف يشبَّه[٣] فيه[٤] شيء[٥] بشيء[٦] بأحد حروف التشبيه ، [٧]وإمّا خيال[٧] يؤخذ[٨] على أنّه نفس[٩] المتخيَّل[١٠] وذلك على جهة التبديل والاستعارة كقولنا[١١] : « هو[١٢] البحر من أى النواحى اتيته » ؛ وهذه الخيالات[١٣] منها قريبة ومنها بعيدة . وهو بيّن أنّ هذه الصناعة ليس تأخذ[١٤] خيالات الشيء[١٥] على أنّه الشيء بعينه . لكن قد يغلط[١٦] كثير من الناس في ذلك فيأخذون[١٧] خيال الشيء [١٨]على أنّه الشيء[١٨] بعينه[١٩] مثل قول ابن[٢٠] دقليس في[٢١] ماء البحر أنّه عرق[٢٢] الأرض اجتمع في مثانتها . وإنّما يُغلَط في هذه الخيالات إذا أُخذت[٢٣] على جهة التبديل ولم يؤتَ[٢٤] فيه[٢٥] بحرف[٢٦] التشبيه[٢٧] . وأكثر[٢٨] ما تغلط[٢٩] هذه الخيالات[٣٠] في الأشياء التي لا يمكن أن تُتصوَّر[٣١] إلاّ[٣٢] بخيالاتها[٣٣] أو

---

(٢) ١) — م ؛ فالخيالات فل .
٢) שני מינים ع ؛ duae species ل.
٣) ידמה ع ؛ assimilat ل .
٤) (كل ما يلى من «فيه» الى «التشبيه») تشبيه م ؛ res alicui rei per una dictionarum assimilationis ل .
٥) الشيء فل ؛ הדבר ع .
٦) بالشيء فل ؛ הדבר ع .
٧) aut simulacrarum sumptuarum ل .
٨) توخذ ب ؛ — ل .
٩) ذات فل ؛ עצם ع ؛ essentia ل.
١٠) خيل م ؛ assimilati ل.
١١) — م ؛ كقوله ب .
١٢) عرق الأرض فل ؛ —ع ؛ terrae sudor est ل .
١٣) industriae ل .
١٤) sumat ل .
١٥) — ل .
١٦) erat ل .
١٧) sumuntur ل .
١٨) — ب .
١٩) — م .
٢٠) بن ب .
٢١) أنّه في ب .
٢٢) — ب .
٢٣) sumuntur ل .
٢٤) يوتى م .
٢٥) فيها ب ، فل .
٢٦) بحروف ب ؛ במלות ع .
٢٧) assimilationis ل .
٢٨) maior autem pars ل .
٢٩) يغلط م ، فل .
٣٠) similitudines sit quando sumuntur secundum modum permutationis ل .
٣١) يتصوّر ب .
٣٢) — ع ، ل .
٣٣) بذيالاتها م ؛ خيالاتها ب ؛ הדמיון בהם ع .

يعسر تصوّرها ، فإنّ هـــذه كثيرة[٣٤] التغليط ، كمن لا يقدر أن يتصوّر موجوداً[٣٥] لا[٣٦] داخل العالم ولا خارجه . ولكن[٣٧] أليق المواضع بهذا[٣٨] التغليط هو كتاب السفسطة.

٣. وهذه الصناعة وإن كانت[١] قياسيّة فليست[٢] تستعمل[٣] القياس بالفعل ولا لها نوع منه تختصّ به بل متى استعملت[٤] قولاً قياسيّاً بالفعل فعلى جهة الغلط ولتشبيهها[٥] بصناعة أخرى .

٤. وأرسطو لمّا رأى أنّ منفعة[١] هذه الصناعة عظيمة الغناء[٢] إذ كانت بها تحرك نفوس الجمهور نحو اعتقاد شيء ما أو لا اعتقاده ونحو الفعل والترك[٣] ، عدّد الأمور التي بها يقدر[٤] الإنسان أن يخيّل شيئاً شيئاً مما يقصد[٥] تخييله[٦] على أتمّ ما يمكن في ذلك الشيء[٧] . فتكون صناعة الشعر هي الصناعة التي بها يقدر[٨] الإنسان أن يخيّل شيئاً شيئاً بأتمّ[٩] ما يمكن فيه . لكن هذه كمالات[١٠] خارجة عن الكمال[١١] الأوّل[١٢] الإنساني .

٥. [١]وعلى الجملة[١] من فهم ما كتبناه في هذه الأقاويل ولم يكن له[٢] معرفة بالطبع أمكنه أن يقف[٣] [٤]على مرتبة[٤] كلّ قول يسمعه في التصديق

---

٣٤) كثرة م ، فل ؛ كثير ب .
٣٥) — م ، فل ؛ موجود ب .
٣٦) الا ب .
٣٧) لكن م ، فل ؛ لاكن ب :
٣٨) بهذه م .

(٣)
١) — ب ، ع .
٢) فليس م ، فل .
٣) يستعمل م .
٤) תעשה ع .
٥) والتشبهها ب ؛ והתדמות ع :
٣) — ع .
٤) יוכל ع ؛ valet ل .
٥) يقصر م .
٦) تخيله م ، فل .
٧) — ع .
٨) ישער ع ؛ estimat ل .
٩) בשלמות ع .
١٠) كماله م .
١١) השלמות ع .
١٢) (هنا انتهت المخطوطة م) ؛ — ل .

(٤)
١) منافعة فل .
٢) العناء م ، فل ؛ הצורך ع ؛ necessitatis ل .

(٥) ١) concludendo autem dicimus quod ل .
٢) — ب .
٣) instituat ل .
٤) — ل .

والتصوّر[٥]. [٦]وهذه المرتبة هي من الشرف[٦] بحيث يكون الإنسان معدّا بها نحو الكمال[٧] الأقصى . فإنّ الإنسان إن كان كماله[٨] إنّما[٩] هو بحصول النظر الصادق له ، وكان بهذا المقدار يحصل معدّا لقبوله ، فبهذا[١٠] المقدار إذاً[١١] يحصل له المرتبة التي يكون بها مستعدّا نحو الكمال[١٢] الأقصى . والله الموفّق للصواب[١٣] .

---

٥) — ع .

٦) in hac autem arte est honor et prestantia ل .

٧) השלמות ع .

٨) שלמותו ع .

٩) اما فل .

١٠) فبهذه ب .

١١) גם כן ع .

١٢) השלמות ع .

١٣) للشواب ب ؛ وفي ع بعد هذا : תם ונשלם תהלה לאל עולם נשלם קצור מלאכת ההגיון תהלה לשוכן ברום חביון ביום שלישי לחדש תשרי שנת חמשת אלפים ומאת ושבע עשרה לפרט ה־יצירה וכתבו לעצמו עוד למי שירצה אחריו עזרא בר שלמה זלהה בן־גרטניך בסרקסטה יגן השם בעדה ؛ وفي ل : Excellus autem Deus est, qui est Deus adiutor, et sustenens, et non est Deus nisi ipse qui semper laudetur. Amen.